Ageing in Contexts of Migration

Population ageing and the globalisation of international migration are challenging the research agendas of social scientists around the world, and posing numerous challenges for policy makers and practitioners whose goal is to formulate and design high-quality and user-friendly policies and services. Both of these phenomena have brought, for example, attention to the fact that more and more people around the world are ageing in countries other than those where they were born. The fact that elderly care sectors around the world need to recruit staff if they are to handle the growing number of older people that will need their services is also something that has been discussed when population ageing and the globalisation of international migration have been debated. The elderly care sector's reliance on people with migrant backgrounds has increased as a result of these phenomena.

This collection is therefore situated at the intersection of ageing and migration studies and takes into account the various issues with which this intersection is concerned. The chapters in this volume are written by established researchers in the field of ageing and migration around the world. The collection explores these issues in three parts:

- Elderly care regimes and migration regimes: national perspectives;
- Ageing in the context of migration: a multifaceted phenomenon;
- Elderly care in the context of migration.

The expert contributions in this volume address the array of issues associated with the study of ageing, old age and elderly care in contexts of migration.

Ute Karl is Associate Professor of Social Pedagogy/Social Work at the Institute for Research and Innovation in Social Work, Social Pedagogy and Social Welfare at the University of Luxembourg.

Sandra Torres is Professor of Sociology and Chair of Social Gerontology in the Department of Sociology at Uppsala University.

Routledge advances in Sociology

Ageing in Contexts of Migration

Edited by Ute Karl and Sandra Torres

Routledge
Taylor & Francis Group

LONDON AND NEW YORK

First published 2016
by Routledge

2 Park Square, Milton Park, Abingdon, Oxfordshire OX14 4RN
52 Vanderbilt Avenue, New York, NY 10017

Routledge is an imprint of the Taylor & Francis Group, an informa business

First issued in paperback 2019

British Library Cataloguing-in-Publication Data
A catalogue record for this book is available from the British Library

Library of Congress Cataloging in Publication Data
Aging in contexts of migration / edited by Ute Karl and Sandra Torres.
– 1 Edition.
   pages cm
   1. Immigrants–Retirement. 2. Older immigrants–Care.
   3. Globalization–Social aspects. I. Karl, Ute, editor. II. Torres, Sandra, 1968– editor.
   HQ1062.A395 2015
   305.26086′912–dc23   2015009431

ISBN: 978-0-415-73806-4 (hbk)
ISBN: 978-0-367-86916-8 (pbk)

Typeset in Times New Roman
by Wearset Ltd, Boldon, Tyne and Wear

Contents

Figures

Tables

Contributors

Anya Ahmed is Senior Lecturer in Social Policy at the University of Salford, UK. Her research interests include migration and gender studies, social gerontology, community and belonging, place and housing and qualitative research methods.

Claudine Attias-Donfut is the former Director of Research at the French National Fund for Retirement and is an Associate to the Edgar Morin Center, CNRS/EHESS (National Center for Scientific Research). Her research interests include ageing, relations between generations, family studies, social policy and migration studies.

Francesco Barbabella is Research Fellow at the Centre for Socio-Economic Research on Ageing, research unit of the Italian National Institute of Health and Science on Ageing (INRCA). His research interests include information and communication technologies in home care, migration of care workforce and comparative analysis of social policies.

Ruxandra Oana Ciobanu is a Marie Curie Post-Doctoral Fellow at the Center for the Interdisciplinary Study of Gerontology and Vulnerability at the University of Geneva. She is also affiliated with the Swiss National Centre of Competence in Research LIVES – Overcoming vulnerability: life course perspectives. Her research interests include ageing migrants, international migration, welfare, transnational processes and qualitative research methods.

Mirko Di Rosa is Research Fellow at the Scientific Directorate of the Italian National Institute of Health and Science on Ageing (INRCA). His research interests include data analysis through the use of quantitative research methods; family care of older people; reconciliation of professional and caring responsibilities; migrant care workers; prevention of elder abuse and neglect; role of technology for improving the quality of life of older people; active ageing and older workers.

Allen Glicksman is Director of Research and Evaluation at the Philadelphia Corporation for Ageing, and Adjunct Associate Professor in the School of Nursing at the University of Pennsylvania. His research interests include older immigrants and refugees, ageing in the Jewish community and the impact of environment on health outcomes in older adults.

Esther Iecovich is Associate Professor of Gerontology/Social Work at the Ben Gurion University of the Negev in Israel. Her research interests include social gerontology, policy on ageing and services for older people, including migrant live-in home care workers in elder care.

Ute Karl is Associate Professor of Social Pedagogy/Social Work at the Institute for Research and Innovation in Social Work, Social Pedagogy and Social Welfare (IRISS) at the University of Luxembourg. Her research interests include social gerontology, migration and gender studies, transition from youth to adulthood and qualitative research methods.

Hans-Joachim von Kondratowitz studied political science, sociology and history in Berlin, Saarbrücken and St. Louis, US. He has been a researcher at Saarbrücken, Berlin, Munich and Ann Arbor, US. He is now a Senior Advisor to the German Center of Gerontology in Berlin. His research interests include the international comparison of long-term care arrangements; elderly and family migration; welfare state and welfare culture comparisons; as well as cultural analyses of ageing.

Johanna Krawietz is Research Associate at the Institute of Social and Organizational Pedagogy, University of Hildesheim, Germany. Her research interests include social gerontology, care work, ageing and transnationalism.

Giovanni Lamura has led the Centre for Socio-Economic Research on Ageing at INRCA since 1992, after a PhD in 'Life course and social policy' at Bremen University (Germany), visiting fellowships in 2006–2007 at the University of Hamburg-Eppendorf (Germany) and in 2010–2011 at the European Centre for Social Welfare Policy and Research in Vienna (Austria). His focus is international research on family and long-term care; work-life balance; migrant care work; prevention of elder abuse; ICT-based support of informal carers; intergenerational solidarity.

Maria Gabriella Melchiorre is Senior Researcher at the Centre for Socio-Economic Research on Ageing, research unit of the Italian National Institute of Health and Science on Ageing (INRCA). Her research interests include ageing well; family care of older people; prevention of elder abuse and neglect; migrant care workers; long-term care; innovative care for older people with chronic conditions; and e-health.

Jolanta Perek-Białas is an Adjunct at the Institute of Statistics and Demography, Warsaw School of Economics and, since 2001, also in the Institute of Sociology of the Jagiellonian University in Kraków, Poland. Her main scientific research interests include socio-economic consequences of population ageing in Poland, and in selected Central and Eastern European countries, active ageing policy, reconciliation of work and care, social exclusion/inclusion of older people and long-term care.

Anne Carolina Ramos is a Research Associate at the Institute for Research and Innovation in Social Work, Social Pedagogy and Social Welfare (IRISS) at the University of Luxembourg. Her main areas of research interest are inter-generational relationships, grandparenthood, migration, and the interfaces between childhood, old age education and care.

Tine Rostgaard is Professor at the Center for Comparative Welfare Studies, at the Department of Political Science, Aalborg University. Her research spans the field of social care for older persons and children, with focus on welfare architecture, quality of care and implications for gender equality.

Krystyna Slany is Professor of Sociology at the Institute of Sociology, Jagiellonian University, Vice-President of the Research Committee on Migration, Polish Academy of Sciences, a member of the Demographic Sciences Committee, Polish Academy of Sciences and a Polish government expert on migration policy. She specializes in the field of social demography, social migration and the sociology of gender and family.

Sandra Torres is Professor of Sociology and Chair in Social Gerontology at Uppsala University, Sweden. Her research – which often lies at the intersection between the sociology of ageing and the sociology of migration and ethnic relations – problematises old age-related constructs, sheds critical light on commonly used methods in health and social care and deconstructs some of the taken-for-granted assumptions that guide policy and practice for the older segments of our populations.

Christina Victor is Professor of Gerontology and Public Health and Vice Dean-Research in the College of Health and Life Sciences at Brunel University London. Her main research interest is social gerontology with specific focus upon ageing in minority communities, loneliness and isolation in later life; health and health inequalities; and the evaluation of services for older people.

Stefanie Visel is Research Associate at the Institute of Social and Organizational Pedagogy, University of Hildesheim, Germany and member of the DFG research training group 'Transnational Social Support'. Her research interests include migration and transnationalisation, care work and labour market policies.

Paul Zahlen is Economic Advisor to the National Statistical Institute of Luxembourg (STATEC).

Maria Zubair is Research Fellow at the School of Sociology and Social Policy and Centre for Dementia at the University of Nottingham. Her research interests fall within the areas of social gerontology, race and ethnicity, and gender studies, with a particular focus on social identities, diversities and inequalities.

A migration lens on inquiries into ageing, old age and elderly care

Carving a space while assessing the state of affairs

Sandra Torres and Ute Karl

Introduction

Carving a space for a book that tackles issues at the intersection of ageing and migration is not an easy task. This book addresses namely an area of inquiry involving two fields that seldom engage in dialogue (i.e. migration research and gerontology). Thus, this edited collection aims to bring together not only the specific angle that migration offers to the study of ageing and old age but also the angle that the study of ageing and old age brings to migration scholarship; a field whose interest on the later stages of life has been relatively lukewarm despite the fact that 'there have been overlaps between migration studies and gerontology for decades' (Warnes and Williams, 2006, p. 1260). This book aims therefore to take on the challenge that the *Journal of Ethnic and Migration Studies* formulated in a special issue in 2006 urging migration scholars to think of the interface of migration and gerontology as 'mutually stimulating and productive' (p. 1261).

Worth noting is perhaps that research at the intersection between migration studies and gerontology seems to be in a consolidating phase as more and more networks that bring scholars from these two fields together are being established. The special issue already mentioned was the result of the scholarly collaborations that were made possible through the *European Science Foundation Research Network on 'International Migration in Europe: Welfare Policy and Practice Implications for Older People'* which met on several occasions during 2001–2003. This research network was also behind a special issue in *Ageing & Society* two years earlier (i.e. in 2004; see vol. 21, part 3) which urged gerontologists, in turn, to note that international migration was generating new questions in their field (Warnes *et al.*, 2004). A more recent initiative from the field of migration can be found in the establishment in 2010 of the committee on *Ageing Migrants: Demography, Welfare and Agency* as part of the *IMISCOE* (International Migration, Integration and Social Cohesion in Europe) European network of migration scholars.

Both of the fields of inquiry with which this book engages seem to have been, in other words, relatively late in their 'discovery' of the topics that this book addresses. It is perhaps because of this that Torres (2006a) has suggested that the study of older migrants has been relegated to the periphery of both, migration scholarship and gerontology. The reason why the first is the case could be that migration scholars tend to often focus on the stages of the life-course when migration tends to occur most often, and that is not old age. The reason why gerontology relegates the ageing and old age of migrants to the periphery of its imagination could, in turn, be that gerontology bases its theoretical frameworks on the idea of continuity and not disruption which is what migration is assumed by these scholars to be (Torres, 2008). Against these backdrops it is perhaps understandable that the ageing of migrants and the implications of migration for ageing, old age and elderly care would be relegated to the periphery of both of these scholarly fields. This book brings, therefore, attention to the space of inquiry that two of the major societal trends we are facing at the moment – population ageing and the globalisation of international migration – have brought to the agenda of the social sciences.

The number of older people with migrant backgrounds has increased in Western societies to such an extent that neither these people's ageing nor their migration experiences can continue to be relegated to the periphery of migration studies (White, 2006) and gerontology (Torres, 2006a, 2012, 2013, 2015; Warnes *et al.*, 2004). Similar observations have been made as far as the recruitment of migrants to the elderly care sector is concerned; migrants have become important sources of late-in-life care support (both formally and informally) over the past few decades (Browne and Braun, 2008). This book aims therefore to bring attention to some of the ways in which migration affects ageing (as a process), old age (as a stage in the life course) and elderly care (as an institutional setting). But before we can move on to present how the book is organised and what the various chapters will offer, it seems appropriate to summarise the body of literature on migration and older migrants, asylum seekers and refugees that can be found in journals of gerontology over the past 15 years, as well as the body of literature on ageing and old age that can be found in journals specialising on migration. It is namely against the backdrop that these literatures offer that we can bring attention to what characterises the state of affairs of these two different fields.

The study of migration, older migrants and elderly care within social gerontology[1]

A look at the social gerontological literature on migration and migrants that has been published in the five main journals in this area over the past 15 years gives us some insight into the focus of this research. In this section we review this literature in a scoping manner in order to give an idea of what characterises the research on migration and migrants that has been published within some of the main gerontological journals. The first thing we would like to draw attention to is the fact that most of the articles on migration and migrants found in these journals are based on empirical findings. This comes perhaps as no surprise considering that gerontology is a 'data-rich and theory-poor' field (Birren and Bengtson,

1988: ix). The few exceptions to these data-rich articles can be found in the pieces that are more theoretically and conceptually driven such as the article by Warnes *et al.* (2004), which draws attention to the fact that the globalisation of international migration challenges the ways in which gerontologists have thought about ageing migrants and formulates a typology of older migrants, and the article written by Blakemore (1999) urging gerontologists to pay attention to the social care and policy implications that the increasing number of older people with migrant backgrounds is bound to entail. In addition to these theoretical/conceptual pieces we have the article that draws attention to the fact that certain migrant populations have been relatively invisible in gerontology research on migrants (as Salari 2002 argues in relation to Middle Eastern immigrants in the US); the article that does an inventory of the disciplinary perspectives on late-in-life migration that can be found in core journals of social gerontology (Walters and Wilder, 2003); the two pieces about the ways gerontologists theorising about older migrants and minorities can move forward (Koehn *et al.*, 2013; McDonald, 2011); and a piece by Torres (2009) arguing that vignette methodology can be useful when trying to shed culture-relevant light on the way in which older migrants make sense of gerontological constructs.

The vast majority of articles on migration and migrants in the main gerontological journals over the past 15 years are, in other words, based on empirical findings on a variety of topics. Most of the work conducted in this period focuses on older migrants; the exception being the articles that draw attention to migrant care workers (e.g. Browne and Braun, 2008; Walsh and Shutes, 2013) and primarily on those that migrated early in life and are ageing with a migrant background. The few exceptions to this statement are the articles that focus on those that have migrated late-in-life (e.g. Cook, 2010; Heikkinen and Lumme-Sandt, 2013). To this end it must also be mentioned that very seldom do the articles reviewed here tend to differentiate between those that have migrated late-in-life (which most of the literature describe as people that have migrated from non-Western to Western societies) and those that are engaged in retirement migration (which the literature describes as form of migration commonly found in North Europeans that migrate to Southern Europe after retirement) (e.g. Ackers and Dwyer, 2004; Gustafson, 2001). Of interest to migration scholars is probably also the fact that most of the articles published in gerontological journals which we have reviewed do not differentiate between *when* migration has taken place and neither do they tend to bring attention to people's *migration motives*. In addition, it is also noted that they very seldom draw attention to the *migration status* that older people with migrant backgrounds have (whether they are labour or family reunification migrants, or are refugees or asylum seekers to name a few).

In terms of the topics touched upon in the gerontological literature reviewed here it seems worth noting that certain topics are particularly salient while others are not. Social support, intergenerational relationships, filial expectations and living arrangements are, for example, some of the topics that have received considerable attention (e.g. Ajrouch, 2005; de Valk and Schans, 2008; Wilmoth,

2001) as is access to health and social care (e.g. Koehn, 2009; Lanari and Bussini, 2012). These themes suggest that the gerontological literature published during the period in question in the publication outlets mentioned regard older migrants as potential elderly care recipients whose needs of help and support in old age demand attention. Contrary to what we had expected a considerable small number of articles focused on some of gerontologists most central concepts such as well-being, successful ageing and life-satisfaction. Although, this could be because these are topics that have been explored before the period in focus here started, it is interesting to note that older migrants and migration as a phenomenon are relatively seldom addressed as potential sources of information that could expand the gerontological imagination (cf. Torres, 2006a, 2012). This is why we think that the chapters in this book will show that there is more to migration and older migrants than meets the gerontological eye.

The study of migration, older migrants and elderly care within migration scholarship[2]

A look at the literature on migration and migrants that has focused on old age and ageing and has been published in the six main journals for migration scholarship over the past 15 years gives us some insight into the focus that this research has had. In this section we review this literature in the same scoping manner used to review the gerontological literature. This will be done in order to give an idea of the themes that have been studied. The first thing to note is that just as it was the case in gerontology, the research published within the migration journals we have reviewed is mostly based on empirical findings. The exceptions to this can be found in the piece by Warnes and Williams (2006) urging migration scholars to think of ageing and old age as a profuse source of information for their field; the piece by Gaines *et al.* (1999) which broadly addresses ageing and migration and the piece by Horn *et al.* (2013) which briefly introduces the area of transnational ageing for a special issue on the topic.

Having stated this, it seems important to note that four research strands[3] characterise the migration scholarship that we have reviewed for this section. The first strand is related to old age in broader terms and focuses on different types of older people whose lifestyles or situation are of interest to migration scholars (such as retired labour migrants, international retirement migration and older people left behind while younger generations migrate for work to name a few). Research in this first strand has addressed not only their present situation but also their life patterns in more general terms. This is work that focuses on international retirement migration (IRM) (especially – though not exclusively – from Northern European countries to Southern European countries (e.g. Božić, 2006; Casado-Díaz, 2006; Remennick, 2003) and the choices that are available to migrants as they age and their effects on well-being (i.e. returning to their home countries, staying in their host countries or establishing residences in both; e.g. Barrett and Mosca, 2013; Baykara-Krumme, 2013; Bolzman *et al.*, 2006; Byron, 1999; Ganga, 2006; Gualda and Escriva, 2014; Klinthäll, 2006; Razum *et al.*,

2005; Rodrigues and Egea, 2006; Yahirun, 2014). In this strand we find also research on how discrimination and/or inequality affect older migrants' lives, including their access to social and health care and the social security system (e.g. Basavarajappa, 2000; Choi, 2006; Dwyer and Papadimitriou, 2006; Ekberg and Lindh, 2013; Forssell, 2013; Grewal *et al.*, 2004; Lee and Angel, 2002; Torres, 2006b) as well as research focusing on the ways in which older migrants are affected not only by specific health problems, but also by their health care attitudes and practices as well as the variety of the factors (including, for example, language use, education, neighbourhood environment and the size of the minority community) that affect different health outcomes (e.g. Chau and Lai, 2011; Lum and Vanderaa, 2010; Park *et al.*, 2014). The first strand of research within migration scholarship that focuses on ageing and old age is, in other words, a strand that is quite broad as far as focus is concerned and tends to be empirically based. What characterises it is, however, that this is work that draws attention to older migrants' present situation.

The second strand brings attention to ageing and old age while focusing on transnational family care and transnational social support. This strand builds on the theoretical concept of transnationalism – which became popular in migration scholarship in the 1990s (cf. Torres, 2013 who discusses the relevance of this phenomenon for the study of ageing and old age specifically) – and brings attention to the fact that social phenomena such as social relations, networks, social support and care in old age can no longer be solely studied from the perspective of national parameters because they stretch across diverse national societies or are embedded in a broader context of migration (e.g. Baldassar, 2007; Kilkey and Merla, 2014; Merla, 2012; Vullnetari and King, 2008; Wilding, 2006; Zhou, 2013; Zontini, 2007). Characteristic of this strand is that older people are seen as both care providers and care receivers and that the research aims to bring to the fore how (intergenerational) family relations are maintained in transnational times, how a sense of belonging and 'familyhood' is constructed, and which forms of social support and care are provided and received over long-distances. Thus, within migration scholarship these issues are explored in terms of the care arrangements that the phenomenon of *migration for care* have brought to the fore (i.e. the (re-)migration to/with the adult children to receive care and the migration of (sometimes retired) adult children to give care) and the *long-distance care arrangements* that transnational families set up to care for their older family members (e.g. Ackers, 2004; Baldassar, 2007; Merla, 2012; Soom Ammann and van Holten, 2013; Wilding, 2006).

The third strand of research within migration studies which our literature review has identified focuses on the provision of elderly care by migrant care workers in domestic and institutional contexts. This strand – which can be found mostly from the 2000s onwards and which brings attention to the idea of global care chains and the care drain that they generate in some national contexts – highlights the multiple intersections between gender, migration and welfare regimes that migrating to care for others, or ending up as a worker in the care sector because of migration earlier in life, bring to fore. This research takes into account the growing care gap for older people in ageing societies which migrant workers are expected to help elderly care sectors in these societies to address (e.g. Um and Lightman, 2011); the work conditions of migrants in the elderly care sector or within domestic settings (e.g. Huang *et al.*, 2012; Lopez, 2012; Ortega *et al.*, 2010) and the caring obligations that can fall on older people as younger generations migrate to care (e.g. Marchetti and Venturini, 2014).

Last but not least we have the strand of research that focuses on the interconnection of migration and ageing societies from a demographic perspective, asking the question of how immigration can delay population ageing (e.g. Keely, 2001; van Nimwegen and van der Erf, 2010; White, 2006). This fourth strand is the one that seems to have generated the least attention within the journals that have been reviewed here.

The rationale for this book

Based on the literature reviews which we have briefly alluded to in the previous sections, this book takes for granted that the context of migration offers gerontologists numerous ways to expand their imagination just as the context of ageing and old age offers migration scholars new angles to explore. Irrespective of what these contexts can offer to these fields it is also taken for granted that the ageing of people that have migrant backgrounds means not only that understandings of ageing and old age are put to test but also that welfare institutions that address the needs of older migrants can in some cases also face challenges as they try to design programmes that cater to these populations (Torres, 2012) and when they try to attract migrants to the elderly care sector now that staff shortages are a given in some parts of the world. Moreover, we take for granted that the migratory life-course offers new possibilities for the generation of research questions that we have yet to address both in gerontology and within migration scholarship.

This collection is organised therefore in three parts in order to draw attention to different angles around which separate agendas for research at the intersection between migration and ageing can be formulated. In focus are: (1) the importance that societal contexts (conceptualised in terms of migration regimes and elderly care regimes) play for the ways in which we think about the intersection of ageing and migration in different countries (as is the case in Part I); (2) results from empirical studies focusing on older migrants specifically and addressing an array of angles from which their situation could be studied (as is the case in Part II); and (3) the ways in which migrants are becoming more involved in elderly care provision around the world (as is the case in Part III).

Part I brings, in other words, attention to the ways in which different societal contexts affect the migrants that can be found in different countries, the ways in which they are ageing and the ways in which they are regarded within the elderly care sectors that cater to their needs. Thus, the chapters in Part I bring attention to the idea that context determines the ways in which migrants are regarded and whether they are deemed to be primarily interesting for these contexts because of their care recipiency, their care provision or both. Worth noting is that some of the chapters in Part I bring attention to both older migrants and migrant care workers (as is the case for the chapter on Sweden by Sandra Torres and the chapter on Poland by Jolanta Perek-Białas and Krystyna Slany), while others bring exclusive attention to older migrants (such as is the case of the chapter on Luxembourg by Paul Zahlen, the chapter on the UK by Anya Ahmed and the chapter on Germany by Hans-Joachim Kondratowitz).

Part II brings attention to the numerous research questions that a focus on older migrants' lives bring to fore. In this Part we find chapters that bring attention to intergenerational issues (such as the chapter that does so from the perspective of data collected in France by Claudine Attias-Donfut); return migration (which is the focus of the state of the art review of the literature by Ruxandra Oana Ciobanu and Anne Carolina Ramos); care and support expectations (which is the focus of the chapter on Bangladeshi and Pakistani elders in the UK by Christina Victor and Maria Zubair); retirement-related issues from a migratory life-course perspective (to which the chapter on post-retirement practices of work of older migrants in Luxembourg by Ute Karl and Anne Carolina Ramos brings attention); and the challenges associated with post-migration adaptation (which the chapter focusing on immigrants from the former Soviet Union to the US by Allen Glicksman touches upon). In focus in this Part is therefore not necessarily who migrants are but rather which research angles does a focus on older migrants offer.

Part III brings attention to the elderly care sector specifically and does so from the perspective of what migrants offer when they are the providers of care. In this Part we find chapters that follow the same context-based knowledge that was used in Part I. This means that this part is organised in terms of different countries emphasising the ways in which different national realities affect the situation of migrants who have been attracted to the care sector as providers. In this part of the book we find a chapter that offers us the state of the art of research on migrant care workers within the elderly care sector (see the chapter written by Esther Iecovich); a chapter that brings attention to the Italian case (see the chapter by Francesco Barbabella, Mirko Di Rosa, Maria Gabriella Melchiorre and Giovanni Lemura); the German case (see the chapter by Johanna Krawietz and Stefanie Visel) and the Danish case (see the chapter by Tine Rostgaard). In these chapters we bring attention to the ways in which migrants are challenging the elderly care sector through the alternative professional identity and work culture they might have, the skills and qualifications they bring with them and the employment opportunities that their presence has created.

Thus, as one of the few edited collections on migration and ageing that are available at the moment, this book brings attention to the variety of issues on which the intersection between migration, ageing, old age and elderly care sheds light. In doing so, the book aims to broaden the angles of study that characterise the literature that we reviewed in previous sections by shifting the reductionist focus we have had so far. As a whole, this edited collection suggests that time has come for research at the intersection between migration and ageing to move beyond the focus that characterises it at present (i.e. who older migrants are and what they need) to a focus that brings attention to theoretical and conceptual profuseness embedded in the study of ageing, old age and elderly care through a migration-aware lens.

Notes

1 This section is based on a review of journal articles in peer-review sources in gerontology. In focus are the main journals in social gerontology that are listed in the Social Science Citation Index (i.e. *Journal of Gerontology: Social Sciences; The Gerontologist; Ageing & Society* and *Journal of Aging Studies*) as well as one journal that specialises in cross-cultural issues (*Journal of Cross-Cultural Gerontology*). The review covers articles published within the last 15 years (1999–2014). The search in question identified 84 articles on the topics in focus here. This section summarises them in a bird's eye view manner in order to give some insight into what this literature has focused on during the period in question and the issues that seem to be relatively disregarded.

2 This section is based on a review of journal articles in peer-review sources within the field of migration. In focus are some of the main journals listed for the ethnic studies area in the Social Sciences Citation Index (i.e. *Journal of Ethnic and Migration Studies, International Migration, Journal of Immigrant and Minority Health* and *Cultural Diversity and Ethnic Minority Psychology*); a newly launched journal specialising in transnational care and social support, transnational networks and transnational ageing (i.e. *Transnational Social Review: A Social Work Journal*) which had a special issue on 'Transnational Ageing' in 2013); and *Global Networks: A Journal of Transnational Affairs*, which is one of the journals that has published articles on the topic in question over the period in question. The review covers articles published within the last 15 years (1999–2014). The search in question identified 83 articles on the topics in focus here.

3 Acknowledged hereby is the fact that three of these strands were first identified by Horn *et al.* (2013).

References

Ackers, L. (2004). Citizenship, migration and the valuation of care in the European Union. *Journal of Ethnic and Migration Studies, 30*, 373–396. doi:10.1080/136918304 2000200759.

Ackers, L. and Dwyer, P. (2004). Fixed laws, fluid lives: the citizenship status of post-retirement migrants in the European Union. *Ageing & Society, 24*, 451–475. doi:10.1017/S0144686X0300165X.

Ajrouch, K. L. (2005). Arab-American immigrant elders' views about social support. *Ageing & Society, 25*, 655–673. doi:10.1017/S0144686X04002934.

Baldassar, L. (2007). Transnational families and aged care: the mobility of care and the migrancy of ageing. *Journal of Ethnic and Migration Studies, 33*, 275–297. doi:10.1080/13691830601154252.

Barrett, A. and Mosca, I. (2013). Social isolation, loneliness and return migration: evidence from older Irish adults. *Journal of Ethnic and Migration Studies, 39*, 1659–1677. doi:10.1080/1369183X.2013.833694.

Basavarajappa, K. G. (2000). Distribution, inequality and concentration of income among older immigrants in canada. *International Migration, 38*, 47–67. doi:10.1111/1468-2435.00098.

Baykara-Krumme, H. (2013). Returning, staying, or both? Mobility patterns among elderly Turkish migrants after retirement. *Transnational Social Review: A Social Work Journal, 3*, 11–29. doi:10.1080/21931674.2013.10820745.

Birren, J. E. and Bengtson, V. L. (eds) (1988). *Emergent Theories of Aging.* New York: Springer.

Blakemore, K. (1999). International migration in later life: social care and policy implications. *Ageing & Society, 19*, 761–774.

Bolzman, C., Fibbi, R. and Vial, M. (2006). What to do after retirement? Elderly migrants and the question of return. *Journal of Ethnic and Migration Studies, 32*, 1359–1375. doi:10.1080/13691830600928748.

Božić, S. (2006). The achievement and potential of international retirement migration research: the need for disciplinary exchange. *Journal of Ethnic and Migration Studies, 32*, 1415–1427. doi:10.1080/13691830600928805.

Browne, C. V. and Braun, K. L. (2008). Globalization, women's migration, and the long-term-care workforce. *The Gerontologist, 48*, 16–24. doi:10.1093/geront/48.1.16.

Byron, M. (1999). The Caribbean-born population in 1990s Britain: who will return? *Journal of Ethnic and Migration Studies, 25*, 285–301. doi:10.1080/1369183X.1999.9976686.

Casado-Díaz, M. A. (2006). Retiring to Spain: an analysis of differences among north European nationals. *Journal of Ethnic and Migration Studies, 32*, 1321–1339. doi:10.1080/13691830600928714.

Chau, S. and Lai, D. W. L. (2011). The size of an ethno-cultural community as a social determinant of health for Chinese seniors. *Journal of Immigrant and Minority Health, 13*, 1090–1098. doi:10.1007/s10903–010–9374–0.

Choi, S. (2006). Insurance status and health service utilization among newly-arrived older immigrants. *Journal of Immigrant and Minority Health, 8*, 149–161. doi:10.1007/s10903–006–8523–3.

Cook, J. (2010). Exploring older women's citizenship: understanding the impact of migration in later life. *Aging & Society, 30*, 253–273. doi:http://dx.doi.org/10.1017/S0144686X09990195.

de Valk, H. A. G. and Schans, D. (2008). "They ought to do this for their parents": perceptions of filial obligations among immigrant and Dutch older people. *Ageing & Society, 28*, 49–66. doi:http://dx.doi.org/10.1017/S0144686X07006307.

Dwyer, P. and Papadimitriou, D. (2006). The social security rights of older international migrants in the European Union. *Journal of Ethnic and Migration Studies, 32*, 1301–1319. doi:10.1080/13691830600927773.

Ekberg, J. and Lindh, T. (2013). Immigrants in the old-age pension system: the case of Sweden. *International Migration.* doi:10.1111/imig.12117.

Forssell, E. (2013). Transnational aging, care and the welfare state. *Transnational Social Review: A Social Work Journal, 3(1)*, 83–99. doi:10.1080/21931674.2013.10820749.

Gaines, A. D., McDonald, P. E. and Wykle, M. L. (1999). Aging and immigration: who are the elderly? *Journal of Immigrant Health* (now: *Journal of Immigrant and Minority Health*), *1*, 99–113. doi:10.1023/A:1021884406146.

Ganga, D. (2006). From potential returnees into settlers: Nottingham's older Italians. *Journal of Ethnic and Migrations Studies, 32*, 1395–1413. doi:10.1080/13691830600928789.

Grewal, I., Nazroo, J., Madhavi, B., Blane, D. and Lewis, J. (2004). Influences on quality of life: a qualitative investigation of ethnic differences among older people in England. *Journal of Ethnic and Migration Studies, 30*, 737–761. doi:10.1080/136918304100016 99595.

Gualda, E. and Escriva, A. (2014). Diversity in return migration and its impact on old age: the expectations and experiences of returnees in Huelva (Spain). *International Migration, 52*, 178–190. doi:10.1111/j.1468–2435.2011.00728.x.

Gustafson, P. (2001). Retirement migration and transnational lifestyles. *Ageing & Society, 21*, 371–394. doi:10.1017/S0144686X01008327.

Heikkinen, S. J. and Lumme-Sandt, K. (2013). Transnational connections of later-life migrants. *Journal of Aging Studies, 27*, 198–206. doi:10.1016/j.jaging.2013.02.002.

Horn, V., Schweppe, C. and Um, S. (2013). Transnational aging: a young field of research. *Transnational Social Review: A Social Work Journal, 3(1)*, 7–10. doi:0.1080/21931674.2013.10820744.

Huang, S., Yeoh, B. S. A. and Toyota, M. (2012). Caring for the elderly: the embodied labour of migrant care worker in Singapore. *Global Networks, 12*, 195–215. doi:10.1111/j.1471–0374.2012.00347.x.

Keely, C. B. (2001). Replacement migration: the wave of the future? *International Migration, 39*, 103–110. doi:10.1111/1468–2435.00181.

Kilkey, M. and Merla, L. (2014). Situating transnational families' care-giving arrangements: the role of institutional context. *Global Networks, 14*, 210–229. doi:10.1111/glob.12034.

Klinthäll, M. (2006). Retirement return migration from Sweden. *International Migration, 44*, 153–180. doi:10.1111/j.1468–2435.2006.00367.x.

Koehn, S. (2009). Negotiating ethnic minority seniors' access to care. *Ageing & Society, 29*, 585–608. doi:http://dx.doi.org/10.1017/S0144686X08007952.

Koehn, S., Neysmith, S., Kobayashi, K. and Khamisa, H. (2013). Revealing the shape of knowledge using an intersectional lens: results of a scoping review on health and health care of ethnocultural minority older adults. *Ageing & Society, 33*, 437–464. doi:http://dx.doi.org/10.1017/S0144686X12000013.

Lanari, D. and Bussini, O. (2012). International migration and health inequalities in later life. *Ageing & Society, 32*, 935–962. doi:10.1017/S0144686X11000730.

Lee, G.-Y. and Angel, R. J. (2002). Living arrangements and Supplemental Security Income use among elderly Asians and Hispanics in the United States: the role of nativity and citizenship. *Journal of Ethnic and Migration Studies, 28*, 553–563. doi:10.1080/13691830220146608.

Lopez, M. (2012). Reconstituting the affective labour of Filipinos as care workers in Japan. *Global Networks, 12*, 252–268. doi:10.1111/j.1471–0374.2012.00350.x.

Lum, T. Y. and Vanderaa, J. P. (2010). Health disparities among immigrant and non-immigrant elders: the association of acculturation and education. *Journal of Immigrant and Minority Health, 12*, 743–753. doi:10.1007/s10903–008–9225–4.

Marchetti, S. and Venturini, A. (2014). Mothers and grandmothers on the move: labour mobility and the household strategies of Moldovan and Ukrainian migrant women in Italy. *International Migration, 52(5)*, 111–126. doi:10.1111/imig.12131.

McDonald, L. (2011). Theorizing about ageing, family and immigration. *Ageing & Society, 31*, 1180–1201. doi:10.1017/S0144686X11000511.

Merla, L. (2012). Salvadoran migrants in Australia: an analysis of transnational families' capability to care across orders. *International Migration*, doi:10.1111/imig.12024.

Ortega, A., Gomes Carneiro, I. and Flyvholm, M.-A. (2010). A descriptive study on immigrant workers in the elderly care sector. *Journal of Immigrant and Minority Health, 12(5)*, 699–706. doi:10.1007/s10903–009–9257–4.

Park, M., Unützer, J. and Grembowski, D. (2014). Ethnic and gender variations in the associations between family cohesion, family conflict, and depression in older Asian and Latino adults. *Journal of Immigrant and Minority Health, 16*, 1103–1110. doi:10.1007/s10903–013–9926–1.

Razum, O., Sahin-Hodoglugil, N. N. and Polit, K. (2005). Health, wealth or family ties? Why Turkish work migrants return from Germany. *Journal of Ethnic and Migration Studies, 31*, 719–739. doi:10.1080/13691830500109894.

Remennick, L. (2003). Retired and making a fresh start: older Russian immigrants discuss their adjustment in Israel. *International Migration, 41(5)*, 153–175. doi:10.1111/j.0020–7985.2003.00264.x.

Rodríguez, V. and Egea, C. (2006). Return and the social environment of Andalusian emigrants in Europe. *Journal of Ethnic and Migration Studies, 32*, 1377–1393. doi:10.1080/13691830600928771.

Salari, S. (2002). Invisible in aging research: Arab Americans, Middle Eastern Immigrants and Muslims in the United States. *The Gerontologist, 42*, 580–588. doi:10.1093/geront/42.5.580.

Soom Ammann, E. and van Holten, K. (2013). Getting old here and there: opportunities and pitfalls of transnational care arrangements. *Transnational Social Review: A Social Work Journal, 3(1)*, 31–47. doi:10.1080/21931674.2013.10820746.

Torres, S. (2006a). Culture, migration, inequality and 'periphery' in a globalized world: challenges for the study of ethno- and anthropo-gerontology. In J. Baars, D. Dannefer, C. Phillipson and A. Walker (eds), *Ageing, Globalization and Inequality: The New Critical Gerontology* (pp. 231–244)*.* Amityville, NY: Baywood Publishing Company.

Torres, S. (2006b). Elderly immigrants in Sweden: 'Otherness' under construction. *Journal of Ethnic and Migration Studies, 32*, 1341–1358. doi:10.1080/136918306 00928730.

Torres, S. (2008). The age of migration: what does it mean and why should European social gerontologists care? *Retraite et Societé (Best of selection 2008)*, pp. 67–90.

Torres, S. (2009). Vignette methodology and culture-relevance: lessons learned through a project on successful aging with Iranian immigrants to Sweden. *Journal of Cross-Cultural Gerontology, 24*, 93–114. doi:10.1007/s10823–009–9095–9.

Torres, S. (2012). International migration: patterns and implications for exclusion in old age. In T. Scharf and N. C. Keating (eds), *From Exclusion to Inclusion in Old Age: A Global Challenge* (pp. 33–49). University of Bristol: The Policy Press.

Torres, S. (2013). Transnationalism and the study of aging and old age. In C. Phellas (ed.), *Aging in European Societies* (pp. 263–281). New York: Springer.

Torres, S. (2015). Ethnicity, culture and migration. In J. Twigg and W. Martin (eds), *Handbook of Cultural Gerontology* (page numbers not yet decided). London: Routledge.

Um, S.-G. and Lightman, E. (2011). Long-term care in South Korea: migrant care workers and transnational social welfare. *Transnational Social Review: A Social Work Journal, 1(1)*, 53–69. doi:10.1080/21931674.2011.10820695.

van Nimwegen, N. and van der Erf, R. (2010). Europe at the crossroads: demographic challenges and international migration. *Journal of Ethnic and Migration Studies, 36*, 1359–1379. doi:10.1080/1369183X.2010.515132.

Vullnetari, J. and King, R. (2008). 'Does your granny eat grass?' On mass migration, care drain and the fate of older people in rural Albania. *Global Networks, 8*, 139–171. doi:10.1111/j.1471–0374.2008.00189.x.

Walsh, K. and Shutes, I. (2013). Care relationships, quality of care and migrant care workers caring for older people. *Ageing & Society, 33*, 393–420. doi:10.1017/S0144686X11001309.

Walters, W. H. and Wilder, E. I. (2003). Disciplinary perspectives on later-life migration in the core journals of social gerontology. *The Gerontologist, 43,* 758–760. doi:10.1093/geront/43.5.758.

Warnes, A. M. and Williams, A. (2006). Older migrants in Europe: a new focus for migration studies. *Journal of Ethnic and Migration Studies, 32,* 1257–1281. doi:10.1080/13691830600927617.

Warnes, A. M., Friedrich, K., Kellaher, L. and Torres, S. (2004). The diversity and welfare of older migrants in Europe. *Ageing & Society, 24,* 307–326. doi:10.1017/S0144686X04002296.

White, P. (2006). Migrant populations approaching old age: prospects in Europe. *Journal of Ethnic and Migration Studies, 32,* 1283–1300. doi:10.1080/13691830600927708.

Wilding, R. (2006). 'Virtual' intimacies? Families communicating across transnational contexts. *Global Networks, 6(2),* 125–142. doi:10.1111/j.1471–0374.2006.00137.x.

Wilmoth, J. M. (2001). Living arrangements among older immigrants in the United States. *The Gerontologist, 41,* 228–238. doi:10.1093/geront/41.2.228.

Yahirun, J. J. (2014). Take me 'home': return migration among Germany's older immigrants, *International Migration, 52,* 231–254. doi:10.1111/imig.12009.

Zhou, R. Y. (2013). Transnational aging: the impacts of adult children's immigration on their parents' later lives. *Transnational Social Review: A Social Work Journal, 3(1),* 49–64. doi:10.1080/21931674.2013.10820747.

Zontini, E. (2007). Continuity and change in transnational Italian families: the caring practices of second-generation women. *Journal of Ethnic and Migration Studies, 33,* 1103–1119. doi:10.1080/13691830701541622.

Part I

Elderly care regimes and migration regimes

National perspectives

1   At the intersection between an elderly care regime and a migration regime

The Swedish case as an example

Sandra Torres

Introduction

Inspired by Kilkey *et al.*'s (2010) assertion that there is a need for research that elucidates the relationship between care regimes and migration regimes, this chapter presents the Swedish case and gives glimpses of research on older immigrants and care workers with immigrant backgrounds. In doing so, the chapter focuses on the context of care – a context that gives us insight into society's moral and political life (Tronto, 2010) as well as its relationship with 'Others' (Narayan, 1995).

The chapter is organised as follows. First, insights into Sweden's elderly care regime and migration regimes are offered in separate sections in order to present the ambitious policies surrounding the terrain that is the elderly care sector. Next, demographics are presented for contextualisation purposes. And finally, a section that sheds light on the debate and the realities of migrants in the Swedish elderly care sector is presented, with concluding remarks meant to problematise the difference between policy ambitions and everyday realities.

The Swedish elderly care regime

The notion of care regimes stems from the feminist critique of Esping-Andersen's (1990) book on several welfare states, and draws attention to the implications that the organisation of care services in different welfare regimes has on gendered power orders (e.g. Anttonen and Sipilä, 1996; Pfau-Effinger, 2005). The idea is that care regimes can be differentiated on the basis of the mixture of formal versus informal care provision, the care expectations that are implicitly placed on families as a result of this mixture and the ways in which the care sector is organised. Focusing on social services, Anttonen and Sipilä (1996) have found, for example, two distinct care regimes: a Scandinavian regime characterised by a strong formal sector, and a southern European regime characterised by strong reliance on the family. Along the same lines – but focusing on the mixture of formal versus informal care – Bettio and Plantenga (2004) distinguish between countries that expect the family to assume responsibility for care (e.g. Italy, Greece and Spain); countries that place care responsibility on the family, but that have different strategies for childcare and elderly care (e.g. Great Britain and the Netherlands); countries that expect a great deal of the family but that provide formal compensation for this (e.g. Austria and Germany); and, finally, countries which allocate a comparatively large amount of resources to the formal care sector (e.g. the Nordic countries).

Thus, although there is no consensus as to which factors should be used to categorise care regimes, and some question whether we can in fact speak of distinctive welfare regimes (e.g. Kasza, 2002), there is some agreement that the Nordic countries have – comparatively speaking at least – a distinct care regime of their own. The notions of universalism and de-familialisation as well as the broad range of public care provisions that are available to large segments of the population are some of the characteristics of this care regime (Bettio and Plantenga, 2004). However, there are some (e.g. Rauch, 2007) who question whether Sweden does in fact qualify as an example of the Scandinavian care regime since there is no elderly care guarantee in this country and restrictive admission tests are actually widely used. Thus, although the Swedish elderly care regime was considered to be a fine example of the kind of egalitarian welfare services that developed in highly industrialised European societies after World War II, the period that started in the mid-1980s brought about dramatic changes in the generosity of the system that gave the Scandinavian care regime its reputation. Korpi (1995) argues that these changes were characterised not only by stagnation of the development of care for the elderly in this country but also by a decrease in the quality as well as the scope of this care regime. Blomberg *et al.* (2000) describe, in turn, the stagnation that has occurred in elderly care specifically as an example of the withdrawal of the welfare state.

Irrespective of whether or not the Swedish elderly care regime is a good example of the Scandinavian social service model, elderly care is – comparatively speaking at least – largely publicly funded in this country. The overall responsibility for care of the elderly in Sweden rests with the state and not with the family, as is the case in some European countries. However, in this regard it must be noted that this does not mean that older people in Sweden have all their care needs met by the state. As Sundström and Johansson (2005) have pointed out: 'informal care is the most common form of assistance that older people in Sweden receive; few rely solely on public services' (p. 8). All older people in Sweden who have permanent residency and are in need of help and support in activities of daily life can, however, apply for assistance from the elderly care sector. The decision on whether or not care services are made available to them is determined after completion of an individual needs assessment process, which is carried out by care managers. This is why Rauch (2007) refers to Sweden's admission tests when questioning the universality of this regime. It is worth noting that in contrast to needs assessment practices in the UK, which give the relatives of older people applying for services the opportunity to have their own needs assessed during this process, the needs assessment process in Sweden focuses only on the older person's needs. This presents challenges when dealing with older people who cannot verbalise their needs, as is often the case when one has immigrated late-in-life, comes from a culture that differs greatly from the Swedish culture, and has not mastered the Swedish language yet (Forssell *et al.*, 2015).

The work of care managers in Sweden is guided by legislation but also by organisational and municipal prerequisites (Dunér and Nordström, 2006). The legal foundations for needs assessment are found in the Social Services Act (SFS no. 2001: 453), which is a framework legislation that emphasises the right of the individual to receive municipal services. This legislation does not specify exactly what this right entails, which is why Rauch (2007) has argued that 'though on a rhetorical level the Swedish Social Services Act (SoL) contains an individual service right, in reality elderly care guarantee is absent' (p. 260). The legislation states that care for older people should be aimed at promoting a life with dignity and a feeling of well-being, but it is up to local municipalities to decide how resources are to be allocated. The legislation also clearly states that only those individuals whose needs cannot be met in any other way can access services, which is why access to elderly care in Sweden is a strongly conditioned right. The discretionary power that care managers in Sweden have has been shown to be particularly challenging when assessing the needs of older people with immigrant backgrounds who express needs that the sector does not always recognise as reasonable (Forssell *et al.*, 2015) and/or have expectations that are not always deemed appropriate (Forssell *et al.*, 2014). This is one of the reasons why welfare scholars question whether Sweden's elderly care regime is in fact as egalitarian and universalistic as its reputation. Research shows that the 'differences in what people are provided with are connected with differences in ethnic background, social class, gender, and the community in which a person resides' (Blomberg *et al.*, 2000, p. 162). Treating Sweden's elderly care regime as a prime example of the Scandinavian social care model or the Nordic elderly care regime is therefore problematic these days.

The Swedish migration regime

Hammar (1985) defines immigrant policy as 'the conditions provided to resident immigrants' (p. 9), while immigration policy regulates who gets to migrate to a country (i.e. the entry categories that a country's immigration policy relies on) and how non-citizens are to be controlled. The conditions that determine whether immigrants are included or excluded from the society that hosts them are often regarded as a country's immigration policy regime (Faist, 1995). A combined look at Sweden's welfare regime and immigration regime shows that although the social democratic regime that characterises this country's welfare regime accords rights on the basis of citizenship, the immigration policy regime is actually far more inclusive since Swedish immigrant policy accords rights on the basis of residence (*ius domicilii*) (Sainsbury, 2006). This is why Sweden is often regarded as 'the model of a tolerant and egalitarian multicultural welfare society, a kind of exceptionalist model for others to follow' (Schierup and Ålund, 2011, p. 47).

Understanding how this situation has arisen requires that we consider how Sweden's immigrant policy has evolved through the years. The first facet of Sweden's migration regime (between 1930 and 1963) was a period when immigration to Sweden exceeded migration from the country, but no immigration policy per se existed (Widgren, 1982). However, immigrant policies began to take shape by the mid-1960s when a variety of efforts to 'incorporate immigrants in a civil community where they could claim individual rights' (Dahlström, 2004, p. 301) was launched.[1] It is perhaps because of the de facto policy implementation despite a lack of formulated policy that the late 1960s and early 1970s were characterised by an intense public debate in the Swedish daily press about the pros and cons of formulating policies for a mixed culture society (*blandkultursamhälle*) or a multicultural society (*flerkultursamhälle*). The advocates of mixed culture argued that the state should neither support the cultural activities of immigrants nor should it force them to assimilate culturally. Instead, immigrants and Swedes should influence one another reciprocally, and the adjustments needed as Sweden's diversity increased should happen voluntarily. The advocates of multiculturalism argued instead that the mixed cultural approach was actually an assimilationist approach in disguise. The state should not make immigrants abandon their cultural identities. It should instead help ethnic communities to prosper.

The second facet of Sweden's immigrant policy comprised the period that ended in 1974–1975 (Widgren, 1982), a period that was characterised by intense public debate but few political stands. It is worth noting perhaps that while public debates were taking place, the government sent a bill to parliament which included the basic design of Sweden's immigrant policy (Dahlström, 2004). Thus, although the debate was actually never settled, assimilationist practices became the adaptation mode in Sweden during the period that ended in the mid-1970s since the Minister of Interior – who formulated most of the policies[2] at that point in time – was an advocate of the mixed culture society. This means that the first two facets of Sweden's immigrant policy were characterised by ambivalence as far as rhetoric was concerned but resolution when it came to practice.

The third facet of immigrant policy was introduced in 1975 when Sweden declared its intention to become a multicultural society and decided that future immigrant and minority policy-making would strive for *equality, freedom of choice* and *partnership*. Equality meant that immigrants were to be guaranteed the same rights, opportunities and obligations enjoyed by native Swedes. The goal of freedom of choice implied that immigrants should have the freedom to decide the degree to which they assimilated, meaning that they were free to choose between preserving their ethnic identity or acquiring Swedish values and traditions. The goal of partnership referred to the expectation and commitment to solidarity and tolerance between Swedes and immigrants. It is worth mentioning that these goals were heavily criticised because they were believed to give rise to unrealistic expectations and did not clearly stipulate the laws and rules of conduct that were characteristic of Swedish society. Thus, a new period of intensive committee- and survey work started once the three goals in question were spelled out. A new bill was passed, for example, which stated that the freedom of choice goal was to be limited by the fundamental norms of Swedish society. In addition, a distinction was made between immigrant policy and minority policy – a distinction that had until then never been made. These and other adjustments meant that that the culture-preserving ambitions of immigrant policies were lowered considerably during this period even though the practices of immigrant policy remained consistently the same (Dahlström, 2004).

The fourth facet of Sweden's immigrant policy was introduced in the late 1990s when new objectives were formulated. Most immigrant policy practices at that point in time had been criticised for stigmatising immigrants and for maintaining the 'us' and 'them' division that characterised Sweden's society (Pred, 1997). Thus, in the late 1990s Sweden's immigrant policy became an integration policy. This meant that immigrants were not to be singled out as beneficiaries of selective programs but were instead meant to be incorporated in the system of universal policies that characterises Sweden's welfare state. A look at the practices of immigrant policy shows, however, that this has not really happened. Sweden continues to operate its immigrant policy in two different ways. Rhetorically speaking, Sweden's immigrant policy has, in other words, undergone numerous transformations over the past four decades. In practice, however, the policies have been very stable (Dahlström, 2004). This is perhaps why Hammar (1999) has asserted that Sweden's immigrant policy has been shaped in a relatively apolitical way. All ministers responsible for immigrant policy have, for example, supported the idea of integration, irrespective of the political party they have been affiliated with. Dahlström (2004) has argued therefore that Sweden's immigrant policy has never had to adapt to either intra-party or voter opinion; a fact that is slowly but surely changing now that the Sweden Democrats – a political party that is clearly anti-immigration and anti-immigrants – have entered the Swedish parliament and have begun to force other parties to take a stand against the generous policies that have been a trademark of Sweden's migration regime over the past few decades.

In short, although the adaptation mode of most facets of Swedish immigrant policy has been integration, and numerous pluralist policies have characterised Sweden's immigrant policy landscape, most Swedish scholars agree that Sweden has not succeeded in becoming a multicultural society in the true sense of the word. The cultural pluralist vision that Sweden prides itself on striving after is currently only affordable in the private spheres of life. Sweden's migration regime seems, in other words, extremely egalitarian and tolerant at first sight because it awards its immigrants numerous social rights; has an encompassing definition of refugees and equal treatment of convention refugees and persons granted asylum for humanitarian reasons; has generous rules for family reunification; offers foreign workers equal access to unemployment and occupational injury benefits at an early date; and offers its immigrants national health insurance, child and housing allowances and social assistance after a short period of residence. Despite this, there is palpable segregation between Sweden's native and immigrant populations (Andersson, 1999). Migration scholars have therefore argued that the Swedish migration regime is filled with

> contradictions between the political rhetoric and an actually existing multiculturalism transformed, through corporatist institutional practices, into a bureaucratically managed 'tower of Babel': a nested hierarchy of ethnonationally defined social collectivities that were monitored and depoliticised through a generous system of public support (but with many conditions attached) to 'migrant organisations', all inserted into a discriminatory and ethnically divided labour force.
>
> (Schierup and Ålund, 2011, p. 48)

Statistics on foreign-born: demographics of relevance to the elderly care sector

In order to contextualise the backdrop that the previous sections have offered, it seems necessary to draw attention to demographics. The proportion of the Swedish population (which totals 9,644,864) that was born in another country was 16 per cent in 2013, while the proportion of older people (65+) in the population at the end of 2012 was 19.4 per cent (Statistics Sweden, 2013). The proportion of foreign-born inhabitants over 65 at the end of 2011 was 11.7 per cent (Statistics Sweden, 2012a). It is worth noting that about half of the foreign-born older population was born in one of the Nordic countries. Nearly one-third of all older foreign-born persons come originally from Finland. Most foreign-born older persons in Sweden have lived a long time in this country and many immigrated before the age of 35 (Statistics Sweden 2012b). Unfortunately, despite the numerous reports written about (and statistics available on) elderly care in Sweden, there is very little information about older foreign-born people.

The situation of elderly care providers with foreign-born background is also not that well-documented, even though the ethnic diversity among staff in the elderly care sector has increased gradually over the past decade. In one of the latest reports on elderly care published by the Swedish Association of Local Authorities and Regions it is stated that the proportion of foreign-born individuals that are employed in the area of elderly care and care for the disabled has increased during the past ten-year period, from 10 per cent to 14 per cent in 2008. The report in question also points out that it was the number of staff born outside the Nordic region and the EU that increased (Swedish Association of Local Authorities and Regions, 2009). The elderly care sector is often the sector believed to have attracted most care workers with these backgrounds. Thus Sweden's elderly care sector is characterised by increasing diversity as far as elderly care recipients and providers are concerned.

The debate and reality of immigrants within the Swedish elderly care sector

Presenting research on the reality of immigrants within the Swedish elderly care sector is not an easy task since there is more research on the debates surrounding immigrants than on their actual situation. This is a little surprising considering that the elderly care sector in Sweden first noted the increasing diversity of its older population in the 1980s when the National Board of Health and Welfare published two reports (see Sachs, 1980; Zetzell, 1980) that drew attention to the number of older people with immigrant backgrounds, and the elderly care sector was urged to take into account that 'ageing in a foreign land' (as one of the reports was entitled) presented numerous challenges. Since then the number of Swedish articles, chapters and reports on older immigrants has steadily grown, even though a representative study on this group of older people has yet to be conducted.

One reason for the growth in the number of publications may be the fascination with 'difference' that is characteristic of the way in which Sweden regards its immigrant population (Koobak and Thapar-Björkert, 2012; Schierup and Ålund, 1991). Thus, when one casts a critical glance at the way in which older immigrants have been talked about in the Swedish elderly care debate (Torres, 2006) as well as the way in which the daily press has written about them over the years (Lindblom and Torres, 2011; Torres *et al.*, 2014), one clearly sees that the rhetoric used makes perfect sense against the backdrop that is Sweden's migration regime. As suggested in the previous section, at the very core of this country's immigrant policy is the idea that immigrants are fundamentally different from Swedes and have 'special needs' that ought to be addressed by the welfare state. The fact that the debates on older immigrants in Sweden have focused on their 'Otherness' is therefore understandable, especially if one takes into account that 'an essentialising and stereotyping *culturalism*, explaining and devising cures to all social problems in terms of "culture" (is at the very core of most) discriminatory institutional practices in Sweden' (Schierup and Ålund, 2011, p. 48; see also Schierup and Ålund, 1991).

With the exception of some of the studies on older Finns conducted in the 1990s (e.g. Leiniö, 1984) and the studies that have been conducted in order to compare the health of older immigrants to the health of the native population (e.g. Solé-Auró and Crimmins, 2008), most of the empirical research on older immigrants in Sweden is based on ethnicity-specific small qualitative studies that have used convenience samples and have often focused on the group that is actually the minority within the category of older migrants on which the debate focuses, i.e. late-in-life immigrants. This means that most research on older immigrants in Sweden is based on samples that are neither representative of the ethnic groups they are based on nor of the larger older immigrant population that most of them claim to be about. This has been problematised on numerous occasions (e.g. Ronström, 2002; Torres, 2006, 2013) since the lack of evidence-based understanding of the situation and needs of older immigrants means that the

Swedish elderly care sector is operating on the basis of stereotypical ideas about who they are and what their needs may be. The fact that the debate in question is often carried on without taking into account that ageing in a country as an immigrant and migrating in old age are two different things also means that the debate is seldom nuanced enough to take into account the variation that is bound to exist in the backgrounds and present situation of older immigrants.

Against this backdrop it is perhaps understandable that some Swedish scholars have argued that it is not uncommon for elderly care planners and providers to regard older immigrants in homogenising ways and to focus on what differentiates them from their Swedish counterparts (i.e. their non-Swedishness or 'Otherness') (e.g. Lill, 2002; Ronström, 2002). However, recently conducted research on the way in which care managers in Sweden regard cross-cultural needs assessment meetings has shown that some of them are aware of the different types of older immigrants there are and regard those who have come late-in-life from countries that are culturally different and who have not mastered the Swedish language as the ones that present the greatest challenges as far as needs assessment practice is concerned (Forssell *et al.*, 2015). There seems therefore to be some awareness amongst elderly care providers that the way in which the debate has been carried on so far is not nuanced enough to capture the reasons behind the challenges that increased ethnic and cultural diversity present to the deliverance of high-quality and user-friendly elderly care.

In contrast to the understandings of older migrants that have permeated the debates about them in this country, we have the understandings of elderly care providers with immigrant backgrounds. They tend to be regarded as assets to the Swedish elderly care sector (Lindblom and Torres, 2011; Torres *et al.*, 2014) since they are believed to be particularly skilful at caring, are expected to be able to provide culture-appropriate care without training, and are regarded as people that are innately patient with and respectful of older people. These taken-for-granted assumptions about them have been found to present challenges when they relate to their Swedish counterparts while working in nursing homes (Torres, 2010). This is why it is possible to say that the Swedish elderly care sector is becoming ethnically differentiated. Against this backdrop it is perhaps understandable that in a recently completed study on the experiences of foreign-born care workers employed within this sector it is stated that although the situation of foreign-born care workers from other Nordic countries is similar to that of Swedish-born care workers, 'being born outside the Nordic countries was associated with an increased risk of having a high work load and not being appreciated by co-workers' (Jönson and Giertz, 2013, p. 809).

In conclusion it is noted that the debate and situation of immigrants within the Swedish elderly care sector indicates that interesting gaps exist in the knowledge that is available about them. Thus, although we are dealing with a very well-developed elderly care sector which used to be regarded as an exemplary model of welfare exceptionalism, there is surprisingly little knowledge about the backgrounds, present situation and the consumption of elderly care amongst older immigrants in this country. The same is also noted of elderly care providers with immigrant backgrounds. The fact that research shows that immigrants are regarded by the sector as 'Others' but in different ways is also interesting to note. Older immigrants, for example, are regarded as 'Others' because they are assumed to have 'special needs' and pose a challenge to the sector. Care workers with immigrant backgrounds, on the other hand, are regarded as 'Others' because they are assumed to have innate 'caring skills' which make them attractive to the sector. This paradoxical way of regarding immigrants (cf. Forssell and Torres, 2012) is understandable considering the ambivalent view of immigrants that has characterised Sweden's attitudes to non-natives since this country became a de facto country of immigration.

In this respect it seems relevant to draw attention to Narayan (1995, p. 136) who has argued that

> while aspects of care discourse have the potential virtue of calling attention to vulnerabilities that mark relationships between differently situated persons, care discourse also runs the risk of being used to ideological ends where these 'differences' are defined in self-serving ways by the dominant and the powerful.

The discrepancies between the debates on immigrants in the Swedish elderly care sector and the realities surrounding their situation suggest that what happens at the intersection of the migration regime and the elderly care regime of this country casts doubts on Sweden's assumed exceptionalism in various ways and raises numerous questions about the discrepancy between political ambition and everyday realities.

Notes

1 Among them are: free language training, information about society and its political institutions in different languages, supplementary language training for immigrant children, programmes to support the activities of different ethnic and religious groups, support for culture and training in immigrants' native languages and the publishing of non-Swedish newspapers and journals (a support that started a decade later but which stems from the same idea; namely that immigrant groups need to be supported by selective programmes if they are to adjust successfully to Swedish society).
2 Such as the establishment of immigrants' rights to interpreter and translator services when dealing with municipalities if they did not speak the Swedish language – a set of services which started in the early 1970s – and the 'native language reform' of 1977 which obliged municipalities to offer training in native languages to immigrant children from pre-school to secondary school.

References

Andersson, R. (1999). 'Divided cities' as a policy-based notion in Sweden. *Housing Studies*, *14*, 601–624. doi:10.1080/02673039982632.
Anttonen, A. and Sipilä, J. (1996). European social care services: is it possible to identify models? *Journal of European Social Policy*, *6*, 87–100. doi:10.1177/0958928796006 00201.

24   *S. Torres*

Bettio, F. and Plantenga, J. (2004). Comparing care regimes in Europe. *Feminist Economics, 10(1)*, 85–113. doi:10.1080/1354570042000198245.

Blomberg, S., Edebalk, P. G. and Petersson, J. (2000). The withdrawal of the welfare state: elderly care in Sweden in the 1990s. *European Journal of Social Work, 3*, 151–163. doi:10.1080/714052821.

Dahlström, C. (2004). Rhetoric, practice and the dynamics of institutional change: immigrant policy in Sweden, 1964–2000. *Scandinavian Political Studies, 27*, 287–310. doi:10.1111/j.1467–9477.2004.00107.x.

Dunér, A. and Nordström, M. (2006). The discretion and power of street-level bureaucrats: an example from Swedish municipal eldercare. *European Journal of Social Work, 9*, 425–444. doi:10.1080/13691450600958486.

Esping-Andersen, G. (1990). *The Three Worlds of Welfare Capitalism*. Cambridge: Polity Press.

Faist, T. (1995). Ethnicization and racialization of welfare-state politics in Germany and the USA. *Ethnic and Racial Studies, 18*, 219–250. doi:10.1080/01419870.1995.9993862.

Forssell, E. and Torres, S. (2012). Social work, older people and migration: an overview of the situation in Sweden. *European Journal of Social Work, 15*, 115–130. doi:10.108 0/13691457.2011.573911.

Forssell, E., Torres, S. and Olaison, A. (2014). Anhörigomsorg mot betalning: Biståndshandläggare om sent-i-livet-invandrares önskemål [Cash for care: care managers on late-in-life immigrants' requests]. *Socialvetenskaplig Tidskrift, 21*, 114–137. Retrieved from http://svt.forsa.nu/Artiklar-SocialVetenskaplig-Tidskrift.aspx.

Forssell, E., Torres, S. and Olaison, A. (2015). Care managers' experiences of cross-cultural needs assessment meetings: the case of late-in-life immigrants. *Ageing & Society, 35*, 576–601. doi:10.1017/S0144686X13000901.

Hammar, T. (ed.) (1985). *European Immigration Policy: A Comparative Study*. Cambridge: Cambridge University Press.

Hammar, T. (1999). Closing the doors to the Swedish welfare state. In G. Brochmann and T. Hammar (eds), *Mechanisms of Immigration Control: A Comparative Analysis of European Regulation Policies* (pp. 169–201). Oxford: Berg.

Jönson, H. and Giertz, A. (2013). Migrant care workers in Swedish elderly and disability care: are they disadvantaged? *Journal of Ethnic and Migration Studies, 39*, 809–825. doi:10.1080/1369183X.2013.756686.

Kasza, G. J. (2002). The illusion of welfare 'regimes'. *Journal of Social Policy, 31*, 271–287. doi:10.1017/S0047279401006584.

Kilkey, M., Lutz, H. and Palenga-Möllenbeck, E. (2010). Introduction. Domestic and care work at the intersection of welfare, gender and migration regimes: some European experiences. *Social Policy and Society, 9*, 379–384. doi:10.1017/S1474746410000096.

Koobak, R. and Thapar-Björkert, S. (2012). Becoming no-Swedish: locating the paradoxes of in/visible identities. *Feminist Review, 102*, 125–134. doi:10.1057/ fr.2012.14.

Korpi, W. (1995). The position of the elderly in the welfare state: comparative perspectives on old-age care in Sweden. *Social Service Review, 69*, 242–273. Retrieved from www.jstor.org/stable/30012851.

Leiniö, T.-L. (1984). *Inte lika men jämlika? Om finländska invandrares levnadsförhållanden enligt levnadsnivå-undersökningarna 1968, 1974 och 1981 [Not the Same but Equal? On Finnish Immigrants' Living Conditions According to the Living Standards' Studies of 1968, 1974 and 1981]*. Stockholm: Institutet för social forskning, Stockholms Universitet.

Lill, L. (2002). Hemvårdsinspektörers möte med äldre invandrare [Home inspectors meet older immigrants]. In F. Magnússon (ed.), *Etniska relationer i vård och omsorg* (pp. 85–106). Lund: Studentlitteratur.

Lindblom, J. and Torres, S. (2011). Etnicitets- och migrationsrelaterade frågor inom äldreomsorgen: en analys av SvD:s rapportering mellan 1995–2008 [Ethnicity and migration-related issues in elderly care: an analysis of articles published 1995–2008 in a Swedish daily newspaper]. *Socialvetenskaplig Tidskrift, 18*, 222–243. Retrieved from http://svt.forsa.nu/Artiklar-SocialVetenskaplig-Tidskrift.aspx.

Narayan, U. (1995). Colonialism and its Others: considerations on rights and care discourses. *Hypatia, 10(2)*, 133–140. doi:10.1111/j.1527–2001.1995.tb01375.x.

Pfau-Effinger, B. (2005). Welfare state policies and the development of care arrangements. *European Societies, 7*, 321–347. doi:10.1080/14616690500083592.

Pred, A. (1997). Somebody else, somewhere else: racisms, racialized spaces and the popular geographical imagination in Sweden. *Antipode, 29*, 383–416. doi:10.1111/1467–8330.00053.

Rauch, D. (2007). Is there really a Scandinavian social service model? A comparison of childcare and elderly care in six European countries. *Acta Sociologica, 50*, 249–269. doi:10.1177/0001699307080931.

Ronström, O. (2002). The making of older immigrants in Sweden: identification, categorization and discrimination. In L. Andersson (ed.), *Cultural Gerontology* (pp. 129–138). Westport, CT: Auburn House.

Sachs, L. (1980). Gamla invandrare i Sverige: en probleminventering [Old Immigrants in Sweden: An Inventory of Problems]. Stockholm: Socialstyrelsens Äldreomsorgsprogrammet, rapport 6.

Sainsbury, D. (2006). Immigrants' social rights in comparative perspective: welfare regimes, forms of immigration and immigration policy regimes. *Journal of European Social Policy, 16*, 229–244. doi:10.1177/0958928706065594.

Schierup, C.-U. and Ålund, A. (1991). *Paradoxes of Multiculturalism: Essays on Swedish Society.* Aldershot, UK and Brookfield, USA: Avebury.

Schierup, C.-U. and Ålund, A. (2011). The end of Swedish exceptionalism? Citizenship, neoliberalism and the politics of exclusion. *Race & Class, 53(1)*, 45–64. doi:10.1177/0306396811406780.

Social Services Act, SFS no. 2001:453. Socialtjänstelag (Swedish Code of Statutes). Retrieved from: www.notisum.se/Rnp/sls/lag/20010453.htm.

Solé-Auró A. and Crimmins E. M. (2008). Health of immigrants in European countries. *International Migration Review, 42*, 861–876. doi:10.1111/j.1747–7379.2008.00150.x.

Statistics Sweden. (2012a). *Population Statistics.* Retrieved from www.scb.se.

Statistics Sweden. (2012b). *Integration: utrikesfödda i pensionsåldern* [Integration: foreign-born persons at retirement age] (Integration Rapport 5). Retrieved from: www.scb.se/statistik/_publikationer/LE0105_2012A01_BR_BE57BR1201.pdf.

Statistics Sweden. (2013). *Population Statistics.* Retrieved from www.scb.se.

Sundström, G. and Johansson, L. (2005). The changing balance of government and family in care for the elderly in Sweden and other European countries. *Australasian Journal on Ageing, 24(s1)*, 5–11. doi:10.1111/j.1741–6612.2005.00100.x.

Swedish Association of Local Authorities and Regions (2009). *Developments in Elderly Policy in Sweden.* Stockholm.

Torres, S. (2006). Elderly immigrants in Sweden: 'Otherness' under construction. *Journal of Ethnic and Migration Studies, 32*, 1341–1358. doi:10.1080/13691830600928730.

Torres, S. (2010). Invandrarskap och tvärkulturella äldreomsorgsmöten [Ethnic 'Otherness' and cross-cultural interaction in elderly care]. In S. Johansson (ed.), *Omsorg och mång-fald* (pp. 67–88). Malmö: Gleerups.

Torres, S. (2013). Healthy aging among immigrants in Sweden: what we know and need to find out. In A. E. Scharlach and K. Hoshino (eds), *Healthy Aging in Sociocultural Context* (pp. 42–50). New York: Routledge.

Torres, S., Lindblom, J. and Nordberg, C. (2014). Daily newspaper reporting on elderly care in Sweden and Finland: a quantitative content analysis of ethnicity- and migration-related issues. *Vulnerable Groups and Inclusion, 5*, doi:http://dx.doi.org/10.3402/vgi.v5.21260.

Tronto, J. C. (2010). Creating caring institutions: politics, plurality and purpose. *Ethics and Social Welfare, 4*, 158–171. doi:10.1080/17496535.2010.484259.

Widgren, J. (1982). *Svensk invandrarpolitik* [Swedish Immigrant Policy]. Lund: Liber Läromedel.

Zetzell, I. (1980) *Äldre invandrare: en bakgrund* [Elderly Immigrants: A Background]. Stockholm: Socialstyrelsen: Äldreomsorgsprogrammet rapport 5.

2 The elderly care regime and migration regime after the EU accession

The case of Poland

Jolanta Perek-Białas and Krystyna Slany

Introduction

Due to its political system, Poland was in the past (till 1989) a rather closed country. Thereafter, however, following the beginning of transformation, and later upon becoming a member of the European Union in 2004 and of the Schengen Area in 2007, Poland entered a new phase in the history of migration. In practice this paved the way for a major increase in mobility within the EU countries; not only do Poles migrate from Poland, but foreigners also migrate to Poland. Poland's geographical location also led to the country becoming the eastern border to the European Union. As a result, once migrants have crossed the Polish border, they have the easy option to travel to Western Europe. However, the acceleration of population ageing will involve depopulation of the country (GUS (Główny Urząd Statystyczny), 2009). Moreover, post-accession emigration (after 2004 and especially of young people) will be of a settlement-related kind, and in the near future will result in a 'generation gap' involving individuals born in the 1970s and 1980s (White, 2011). It will also lead to a permanent decrease in the size of the coming generations and an ageing population. The contemporary migration of Poles will, in turn, have far-reaching consequences in the field of population-related processes, and even if a given share of migrants does come back to the country in the future, the European Union enlargement will always be reflected in Poland's population age structure (Lesińska *et al.*, 2014).

This chapter will present the unique Polish situation as far as migration, ageing and elderly care are concerned. One of the special features of the Polish case is that, on the one hand, we have the modernisation character of the changes (which has been noticeable in the transformation of family and its ties, being in the past a guarantee of stabilisation and security), while, on the other hand, we have the great mobility that came with entry to the EU which has created many chances for Poles to be part of the European labour market. Thus, the migration of (mostly young) Poles and their families has substantially changed the situation as far as migration, ageing and elderly care are concerned since it has modified social expectations in relation to elderly care and also in terms of the options that people have as far as reliance on family members for care is concerned. The chapter comprises an introduction and a presentation of the demographic situation in Poland with a focus on migration and ageing. Later, we discuss the relationship between migration and the impact this phenomenon has on the elderly care regime in Poland. We will also discuss the Polish migrants that have left the country (as well as their ageing parents and relatives), and the new challenges that this poses against the emerging literature on transnationalism and care. The chapter concludes with policy recommendations.

Demographic context: ageing and migration

In 2011 Poland's population amounted to more than 38 million inhabitants of whom about 13.6 per cent were people over 65 years of age. An increase in the percentage of older people in the total population is expected (up to 23 per cent of people aged 65+ in 2035) which is why the topic discussed here is timely (GUS Baza Demografia, 2014). The demographic change is a result of a low fertility rate (TFR 1.3) and increased life expectancy (for men –72 and for women –81).[1] As already suggested, migration (especially migration out of Poland) will have a crucial impact on how we think of population ageing in Poland (Okólski, 2012). According to Eurostat data (Eurostat Database, 2013), the old age dependency ratio (population 65 and over compared to population 15 to 64 years old) for Poland is still lower than for the EU-27 overall. In 2011, it was 18.9 for Poland, whereas for the EU-27 it was 26.2, but according to projections by around 2050 the indicator will be higher for Poland – reaching 53 – than for the EU-27 – which is expected to be 50. The overall population size will be about 35.993 million in 2035 based on projections of the Central Statistical Office (GUS, 2009). Projections based on data before the National Census from 2011 show that the population structure will change further as there will be around 4.5 million people below 15 years old, about 23 million aged 15–64 and about 8.35 million people aged 65+ by 2035 (GUS Baza Demografia, 2014). Furthermore, based on the results of the last National Census from 2011, in May 2011 about 2.017 million permanent inhabitants of Poland were abroad for a temporary period (for more than three months) (GUS, 2013). If emigrants and their children do not come back to Poland, the effect will be even stronger. On 1 April 2011, about 1.565 million permanent inhabitants of Poland were temporarily abroad for at least one year (Fihel and Solga, 2014). These results could be compared with data from the Labour Force Surveys and National Census from 2002, where in between estimations it was shown that in the 2004–2010 period there were about one million emigrants (in 2004), whereas there were around 2.270 million in the peak year, 2007 (Fihel and Solga, 2014). Taking into account the period of migration, a trend of feminisation of migration from Poland could be noticed. Women migrate more often (about 52 per cent) than men (see Figure 2.1), although today the difference between migrating men and women is smaller than it was in 2002 (about 2 per cent less).

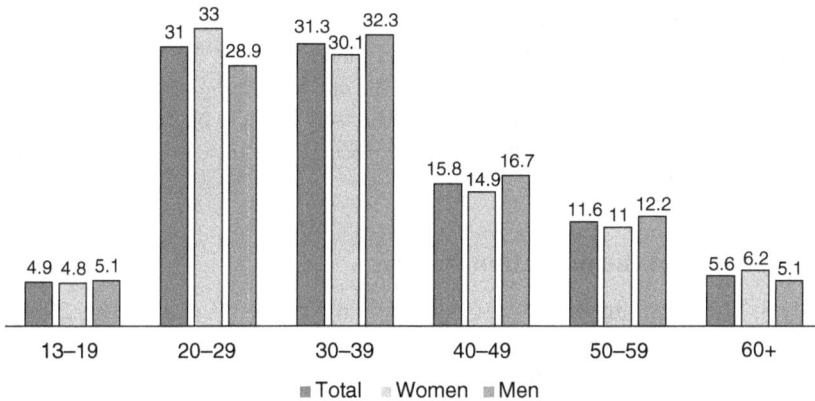

Figure 2.1 Poland: Structure of Polish migrants based on data from National Census of Population and Housing of 2011 (source: Own calculation and preparation of the graph based on data from www.stat.gov.pl/gus/5840_14242_PLK_HTML. htm, accessed 23 August 2013).

The main feature of migration is the mobility of women from rural areas; in 2002 this had increased by about 107 per cent compared to 1988 (GUS, 2010a). Based on the last National Census of Population from 2011 (GUS, 2013), more often young people age 20–39 migrate (about 62 per cent), but women age 60+ also decide to leave the country to find work, including in other countries' care sectors. Available data further shows that the majority of migrants from Poland have at least secondary education (67 per cent), and a substantial group of them have jobs below their skills obtained in the education systems in their country of origin (brain waste). It should be noted that international mobility is also undertaken by poorly educated individuals and older individuals (females), who represent a relatively large group in Polish society (about 33 per cent).

The exact number of immigrants in Poland is difficult to estimate owing to outdated and incomplete statistics, for example not including illegal immigration. According to the Central Statistical Office (GUS, 2013) in 2011, there were about 55,400 people with non-Polish passports, an additional 2,000 without nationality identification and 8,800 with no recognised citizenship, giving a total of 66,200 without Polish citizenship. The Central Statistical Office found that there were 40,100 migrants in Poland temporarily, for more than three months in 2011. They came from Ukraine (7,000), Germany (3,900), the UK (2,200), Belarus (1,800), Russia (1,300), Armenia (1,100), China (1,100) and Bulgaria (1,000) (GUS, 2013). Data from the National Census showed further that in 2011 there were about 56,300 foreigners, including 40,097 staying more than three months and about 12,000 more than one year (GUS, 2013). However, there is also data showing that in Poland there are about 97,000 migrants, albeit many of them not registered (Cianciara *et al.*, 2012).

The rapid population ageing in Poland and the sharp increase in people aged 85+ creates a serious challenge for elderly care, especially in the context of migration of the young generations from Poland. This is best illustrated by looking at the potential support ratio (population 15–64/population 65+), which in 2011 in Poland equalled 5.1 and in 2030 will be 2.7. Moreover, the care potential ratio (population 50–64/population 85+) was 14.8 in 2011, while in 2030 it will be 9.8.

Elderly care and the migration regime

Family is the most important care provider in Poland (Czekanowski, 2006). Polish society's strong expectations to care for older dependent parents and relatives stem from traditions, religion (Catholic) and values, as it is considered natural for children to care for their parents and grandparents as they age (Eurobarometer, 2007; Drożdżak *et al.*, 2013; Perek-Białas and Racław, 2014). The majority of care is provided by daughters looking after their parents. Often, wives or husbands become the first caregiver to elderly people in need of care (Bojanowska, 2008). However, the organisation of elderly care is also dependent upon the social policy model or welfare/elderly care regime as gerontologists often refer to it – a regime that changed after 1989 (Łuczak, 2013). In the communist era, the State was responsible for securing just the basic needs. Concerning elderly care, the family was left with that duty as it was treated as a social norm due to the fact that children who inherited the wealth of their parents were responsible for caring for dependent parents. Poland's welfare regime is currently described as being more hybrid, and less redistributive and collective than neoliberal and individualistic models of welfare tend to be (Księżopolski, 2013). This means that citizens have become more and more responsible for securing care for their relatives. Even if there are more options for care arrangements (including private care in care homes and also at migrants' own homes), the cost of care is relatively high, and many are unable to afford these options. Moreover, some services (like daily care centres) are not widely available, especially in rural areas.

Thus the Polish family is also changing. The country follows the same demographic trends (such as decreased fertility, postponing the first marriage, postponing the decision about having the first child or fewer children, couples' instability) as previously noticed in Western European countries and explained in the second demographic transition theory (van de Kaa, 1988; Kotowska, 1999; Slany, 2002). As a result there are and will be less children who could (and would) care for their ageing parents. Motivation for family members to undertake caring duties depends on family ties, relations and the possibilities that people have to reconcile work and care responsibilities (Stypińska and Perek-Białas, 2014), as well as on a lack of jobs, which can motivate people to undertake informal family elderly care and as a result lead to inactivity in the labour market. To this end we must add that the younger generation of women (aged up to 30) are also more economically active than previous generations and may therefore be less willing to take on caring responsibilities for the elderly (Titkow *et al.*, 2004; Kotowska, 2009; Perek-Białas and Racław, 2014).

Perek-Białas and Racław (2014) claim that parallel to this decrease in the number of family members willing and able to care for older persons, the importance of paid care work is growing (cf. Racław, 2011). Already some wealthy families purchase care through officially registered private companies, while others employ informal carers in the 'shadow economy' (including migrants), without paying social security taxes and insurance. Currently, it is difficult to estimate how many Polish families are solving the care challenges in their everyday life in this way due to insufficient data about these phenomena (GUS, 2010b).

Migration regime

Even though Poland is still a country of net emigration, an increasing number of immigrants has already been observed. In fact, 1989 is treated as a turning point in the history of migration movement to and from Poland because of the transformation and changes in the political system that took place then as well as the consequences that the opening of the borders entailed. It was namely then that Poland became not only a sending country but also a receiving one, as well as a transit country for migrants aiming to enter Western Europe. After 1989, repatriates from the Polish diaspora in the former Soviet Union republics started to come back to Poland, including migrants aiming to settle in the country for economic reasons (Grzymała-Kazłowska and Łodziński, 2008; Łodziński and Nowicka, 1998).

At the beginning of the 1990s, Poland was not prepared for accepting an inflow of migrants, as it had had little experience with this phenomenon and lacked adequate laws to regulate issues of migration (MSW (Ministerstwo Spraw Wewnętrznych), 2012). At that time there was not enough interest in migration policy, and little public discourse on it. Something else worth noting is that Poland's migration policy was and still is dependent on the European perspective on this phenomenon. This means that Poland's migration regime was originally primarily dictated by the negotiations of Polish membership in the Schengen Area and European Union, and the protection of the eastern border that these entailed. This meant that the questions of whether Poland needed migrants, how they found themselves in the labour market and how they should be integrated were questions that did not seem relevant to the Polish case at that time (Slany, 2008). Many female migrants are, however, working nowadays in jobs in the agricultural and service sectors. The services performed by migrants are related to housing services (like cleaning) and caring, including elderly care (Slany *et al.*, 2010). Their migration and their involvement in this part of the Polish labour market is not that regulated and since there is a lack of services, and thus a lack of professionals in some sectors of the economy, female migrants fill these gaps. In some services there is a great demand for migrant work. This is especially the case in the care sector.

It is difficult to analyse not only migration in and by itself, but also the consequences that this phenomenon has as far as population ageing is concerned (this is the case in the country receiving the migrants as well as in their country of origin). Each assessment of migration effects presented at the aggregate level (the national economy level) is vulnerable to simplifications and excessive generalisations (Lesińska *et al.*, 2014). This is one of the reasons why analyses such as the one we briefly provide here should not just address the national level, regional experiences have to be taken into account as well.[2]

Migrant care workers in Poland[3]

Some studies (mostly qualitative) have been carried out on labour migrants in Poland employed unofficially in the elderly care sector (Lasota, 2008; Krajewska, 2012). Most often it is female immigrants from Ukraine and Belarus who are employed in these jobs (Krajewska, 2012), as they are willing to work for less. On the other hand, Poles go to Western European countries to be employed in long-term care services (Szczygielska, 2013). Previous research suggests that there are many problems related to the elderly care jobs that are performed by migrants (Kindler and Napierała, 2010; Slany *et al.*, 2010). As there are no clear policy or regulations in Poland (Krajewska, 2012), migrants look for work through informal channels, which at once creates a situation in which the work that people perform becomes hidden since it is not officially registered. Further risks are associated with the fact that migrant care workers are overloaded with household chores and have no or little free time (if employed in-home), and are socially isolated. Even though they may be at risk of abuse if the people they care for make verbal and/or physical attacks, they are unlikely to quit their jobs because of the economic pressure to earn money to support their family left at home (Lasota, 2008; Krajewska, 2012). There is, in other words, some evidence already which indicates that Poland's migrant care workers face similar challenges to the ones that research on migrant care workers elsewhere have disclosed (see Iecovich's Chapter 11 in this book, for example).

Polish migrants in care sectors abroad

There is evidence to suggest that Polish women go abroad (León, 2014) to work in the long-term care sector and receive higher pay than they could get in Poland for similar work in the same sector. One of the studies conducted by Małek (2011) presents the work of migrants in various jobs, including the elderly care sector in Italy and argues that the perception of care is often idealised amongst Polish care workers. Many fail, for example, to understand that caring for frail and dependent older people requires difficult and constant physical (and emotional) contact between care provider and care recipient (Małek, 2011). The work that migrant care workers perform is therefore arduous and demanding (Lutz, 2011; Rosińska-Kordasiewicz, 2008). Similar findings have been found in the research carried out by Szczygielska (2013), who has conducted interviews with 22 female migrant workers who worked in Italy, Germany, France, US, Greece and Sweden, among whom were a few carers for elderly people. Here, however, it was found that there could be good relations between a foreign carer and a cared-for person and his/her families. But there were also cases where this job was treated as any other job and migrant carers were treated in a humiliating way, as servants.

In another project – not directly focusing on migrant care workers but on working caregivers, Carers@Work[4] – 58 interviews were conducted, among them 14 in Witnica and the surrounding areas. Witnica is a small town of 6,000 inhabitants located near the Polish-German border. In this project, we found carers who have double caring duties, i.e. people with caring responsibilities for their relatives in Poland (elderly parents) and in the elderly care sector in Germany (thus making them part of the elderly care system there). The analysis of these interviews clearly shows that the women, who undertake such cross-border work for financial reasons, tend to be those who also find it difficult to secure care for their own parents. Evidently, the lack of jobs in their place of residence has created an incentive to go to Germany to work. One of the women interviewed in this project said the following, for example:

As it is said, I would like to work in our village [Polish], but everything makes me look for the better job for myself, and for money and that's why I left the country. I started to go to Germany. Yes, only money convinced me to go. [...] So, I underline it once again, finances are the most important factor.

(R51, Carers@Work project)

This respondent managed to maintain a schedule whereby she worked four weeks in Germany caring for older people and then spent four weeks at home in order to take care of her parents. Additionally, in this interview it was possible to see something which could create an additional problem between these women's parents (who need support and care from time to time) and the work these women perform in Germany in order to make ends meet. The mother of this respondent is very much against the situation since it affects her relationship with her daughter:

Mother is very conscious that I am going out. It is true. She was crying today. [...] Mum because of just this split off, as I am leaving, she is conscious. Father not. Maybe he is not showing it, but mother very much.

(R51, Carers@Work project)

Thus the interviews in this project suggest we may have a possible future trend: that migrant care workers who also have their own parents who need care in Poland (a country that lacks effective organisation of elderly care services) will have to split their time between the 'informal' care sector in other countries (i.e. the care they perform for elderly abroad as migrant care workers) and informal caring responsibilities (i.e. the ones they need to perform for their own parents). Women who could care for their parents have to go abroad to care for other people's parents due to financial reasons. The caring that these women perform is, however, different from the care they provide to close family members (like parents). When family members' care needs intensify (and one's support networks are not available), these workers may be more than willing to come back to Poland immediately, leaving behind the elderly people they care for abroad.

Transnational care in migration families

We outlined earlier that migration from Poland has a substantial impact on the demographic situation of the country, but also on families and the role that family members (parents, grandparents) who stayed in the country play as far as care for older people is concerned. The question of who will take care of elderly parents when adult children (sometimes all) migrate, and public institutions remain inefficient in this field, is of key importance in terms of population ageing and migration. There are already studies on transnational care in migrating families including elderly parents in Poland (Krzyżowski and Mucha, 2014). In his studies, Krzyżowski (2013) for example, refers to the transnational perspective, which facilitates observations of numerous practices in terms of care for elderly parents. He found that three explanations should be given for the stereotypes about the care for elderly people in the context of adult children's migration. First, inter-generational transfers are not one-way, and they are not always necessary – parents equally often help their children working abroad, and not all older parents require intensive care. Second, the dynamics of obligations at various stages of a transnational family's life should be taken into account. And third, care obligations towards elderly parents (and methods of care and support delivery) are adjusted to the possibilities of migrating children (Krzyżowski, 2013). The studies indicate various meanings assigned to economic support, which is the most common form of assistance provided by migrants to their elderly parents. To migrants (females in particular), financial support represents compensation for the lack of their physical presence, assistance with maintaining personal hygiene of parents (mothers in particular) and practical help in housework at the parents' home in Poland.

Conclusion

It should be stressed that Poland before 1989 was a closed country where migration out of and into the country was not possible to the same extent as afterwards. As a result, there are comparatively fewer migrants from other countries in Poland than in other European countries. This is why this chapter has not focused on the ageing of migrants as chapters on ageing and migration tend to focus on. However, the role of migrants in Poland does have relevance to ageing since we have begun to see that they can and already contribute to a 'shadow economy' that is growing as far as the elderly care sector is concerned. Perek-Białas and Racław (2014) claim that although the family will remain the most important institution providing long-term care in Poland, the private sector will also gain an increased presence (Racław, 2011) as will migrants from other countries. This has already happened in some European countries (for the Italian case, see for example Drozdzak *et al.*, 2013 and Barbabella *et al.*'s Chapter 12 in this book). We deem this therefore plausible in the Polish case as well.

Discussions about ageing and elderly care in Poland cannot be isolated from contemporary migration dynamics (Slany *et al.*, 2014). Migration of Polish women to work as informal caregivers in other EU countries (Bettio *et al.*, 2006; relevant chapters in Léon, 2014) implies short-term deficits of family caregivers in Poland, which is only partially compensated by an inflow of migrants from poorer countries (like Ukraine and Belarus). However, it is difficult to obtain analysis from representative surveys on this topic, which is why just a few cases from qualitative research were outlined here. For more results it is worth recalling the output of the FeMiPol project (Slany *et al.*, 2010). Poland is already experiencing, and will continue to experience even more, migrant carers from the East who regard Poland as an attractive place to work. As a result, it can be predicted that fewer and fewer women from Poland will be interested in working in this sector, not only because of the better economic possibilities that are available to them abroad. Since families continue to play an important role in Polish elderly care, we expect that those who go abroad to work for an elderly foreign person (instead of doing the same job for a family member) will face difficulties.

It is important to explain to the society that migrants can make a significant contribution to the elderly care sector. There is a need for a political framework for such measures, which allow for equal treatment for various actors in this situation (migrant carer workers – older person – families from sending and receiving counties). Not regulating this issue at all fails to solve the challenges that Poland faces as far as population ageing and migration are concerned.

Notes

1 The fertility rate decreased from 1.99 in 1990 to 1.29 in 2013, while life expectancy for males increased between 1990 and 2013 from 66.2 to 73.1 years and for females from 75.24 to 81.1 years (GUS Baza Demografia, 2014).
2 Such an analysis cannot be made here, but a regional analysis for Poland with the relations of ageing and migration can be found in many OECD reports, e.g. www.oecd-ilibrary.org/industry-and-services/oecd-local-economic-and-employment-development-leed-working-papers_20794797 or reports from www.adapt2dc.eu.
3 A comprehensive overview of migrant workers in Poland was made in the FeMiPol project, more details can be found at www.femipol.uni-frankfurt.de.
4 The project was carried out by a scientific consortium consisting of six universities in four European countries: Germany, Italy, UK and Poland. More detailed information can be found online at www.carersatwork.tu-dortmund.de/en/index.php. The Polish part was carried out by Justyna Stypińska and Jolanta Perek-Białas (project coordinator) at the Jagiellonian University, and interviews in Witnica were carried out by Katarzyna Wojnicka.

References

Bettio, F., Simonazzi, A. and Villa, P. (2006). Change in care regimes and female migration: the 'care drain' in the Mediterranean. *Journal of European Social Policy, 16*, 271–285. doi:10.1177/0958928706065598.

Bojanowska, E. (2008). Opieka nad ludźmi starszymi [Elderly care]. In P. Szukalski (ed.), *To idzie starość* [This Old Age is Coming] (pp. 87–101). Warszawa: Instytut Spraw Publicznych.

Cianciara, D., Dudzik, K., Lewczuk, A. and Pinkas, J. (2012). Liczba, charakterystyka i zdrowie imigrantów w Polsce [Number, characteristics and health of immigrants in Poland]. *Problemy Higieny i Epidemiologii, 93*, 143–150. Retrieved from www.phie. pl/pdf/phe-2012/phe-2012-1-143.pdf.

Czekanowski, P. (2006). Family carer of the elderly. In B. Bień (ed.), *Family Caregiving for the Elderly in Poland* (pp. 85–112). Białystok: Trans Humana.

Drożdżak, Z., Melchiorre, M. G., Perek-Białas, J., Principi, A. and Lamura, G. (2013). Ageing and long-term care in Poland and Italy: a comparative analysis. In R. Ervik and T. S. Lindén (eds), *The Making of Ageing Policy: Theory and Practice in Europe* (pp. 205–230). Cheltenham, UK: Edward Elgar Publishing.

Eurobarometer (2007). *Health and Long-Term Care in the European Union* (Special Eurobarometer 283/Wave 67.3). Retrieved from http://ec.europa.eu/public_opinion/ archives/ebs/ebs_283_en.pdf.

Eurostat Database (2013). Retrieved from http://ec.europa.eu/eurostat/data/database.

Fihel, A. and Solga, B. (2014). Demograficzne konsekwencje migracji [The demographic consequences of migration]. In M. Lesińska, M. Okólski, K. Slany and B. Solga (eds), *Dekada członkostwa Polski w UE: społeczne skutki emigracji Polaków po 2004 roku* [Ten Years of Polish Membership of the EU: Social Consequences of Polish Migration after 2004] (pp. 87–108). Warszawa: Wydawnictwo Uniwersytetu Warszawskiego.

Grzymała-Kazłowska, A. and Łodziński, S. (eds) (2008). *Problemy integracji imigrantów: koncepcje, badania, polityki* [The Problems of Migrants' Integration: Concepts, Research, Policies]. Warszawa: Wydawnictwo Uniwersytetu Warszawskiego.

GUS (Główny Urząd Statystyczny) (2009). *Prognoza ludności na lata 2008–2035* [Population projections for 2008–2035]. Retrieved from http://stat.gov.pl/cps/rde/xbcr/ gus/L_prognoza_ludnosci_na_lata2008_2035.pdf.

GUS (Główny Urząd Statystyczny) (2010a). *Główne kierunki emigracji i imigracji w latach 1966–2008* [The main directions of in and out-migrations in 1966–2008]. Retrieved from http://stat.gov.pl/obszary-tematyczne/ludnosc/migracje-ludnosci/glowne-kierunki-emigracji-i-imigracji-w-latach-1966-2008,4,1.html.

GUS (Główny Urząd Statystyczny) (2010b). *Praca nierejestrowana w Polsce w 2010 r.* [Unregistered employment in Poland in 2010]. Retrieved from http://stat.gov.pl/cps/ rde/xbcr/gus/pw_praca_nierejestrowana_w_2010.pdf.

GUS (Główny Urząd Statystyczny) (2013). *Migracje zagraniczne ludności: Narodowy Spis Ludności i Mieszkań 2011* [The foreign migration of citizens: The National Census of Population and Housing 2011]. Retrieved from www.stat.gov.pl/cps/rde/xbcr/gus/L_ migracje_zagraniczne_ludnosci_NSP2011.pdf.

GUS Baza Demografia, Główny Urząd Statystyczny [Central Statistical Office Demographic Database] (2014). Retrieved from www.stat.gov.pl and http://demografia.stat. gov.pl/bazademografia.

Kindler, M. and Napierała, J. (eds) (2010). *Migracje kobiet: przypadek Polski* [The Migration of Women: The Case of Poland]. Warszawa: Wydawnictwo Naukowe Scholar.

Kotowska, I. E. (1999). *Przemiany demograficzne w Polsce w latach 90. w świetle koncepcji drugiego przejścia demograficznego* [Demographic Changes in the 1990s in the Theory of the Second Demographic Transition]. Warszawa: Szkoła Główna Handlowa.

Kotowska, I. E. (ed.) (2009). *Strukturalne i kulturowe uwarunkowania aktywności zawodowej kobiet w Polsce* [The Structural and Cultural Economic Activity of Women in Poland]. Warszawa: Wydawnictwo Naukowe Scholar.

Krajewska, A. (2012). 'Polityka braku polityki': imigrantki w polskim sektorze opieki nad osobami starszymi ['The policy of no-policy': immigrants in the Polish elderly care sector]. *Societas/Communitas, 1(13)*, 57–78.

Krzyżowski, Ł. (2013). *Polscy migranci i ich starzejący się rodzice: Transnarodowy system opieki międzygeneracyjnej* [Polish Migrants and their Ageing Parents: Transnational System of Intergenerational Care]. Warszawa: Scholar.

Krzyżowski, Ł. and Mucha, J. (2014). Transnational caregiving in turbulent times: Polish migrants in Iceland and their elderly parents in Poland. *International Sociology, 29*, 22–37. doi:10.1177/0268580913515287.

Księżopolski, M. (2013). Polish social policy at the turn of the 20th century. In P. Michoń, J. Orczyk and M. Żukowski (eds), *Facing the Challenges: Social Policy in Poland after 1990* (pp. 37–49). Poznań: Poznań University of Economics Press.

Lasota, E. (2008). Praca domowa imigrantek a proces urynkowienia ról społecznych Polek [The homework of migrants and the process of marketization of social roles of Poles]. In K. Slany (ed.), *Migracje kobiet: Perspektywa wielowymiarowa* [The Migration of Women: Multidimensial Perspective] (pp. 221–238). Kraków: Wydawnictwo Uniwersytetu Jagiellońskiego.

León, M. (ed.) (2014). *The Transformation of Care in European Societies*. London: Palgrave Macmillan.

Lesińska, M., Okólski, M., Slany, K. and Solga, B. (eds). (2014). *Dekada członkostwa Polski w UE: Społeczne skutki emigracji Polaków po 2004 roku* [Ten Years of Polish Membership of the EU: Social Consequences of Polish Migration after 2004]. Warszawa: Wydawnictwo Uniwersytetu Warszawskiego.

Łodziński, S. and Nowicka, E. (1998). Cudzoziemcy w Polsce: sytuacja prawna i społeczna [The foreigners in Poland: legal and social situation]. In H. Grzymała-Moszczyńska and E. Nowicka (eds), *Goście i gospodarze* [The Visitors and Hosts] (pp. 17–51). Kraków: NOMOS.

Łuczak, P. (2013). Long-term care in Poland. In P. Michoń, J. Orczyk and M. Żukowski (eds), *Facing the Challenges: Social Policy in Poland after 1990* (pp. 169–179). Poznań: University of Economics Press.

Lutz, H. (2011). *The New Maids: Transnational Women and Care Economy*. London: Zed Books.

Małek, A. (2011). *Migrantki-opiekunki: Doświadczenia migracyjne Polek pracujących w Rzymie* [The Migrants-Carers: The Migration Experience of Poles Working in Rome]. Kraków: Wydawnictwo Uniwersytetu Jagiellońskiego.

MSW (Ministerstwo Spraw Wewnętrznych) (2012). *Polityka migracyjna Polski – stan obecny i postulowane działania* [The migration policy of Poland – current situation and recommended actions]. Retrieved from http://bip.msw.gov.pl/portal/bip/227/19529/Polityka_migracyjna_Polski.html.

Okólski, M. (2012). Modernising impacts of emigration. *Studia Socjologiczne, 3(206)*, 49–79. Retrieved from http://yadda.icm.edu.pl/yadda/element/bwmeta1.element.cejsh-1c8baff9-7c1c-4c67-95a1-3e6709f7e87a.

Perek-Białas, J. and Racław, M. (2014). Transformation of elderly care in Poland. In M. Léon (ed.), *The Transformation of Care in European Societies* (pp. 256–275). London: Palgrave Macmillan.

Racław, M. (2011). Opiekunowie nieformalni – 'niewidoczne' podmioty [Informal caregivers – 'invisible' actors]. In M. Racław (ed.), *Publiczna troska, prywatna opieka: Społeczności lokalne wobec osób starszych* [Public Concerns, Private Care: Local Community towards Older Persons] (pp. 275–286). Warszawa: Instytut Spraw Publicznych.

Rosińska-Kordasiewicz, A. (2008). Służąca, pracownik, domownik: Polki jako pomoce domowe w Neapolu w kontekście retradycjonalizacji instytucji [Servant, Worker, Family Member: Polish Women as Domestic Workers in Naples]. *Kultura i Społeczeństwo, 2*, 79–109.

Slany, K. (2002). *Alternatywne formy życia małżeńsko-rodzinnego w ponowoczesnym świecie* [Alternative Forms of Married and Family Life in the Postmodern World]. Kraków: NOMOS.

Slany, K. (ed.) (2008). *Migracje kobiet: Perspektywa wielowymiarowa* [The Migration of Women: Multidimensional Perspective]. Kraków: Wydawnictwo Uniwersytetu Jagiellońskiego.

Slany, K., Kontos, M. and Liapi, M. (eds) (2010). *Women in New Migrations: Current Debates in European Societies.* Cracow: Jagiellonian University Press.

Slany, K., Ślusarczyk, M. and Krzyżowski, Ł. (2014). *Wpływ współczesnych migracji Polaków na przemiany więzi społeczne, relacje w rodzinie, i relacje międzygeneracyjne* [Impact of modern migration of Poles on changes of social ties, family and intergenerational relations]. Expertise for Research Committee on Migration, Polish Academy of Sciences. Retrieved from www.kbnm.pan.pl/raporty-i-ekspertyzy-komitetu.

Stypińska, J. and Perek-Białas, J. (2014). Working carers in Poland – successful strategies of reconciliation of work and care of an older adult. *Anthropological Notebooks, 20(1)*, 87–104. Retrieved from www.drustvo-antropologov.si/AN/PDF/2014_1/Anthropological_Notebooks_XX_1_Stypinska.pdf.

Szczygielska, I. (2013). *Migracje zarobkowe kobiet i ich wpływ na funkcjonowanie rodzin* [Earning Migration and its Influence on Functioning of Families]. Warszawa: Wydawnictwa Uniwersytetu Warszawskiego.

Titkow, A., Duch-Krzystoszek, D. and Budrowska, B. (2004). *Nieodpłatna praca kobiet: Mity, realia, perspektywy* [Women's Unpaid Work: Myths, Reality, Perspectives]. Warszawa: Instytut Filozofii i Socjologii Polskiej Akademii Nauk.

van de Kaa, D. (1988). Europe's second demographic transition. *Population Bulletin, 42(1)*, 1–59.

White, A. (2011). *Polish Families and Migration since EU Accession.* Bristol: Policy Press.

3 Elderly migrants in Luxembourg
Diversity and inequality

Paul Zahlen

Introduction

The scholarly literature on elderly migrants mainly focuses on the question of ageing and the challenges (such as health, pensions as well as on the question of social integration of migrant minorities) that the ageing of migrants entail (see, for example, Baykara-Krumme *et al.*, 2012). It is generally accepted that immigrants or ethnic minorities, and particularly elderly migrants, have special needs in terms of education, welfare, health or housing (White, 2006). The scholarly literature on migration in Luxembourg is largely dominated by history, linguistics and socio-linguistics. Historians generally emphasise the essential role of immigrants in the economic expansion of the Luxembourgish economy (see, for example, Pauly, 2010; Zahlen, 2012), while linguists tend to focus on the roles and impact of the native language (Luxembourgish) as well as on the country's multilingualism (Fehlen, 2007). Only a few studies have taken a more encompassing sociological approach (Fehlen, 2010; Hartmann-Hirsch and Ametepe, 2011). In this context, some interesting work has been carried out on specific migration components, especially on the Portuguese and Italian immigration waves (see, for example, Beirao, 1999; Correia, 2013; Gallo, 1987).

Migration is implicitly analysed in Luxembourg – as in other countries – as a question of social and political integration of one minority or of several minorities into a large homogeneous cultural or ethnic majority. In most of the EU-countries, this view might be appropriate. However, approaching the question of migrants and elderly migrants in Luxembourg as a 'minority question' may be misleading. In fact, people with a migration background make up more than 60 per cent of the inhabitants of Luxembourg. Furthermore, on the basis of the Swedish case, Torres (2006) argues that, apart from the non-national background, the various groups which constitute the 'elderly migrants' have little in common. This may be also applied to the Luxembourgish case. Elderly migrants in Luxembourg constitute a group which is extremely diverse and cannot be treated as a single, uniform group with the same needs. In order to further explain this chain of thought this chapter is not only dedicated to those in the 65+ age category, generally considered as the 'elderly', but also to the cluster of people in transition from labour to retirement. Their socio-economic status in working life determines largely their status as an elderly migrant. The terms 'foreigners' (non-nationals) and 'migrants' are used interchangeably in the sections that follow.

Migration: no longer a 'minority' question in Luxembourg

Labour migration is one of the main demographic, social and economic characteristics of Luxembourg. Massive immigration flows date back to the end of the nineteenth century and the rapid expansion of the iron-and-steel industry at that time. The economic, social and political crises of the twentieth century – World War I and II, the Great Depression, the economic slump between the mid-1970s and the mid-1980s – only temporarily slowed down migration inflows. Between 1960 and 2013, domestic employment grew at an average rate of 2.0 per cent per year compared to the 0.5 per cent average in the EU-15 countries. From the mid-1980s onwards, employment growth even accelerated in Luxembourg: from 1985 to 2013, the annual growth rate of employment reached 3.1 per cent on average. This rate exceeds more than four times the employment growth rate of the EU-15 (0.7 per cent on average from 1985 to 2013). Luxembourg had to rely on labour migration, i.e. immigration of non-nationals, and on cross-border workers as the growing labour demand could not be satisfied by the available resident work force. The most recent available figures (which are from the third trimester of 2013) show that workers of Luxembourgish nationality make up only 29 per cent of the total workforce. Another 27 per cent of all salaried workers were foreigners living in Luxembourg while 44 per cent were cross-border workers. As a result, migration is at the core of the social structure of the Grand-Duchy and thus has to be analysed in terms of diversity, inequality, social structure and living conditions in general.

A strong Portuguese component, but an ongoing diversification of migration

In 1961, the total population of Luxembourg stood at 273,400 inhabitants, of whom 41,500 were foreigners (13 per cent of the total population). According to the census data of 2011, the number of foreign residents reached 220,522 out of 512,353 residents – 43 per cent of the total population. In 2011, 61 per cent of the total population had a migration background, i.e. people who migrated themselves or of whom one or the two parents migrated to Luxembourg. From the end of the 1960s onwards, Portuguese migrants have replaced the Italians as the principal migration group. The rotational pattern of migration has been substituted by family migration. Regarding the period between the censuses of 2001 and 2011, the number of non-national residents grew by 36 per cent (from 162,285 to 220,522). The number of Portuguese people living in Luxembourg rose from 58,657 in 2001 to 82,363 in 2011, a slightly higher increase (+40 per cent) than the average rate of non-nationals. In 2011, Portuguese nationals represented more than a third (37 per cent) of the total non-national population living in Luxembourg. Approximately the same percentage could be observed in 2001 (36 per cent of the foreigners were Portuguese). The number of nearly all migrating nationals progressed in absolute terms from 2001 to 2011: the number of Belgians living in Luxembourg grew by 14 per cent and the number of Germans by 20 per cent. French nationals were even 57 per cent more numerous in 2011 than in 2001. Overall, the number of people who migrated to Luxembourg from the neighbouring countries grew slightly slower (35 per cent) than the average of all non-nationals (36 per cent). By contrast, the Italians are one of the rare nationalities whose number decreased (–4 per cent from 2001 and 2011). On the other hand, migration from other EU-countries (EU-27 except the five above-mentioned countries) developed much faster (+164 per cent). So did the migration from African countries (+108 per cent), from North and South America (+73 per cent), Oceania (+78 per cent) and Asia (+92 per cent). Nevertheless, the relative size of the non-EU migrant components remains rather small. Foreigners with an African nationality constitute only 1.1 per cent of the total population; the corresponding percentage is 0.7 per cent for people from North and South America and 1.0 per cent for people from Asia. In other words, Luxembourg remains the EU-country in which the percentage of non-EU migrants is the lowest; approximately 87 per cent of all foreigners living in Luxembourg have an EU-27 nationality. The corresponding percentages of EU nationals in the foreign population are 68 per cent in Belgium and merely 35 per cent in France and Germany while the average percentage on the EU level is 38 per cent.

Immigration rejuvenates the age structure, but the ageing of migrants is on its way

As most of the migrants are of working (and child-bearing) age, it is obvious that immigration tends to bring down the average age of the Luxembourg population. In 2011, 14 per cent of the total population in Luxembourg were aged 65 and over; a rate hardly higher than ten years earlier (13.9 per cent). This figure varies strongly across EU countries: in 2011, 21 per cent of the total German population were aged 65 and over, while the percentage in Belgium and France was 17 per cent. Only in Cyprus and in Slovakia is the percentage of people aged 65 and over somewhat lower (13 per cent) than in Luxembourg. In 2011, nearly 20 per cent of the population of Luxembourg were aged 65 and over. On the other hand, the corresponding figure was only 7 per cent for non-nationals. The old-age dependency rate (ratio 65+ aged/15–64 aged) is a complementary indicator on ageing. In Luxembourg, the dependency rate stood at approximately 22 per cent in 1995 and has not significantly increased since then. In Germany, however, the dependency rate increased from 25 per cent to 35 per cent in the same period. Nonetheless, it is important to acknowledge that with increasing age, the share of migrants in the population diminishes: non-nationals make up 21 per cent of the age group 65 and over in Luxembourg, but only 12 per cent of the age group 85 and over. This can be explained with the general path of immigration: the largest inflow of migrants

Table 3.1 Luxembourg: Residents aged 65 and over by nationality in 2001 and 2011

Rank 2011 (Rank 2001)	Nationality	Number in 2001	Number in 2011	Percentage of 65+ by nationality 2001	Percentage of 65+ by nationality 2011	Percentage of total population aged 65+ in 2001	Percentage of total population aged 65+ in 2011	Variation from 2001 to 2011 (%)
1 (1)	Luxembourg	51,738	56,363	18.7	19.3	84.7	78.6	8.9
	Non-nationals	9,332	15,379	5.8	7.0	15.3	21.4	64.8
2 (2)	Italy	2,756	3,917	14.5	21.7	4.5	5.5	42.1
3 (6)	Portugal	976	3,015	13.7	3.7	1.6	4.2	208.9
4 (3)	France	1,408	2,013	7.0	6.4	2.3	2.8	43.0
5 (5)	Germany	1,306	1,851	13.0	15.4	2.1	2.6	41.7
6 (4)	Belgium	1,329	1,768	9.0	10.4	2.2	2.5	33.0
7 (7)	Netherlands	407	572	11.0	14.7	0.7	0.8	40.5
8 (9)	United Kingdom	114	278	2.6	5.1	0.2	0.4	143.9
9 (8)	Spain	145	271	5.2	7.4	0.2	0.4	86.9
10 (16)	China	49	133	4.6	8.3	0.1	0.2	171.4
11–95 (11–73)	Others	842	1,561	3.0	3.5	1.4	2.2	85.4
Total		61,070	71,742	13.9	14.0	100.0	100.0	17.5

Source: STATEC. Census 2011. www.statistiques.public.lu/fr/population-emploi/rp2011/index.html.

(generally people in working age) did occur from mid-1985 and onwards and these cohorts have not yet reached the oldest-old age groups.

However, these figures merely give a partial view on the ageing of migrants. In fact, the share of the aged 65 and over is growing faster among migrants than among Luxembourgers. In 1961, only 7 per cent of the population aged 65 and over were foreigners. In 2001, the figure reached 15 per cent and in 2011 it peaked at 21 per cent. Between 2001 and 2011, the number of non-nationals aged 65 and over went from 9,332 to 15,679 (+65 per cent). Elderly nationals are clearly more numerous (56,363 in 2011), but, between 2001 and 2011, the relative increase (+9 per cent) was much lower than for non-nationals. In other words, migration rejuvenates the global age structure of Luxembourg. Nevertheless, the weight of foreigners among the elderly will continue to increase. Ageing also impacts the workforce: in 1995, 12 per cent of all foreign employees living in Luxemburg were aged between 55 and 64; in 2010, the percentage reached nearly 18 per cent. In comparison, the share of working Luxembourgers aged between 55 and 64 years increased from 17 per cent in 1995 to 25 per cent in 2010.

Treating migrants as one uniform group impedes us from highlighting the different national characteristics and the diversity in terms of ageing. Italians, the main immigration component until the 1960s, are commonly older than Luxembourgers. Nearly 22 per cent of the Italians living in Luxembourg are aged 65 and over. In comparison, only 4 per cent of the Portuguese and 6 per cent of the French belong to the 65 and over age group. The corresponding figures for Germans (15 per cent) and Belgians (10 per cent) are closer to the percentage of the Luxembourgers. Moreover, the number of different nationalities among the aged 65 and over increases significantly from 73 in 2001 to 95 in 2011, reflecting the diversification of immigration.

Older migrants on the top and on the bottom of the social structure

The education level offers a first insight into the complex social fabric of Luxembourg. Luxembourgers in the working age category of 55 to 64 years are overrepresented among medium educated people; 38 per cent of nationals aged 55–64 have an upper secondary education level, compared to 22 per cent of foreigners belonging to this same age group. On the other hand, foreigners are overrepresented among residents having a lower education level (46 per cent of the foreigners aged 55–64 have a low education level compared to 36 per cent of Luxembourgers) and among people having a higher education level (28 per cent of non-nationals aged 55 to 64 years own a tertiary education degree, compared to 22 per cent of Luxembourgers). Thus, analysing migrants as a homogeneous group is also misleading in this case. The low education level is far more present among Portuguese and Italians aged 55–64 (87 per cent and 53 per cent, respectively, have a primary or lower secondary education level) than among migrants from the neighbouring countries (12 per cent for Belgians, 20 per cent for French

Table 3.2 Luxembourg: Education level of residents aged 55 to 64 and 65 and over by nationality, 2011 (%)

Nationality	Aged 55–64				Aged 65+			
	Primary and lower secondary	Upper secondary	Tertiary	Other	Primary and lower secondary	Upper secondary	Tertiary	Other
Luxembourg	35.8	38.3	22.4	3.5	54.3	27.5	14.5	3.6
Non-nationals	46.0	21.9	28.0	4.1	52.9	20.2	18.8	8.1
Belgium	12.4	29.7	55.9	2.0	33.1	29.7	33.6	3.6
France	19.6	38.0	38.8	3.5	35.1	33.6	26.9	4.4
Germany	13.1	38.5	44.1	4.3	34.0	33.7	25.9	6.4
Italy	52.5	26.5	17.8	3.3	74.5	11.2	7.5	6.8
Portugal	86.7	6.0	2.6	4.7	79.9	4.2	1.1	14.8
Other EU-27	12.6	25.5	58.0	3.9	27.7	26.8	39.4	6.0
Other non-EU-27	36.8	26.4	29.8	7.0	39.1	21.5	23.0	16.4
Total	39.3	32.7	24.3	3.7	54.0	26.0	15.4	4.6

Source: STATEC. *Census 2011*. www.statistiques.public.lu/fr/population-emploi/rp2011/index.html.

and 13 per cent for Germans). The percentage of migrants from other EU-countries with a weak education level is also rather low (13 per cent of the aged 55 to 64), while the corresponding percentage for foreigners from outside the EU-27 is much higher (37 per cent have a low education level). More than half of the Belgians and of people from 'other EU-27'-countries living in Luxembourg own a tertiary education degree. In comparison, less than a quarter of Luxembourgers graduated from a higher education structure and merely 3 per cent of Portuguese aged from 55 to 64 years.

It is obvious that the education level of nationals, as of non-nationals is increasing. Between the census years 2001 and 2011, the percentage of people with a tertiary education diploma grew from 20 to 30 per cent (Allegrezza *et al.*, 2014). This pattern also appears when comparing the 2011 census data of the 55–64 year olds to that of the 65+ age group. Only 15.4 per cent of all people living in Luxembourg aged 65 and over have a tertiary education level. The corresponding percentage reaches 24.3 per cent for the 55–64 age group. In 2011, more than half of the Luxembourgers aged 65 and over (54.3 per cent) have only a primary or lower secondary education qualification. Overall, regarding migrants aged 65 and over, the percentage is very similar (52.9 per cent). However, there are huge differences among nationalities. About three quarters of Portuguese (79.9 per cent) and Italians (74.5 per cent) aged 65 and over have a low education level; however, Belgians, French and Germans and people from other EU nations frequently have a higher education. Finally, it should be highlighted that the Portuguese community is the only immigration group amongst whom the education level did not significantly increase from the 65 and overs to the 55–64 year olds.

Some evidence for a segmented labour market

Segmented labour markets are characterised by various sub-groups with little or no crossover capability. The term is often used as a synonym for a 'dual' labour market, with, on the one hand, the primary sector (well-paid, highly-skilled jobs and good working conditions) and the secondary sector (low-skilled, low-paid jobs and insecure working conditions) on the other hand. Unfortunately, data on the crossover capability do not exist for Luxembourg. As a consequence, we have to rely on the 2011 census data, which analyse employment of older migrants, differentiating between nationalities and economic sectors. Foreigners aged between 55 and 64 living in Luxembourg are largely overrepresented in the construction sector. Overall, they represent more than 70 per cent of the employment in that specific sector. Moreover, the share of Portuguese among those construction workers exceeds 50 per cent. Nearly a third of all Portuguese migrants in that age group work in the construction sector. Inversely, foreigners are underrepresented in the public and para-public sector (public administration, education, health services, social work) in which Luxembourgers represent 84.1 per cent of all employees.

Around 42 per cent of all Luxembourgers in that specific age group work in the public and para-public sector, while French, Belgian and German migrants

Table 3.3 Luxembourg: Employment of residents aged 55 to 64 by nationality and by economic branch, 2011 (%)

	Luxembourg	Non-nationals	Portugal	France	Italy	Belgium	Germany	Other nationalities
Agriculture	94.5	5.5	1.8	0.2	0.2	1.0	0.3	2.0
Manufacturing industry	69.9	30.1	12.7	4.2	3.5	3.3	1.7	4.7
Construction	30.0	70.0	51.0	4.3	4.3	2.7	1.9	5.9
Wholesale and retail trade, transport, accommodation and food service activities	59.2	40.8	11.6	6.7	5.4	5.6	3.6	7.9
Information and communication	70.7	29.3	3.8	7.6	1.7	5.7	3.0	7.6
Financial and insurance activities	59.5	40.5	2.3	8.3	2.8	9.0	5.1	13.1
Real estate activities	58.1	41.9	14.5	7.0	4.1	7.0	3.5	5.8
Professional, scientific and technical activities; administrative and support service activities	48.7	51.3	16.3	8.5	3.5	8.4	3.8	10.8
Public administration, defence, education, human health and social work activities	84.1	15.9	5.2	2.7	1.4	1.9	1.7	2.9
Arts, entertainment and recreation; other service activities	24.6	75.4	8.2	9.6	10.7	9.0	4.8	33.0
Total	61.5	38.5	11.1	5.6	4.0	4.9	2.9	10.0

Source: STATEC. *Census 2011.* www.statistiques.public.lu/fr/population-emploi/rp2011/index.html.

are overrepresented in the financial and insurance services. Regarding the sector 'arts, entertainment and recreation, other service activities', which is a very heterogeneous sector including international and European institutions, Luxembourgers are largely underrepresented. Foreigners make up three-quarters of the employees aged between 55 and 64 of this sector which includes maintenance jobs such as cleaning.

Overall, one observation prevails: the lower the average wage in an economic sector, the higher the share of migrants. In the sectors 'activities of households as employers', 'administrative and support service activities', 'accommodation and food services' as well as in the construction sector, the share of migrants is much higher than in other economic domains. The average wage in these sectors is much lower than the total average wage. Furthermore, Portuguese migrants are overrepresented in these economic sectors. On the other end of the scale, in the education sector, the public administration and the 'water supply and distribution' services, the average wage is much higher than the standard, regular one. Moreover, the share of Luxembourgers in these branches greatly exceeds their appearance in the overall economy. Nonetheless, two sectors with a different profile have to be mentioned. In the finance and insurance services, the specialised and technical services as well as in 'research and development' activities – sectors for which a highly-skilled workforce is crucial – the share of foreigners

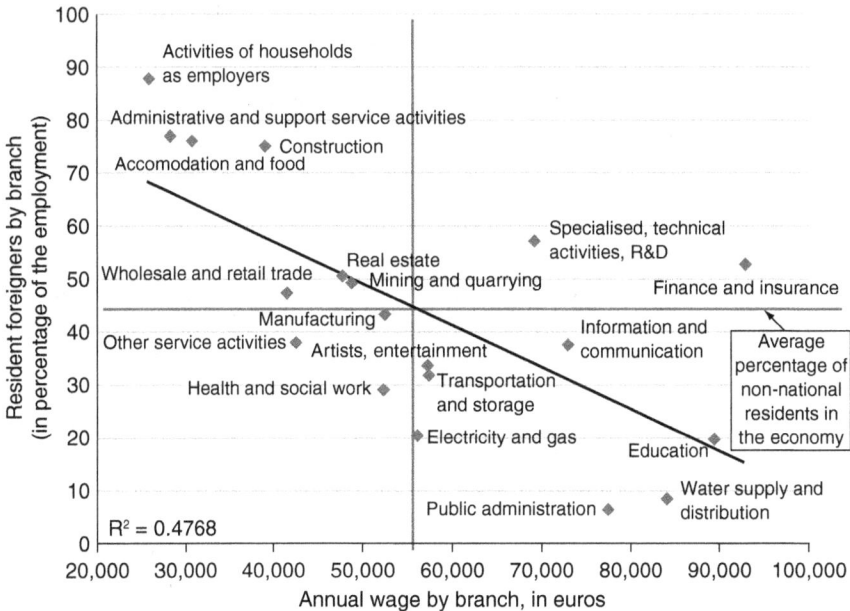

Figure 3.1 Luxembourg: Share of resident non-nationals and average wage by economic branch, 2011 (sources: STATEC. *Census* 2011 and STATEC. *National accounts* 2011; www.statistiques.public.lu).

is high, but the wages are also higher than average. However, Portuguese migrants are underrepresented in these sectors.

Clearly, as the figures are based on the 'national employment' (i.e. without cross-border workers), the complexity of the Luxembourgish labour market is not entirely reflected. Furthermore, the determinants of wages are multiple and diverse: human capital, productivity, working hours and institutional settings. The interpretation of the differences of the level of wages by branches is not straightforward. Nevertheless, it is obvious that, all in all, Portuguese migrants are frequently located at the lower end of the social structure, whereas migrants from the neighbouring countries are commonly represented in the middle and upper regions of the social ladder. In 2011, the monthly median wage of Belgian residents stood at €4,300 and that of Luxembourgers and Germans at €3,800. The median wage of French residents was only slightly lower (€3,600). In contrast, the median wage of Portuguese stood at around €2,350, while the average wage of resident workers from other national backgrounds (€2,800) is located somewhat higher. Nonetheless, the average hides significant differences in the distribution of wages among workers with 'other nationalities'.

Migrants stay longer on the labour market, but are also more frequently unemployed

Around 42 per cent of all migrants (male and female), aged from 55 to 64, are employed, compared to 34 per cent of the Luxembourgers in the same age group. Nevertheless, migrants are also far more frequently unemployed than Luxembourgers: 3.9 per cent of non-nationals aged 55–64 are unemployed. 1.6 per cent of Luxembourgers in the corresponding age group are in the same situation. Additionally, migrants aged 55 to 64 are underrepresented among people working exclusively in their own household; 15 per cent of them work in their own household, compared to 20 per cent of Luxembourgers.

As foreigners stay longer in the labour market, they are less frequently retired (33 per cent) than Luxembourgers (40 per cent) in the age group 55 to 64. However, as for the level of education, the heterogeneity of the activity status of migrants has to be acknowledged. Additionally, the differences between women and men are important in this context. The share of British men aged 55 to 64 in employment (71.1 per cent) greatly exceeds the corresponding share for foreigners as a whole (48.3 per cent) and that of Luxembourgers as well (39.6 per cent). For Dutch, German and Belgian men, the share of employed people (more than 60 per cent) is also significantly superior to that of Luxembourgers and migrants taken together.

Male Portuguese aged between 55 and 64 are less frequently employed (35.6 per cent) than Luxembourgers (39.6 per cent) and other migrants. One of the reasons for this fact is probably that many Portuguese workers are employed in the construction industry, a sector known for its rigorous working conditions, which consequently leads often to a relatively early retirement. On the other hand, Portuguese are also more often unemployed. Overall, women (migrants or

Table 3.4 Luxembourg: Activity status of residents aged 55 to 64 by gender and by nationality, 2011 (%)

	Men				Women			
	Employed	Unemployed	Occupied in one's own household*	Pension recipients	Employed	Unemployed	Occupied in one's own household*	Pension recipients
Luxembourg	39.6	1.5	1.7	50.4	27.7	1.7	37.7	28.7
Non-nationals	48.3	4.4	1.6	38.7	35.2	3.4	30.5	26.0
Italy	40.5	3.8	1.5	45.7	28.0	3.1	38.0	27.6
Belgium	63.0	3.5	1.1	28.3	38.5	1.8	33.9	21.5
United Kingdom	71.1	4.0	1.4	21.7	50.0	0.8	25.2	21.4
Spain	56.3	2.6	3.2	33.7	39.8	2.9	31.6	25.1
Netherlands	61.0	2.9	1.4	30.0	39.4	0.8	31.7	25.9
Germany	60.7	4.2	2.7	27.0	35.2	3.6	33.9	22.6
Portugal	35.6	4.8	1.4	50.5	34.5	3.6	24.7	31.8
France	53.5	4.3	1.1	34.6	35.2	4.3	32.3	23.7
Other	59.6	6.0	2.8	22.4	35.8	4.5	32.6	19.0
Total	42.8	2.6	1.6	46.2	30.2	2.2	35.3	27.8

Source: STATEC. *Census 2011*. www.statistiques.public.lu/fr/population-emploi/rp2011/index.html.

Note
* The category of 'occupied in one's own household' refers to those who exclusively provide unpaid household work in their own household, and it includes also those receiving widow's pensions.

not) are less frequently in employment than men. However, similar to male migrants, the share of female migrants aged 55 to 64 in employment is higher (35.2 per cent) than that of female Luxembourgers (27.7 per cent). Furthermore, the differences between female migrant groups are significant; 50.0 per cent of British women aged 55 to 64 are working compared to 35.2 per cent of all female migrants. Nearly 40 per cent of women with Spanish, Belgian and Dutch citizenship are in employment. The percentage for Portuguese women who are working is lower (34.5 per cent), but still superior to that of Luxembourgish women (27.7 per cent). Inversely, Portuguese women are less likely to be occupied exclusively at home (24.7 per cent) than Luxembourgish women (37.7 per cent) and foreign women as a whole (30.5 per cent).

Non-EU nationals and Portuguese, the most vulnerable immigration groups

The earnings replacement rate of old-age pensions is very high in Luxembourg, compared to most of the other EU-countries. As a consequence, the living standard of the 65+ age group, and particularly of pensioners, in Luxembourg is far better compared to the average living standard of the elderly in most of the other EU-countries. The median income of this age group in Luxembourg is around 2 per cent higher than the median income of the total population aged 16 and over. Inversely, in the euro zone, the median income of the aged 65 and over is around 10 per cent lower than the total median income, in Belgium it is even 20 per cent lower. The risk-of-poverty rate (60 per cent of median income threshold) of the population aged 65 years and over in Luxembourg (around 5–6 per cent) is three times lower than in the other EU-27 countries, where approximately 15 per cent of the population are living with an income located under the 60 per cent poverty threshold.

In general, the income level of all foreigners living in Luxembourg, taken as a whole, is lower than that of Luxembourgers. However, there are big discrepancies between nationalities, especially among the elderly (65 and over). In 2010, the median income of Portuguese aged 65 and over is situated at approximately €1,800 per month, whereas the median income of Luxembourgers in that same

Table 3.5 Luxembourg: Median disposable income by nationality and by age group, 2010 (in euros per month)

Nationality	Aged 16–24	Aged 25–49	Aged 50–64	Aged 65 and over
Luxembourg	2,508	3,243	3,177	2,872
Foreigners EU-27	2,046	2,520	2,687	2,303
Portugal	*1,795*	*1,978*	*2,236*	*1,796*
Other EU-27	*2,647*	*3,389*	*3,008*	*2,581*
Non-EU nationals	1,644	1,754	1,436	2,033

Source: STATEC. *EU-SILC, 2010.*

age group reaches nearly €2,900. For other EU-nationals, except Portuguese, the median income (€2,300) is closer to that of Luxembourgers. The income level of non-EU nationals (€2,000), is also higher than that of the elderly Portuguese, but lower than the amounts of Luxembourgers and other EU-nationals. However, as we have seen above, the group of non-EU nationals is rather diverse and the individuals of this group are located on the top and the bottom of the social ladder. Unfortunately, the sample size of the EU-SILC survey in Luxembourg, on which these figures on income are based, does not allow a more detailed dis-aggregation by nationality.

Social capital and political integration of migrants

The exclusion of migrants from political participation may have negative con-sequences for democracy and democratic processes as this exclusion could lead to or perpetuate the perception of migrants and their descendants as 'outsiders' of a territorial or national community. Political marginalisation could also hamper the social and economic integration of migrants as their needs are not specifically addressed (Jones-Correa, 2005). Figures based on the European Social Survey (cumulated waves 2001–2004) show a wide gap between natives and foreigners concerning political and civic engagement, a synthetic indicator based on several variables of concrete political engagement forms.[1] Moreover, the participation of migrants in political and civic associations[2] is far less developed than that of Luxembourgers. Regarding the indicators of political and civic participation, older Portuguese migrants have the weakest scores.

Another strand of the literature on integration of migrants within a community stresses the role of social capital (Morales and Giugni, 2011), a concept which catches possible positive outcomes of organisational networks (for example, socio-cultural associations) and social ties. These ties are supposed to strengthen the feeling of attachment to a community and mutual trust (see, for example, Putnam, 2000). As for political engagement and membership in political associ-ations, foreigners participate less in sociocultural associations[3] than Luxem-bourgers. Portuguese citizens, for example, are located at the bottom of the scale. A similar pattern appears for the 'trust in others'[4] indicator. Among Portuguese people aged 50 and over, interpersonal trust is far less developed than for the entire group of foreigners. However, foreigners in general are less trusting in others than Luxembourgers. Finally, voter turnout is generally considered as a strong indicator of political participation. Under certain conditions, foreigners living in Luxembourg are allowed to vote on the local level, but the participation in national elections is limited to Luxembourgish citizens who represent less than 60 per cent of the total population aged 18 and over.

Political participation and integration can be measured, on the one hand, by objective or behavioural indicators such as membership in political and civic organisations or political and civic engagement, and on the other hand by sub-jective indicators such as confidence in institutions which may have an impact on the capacity of these institutions to act as mediators between individuals,

52   P. Zahlen

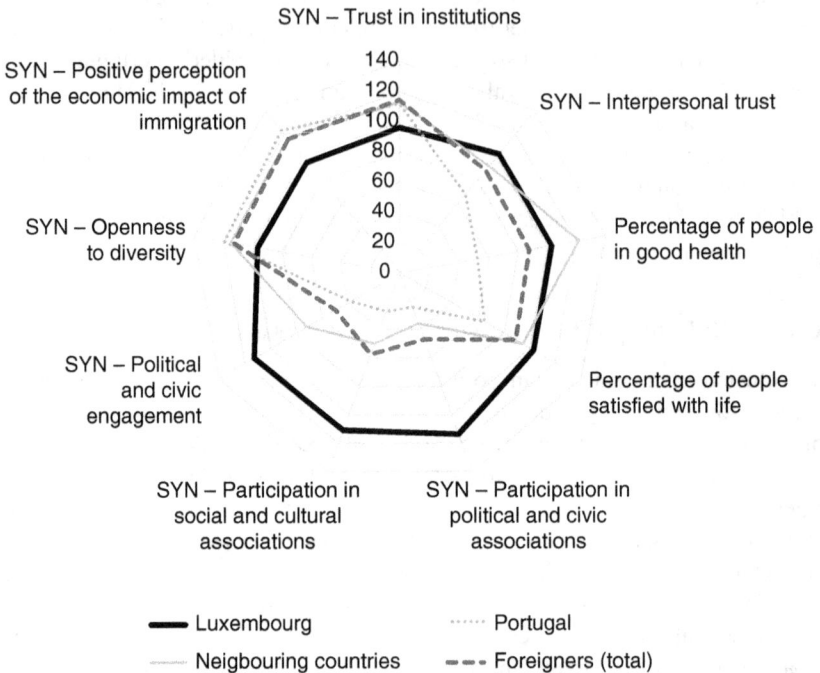

Figure 3.2 Luxembourg: Indicators of well-being, social capital and political participation by nationality for the 50+ age group (difference to the mean of the total
population) (source: European Social Survey (wave 2004, own calculations)).

Note
SYN=synthetic indicator.

groups (e.g. ethnic groups) or different interests. In other terms, the horizontal
dimension of integration can be complemented by a vertical dimension, the
State-citizen relationship (Chan *et al.*, 2006). Contrary to political participation
and political and civic engagement, foreigners are more trustful in institutions
than Luxembourgers. Moreover, there are no large discrepancies among nationality groups.

The literature on social cohesion indicators introduces other possible types of
analysis concerning the social and political integration of migrants. Beyond
objective and behavioural indicators, such as participation in associations, the
feeling of belonging to a community has to do with shared values, but also with
attitudes related to tolerance as well as respect for difference (Jenson, 1998).
Foreigners aged 50 and over are more open to diversity[5] and have a more
positive perception of the economic impact of immigration[6] than Luxembourgers
in the same age group. Interestingly, there are no fundamental discrepancies
between Portuguese people and migrants originating from other countries in two
specific aspects: trust in institutions and the (positive) perception of immigration.

In all other dimensions, the scores in terms of civic, cultural and political participation are lower for the Portuguese community. As a result, in Luxembourg, institutions seem to be at the core of the factors contributing to a cohesive society in Luxembourg.

Finally, subjective well-being is increasingly considered as an important indicator regarding quality of life. In this respect, the disparities between elderly foreigners, especially Portuguese, and elderly natives are significant. Luxembourgers commonly consider themselves in good health in comparison to foreigners. Especially Portuguese have a far more pessimistic appreciation of their health, while migrants from the neighbouring countries are even more optimistic than Luxembourgers in this respect. Furthermore, Luxembourgers are more satisfied with their life than foreigners; Portuguese are the most dissatisfied group.

Conclusion

Overall, migrants in Luxembourg can be considered a very heterogeneous group, even if the Portuguese component makes up more than a third of the non-nationals living in Luxembourg and a fifth of the population aged 65 and over in the country. Economic inequalities between migrants are one of the aspects of this heterogeneity. Disparities among the elderly reflect the inequalities among people of working age. Portuguese are located at the weaker end of the social ladder, while Luxembourgers frequently have a medium social status. The other EU-nationals are commonly situated in the middle or on the top of the social structure, while the education attainment and the structure of the household income of non-EU nationals suggest that they are located at the bottom as well as at the top of the social structure.

Discrepancies in political participation, in social capital and in subjective well-being largely reflect these socio-economic differences. However, more scientific work has to be done concerning the participation of elderly migrants in society. Some authors make the useful distinction between bonding and bridging social capital (see, for example, Paxton, 1999). Bonding social capital may be defined as the 'strong ties' within a community, including an ethnic community. Strong relationships may favour the integration of migrants within a community. However, if these ties are restricted to an ethnic or a neighbourhood community, this form of social capital 'does not necessarily result in collective action', as Larsen *et al.* (2004, p. 66) explain. Bridging social capital on the other hand, defined as 'weak ties' by Granovetter (1973), may allow mobilising the necessary resources outside the community in order to promote societal change. These are noteworthy aspects, which need to be further analysed in the unique case of Luxembourg.

Notes

1 The 'political engagement' items are: contact with a politician; work in a political organisation; wearing a badge or a sticker, signing a petition; participation in a demonstration; boycott of products. The synthetic indicator is based on the mean percentage of actions people say they have realised in the last 12 month.

2 The 'political and civic participation' items are: membership in a trade union, in a professional association, in a humanitarian association, in an environmental association, in a political party. The synthetic indicator is based on the mean percentage of associations that people say they are members of.

3 The 'socio-cultural participation' items are: membership in a sports association, in a cultural association, in an educational association, in a social club, in another association. The synthetic indicator is based on the mean percentage of associations that people say they are members of.

4 The indicator is based on the following questions of the European Social Survey: 1. Generally speaking, would you say that most people can be trusted, or that you can't be too careful in dealing with people? 2. Do you think that most people would try to take advantage of you if they got the chance, or would they try to be fair? 3. Would you say that most of the time people try to be helpful or that they are mostly looking out for themselves? The synthetic indicator is based on the mean percentage of attributes recognised in other people.

5 The indicator is based on the following questions of the European Social Survey: 1. It is better for a country if almost everyone shares the same customs and traditions (opposite sign). 2. Cultural life is generally enriched by people coming to live here from other countries. 3. The country is made a better place to live by people coming to live here from other countries. The synthetic indicator is the mean percentage of assertions people agree with (opposite sign for the first assertion).

6 The indicator is based on the following questions of the European Social Survey: 1. People who come to live here generally help to create new jobs. 2. On balance, people who come put in more than they take out. 3. It is generally good for the country's economy that people come to live here from other countries. The synthetic indicator is the mean percentage of assertions people agree with.

References

Allegrezza, S., Ferring, D., Willems, H. and Zahlen, P. (eds) (2014). *La société luxembourgeoise dans le miroir du recensement de la population* [Luxembourg Society in the Mirror of the Population Census]. Luxembourg: Editions Saint-Paul.

Baykara-Krumme H., Motel-Klingebiel, A. and Schimany, P. (eds) (2012). *Viele Welten des Alterns: Ältere Migranten im alternden Deutschland* [Many Worlds of Ageing: Elderly Migrants in Ageing Germany]. Wiesbaden: Springer VS.

Beirao D. (1999). *Les Portugais du Luxembourg: des familles racontent leur vie* [The Portuguese in Luxembourg: Families Recount Their Life]. Paris: L'Harmattan.

Chan, J., To, H. and Chan, E. (2006). Reconsidering social cohesion: developing a definition and analytical framework for empirical research. *Social Indicators Research, 75*, 273–302.

Correia, S. (2013). *Les Portugais du Luxembourg: questions sur la transmission intergénérationnelle de la langue et de la culture d'origine* [Portuguese in Luxembourg: Questions about the Intergenerational Transmission of the Language and Culture of Origin]. Luxembourg: Éditions d'Letzeburger Land.

Fehlen, F. (2007). Multilingualismus und Sprachenpolitik [Multilingualism and the politics of language]. In W. Lorig and M. Hirsch (eds), *Das politische System Luxemburgs* [The Political System of Luxembourg] (pp. 45–61). Wiesbaden: Springer VS.

Fehlen, F. (2010). La transnationalisation de l'espace social luxembourgeois et la réponse des autochtones [Transnationalization of Luxembourg social space and the response of the indigenous]. In M. Pauly (ed.), *30 ans de migrations – 30 ans de recherches – 30 ans d'ASTI* [30 Years of Migration – 30 Years of Research – 30 Years of ASTI] (pp. 150–165). Luxembourg: Binsfeld.

Gallo, B. (1987). *Les Italiens au Grand-Duché de Luxembourg: un siècle d'histoire et de chroniques sur l'immigration italienne* [Italians in the Grand Duchy of Luxembourg: a Century of History and Chronicles on Italian Immigration]. Luxembourg: Saint-Paul.

Granovetter, M. (1973). The strength of weak ties. *American Journal of Sociology, 78*, 1360–1380.

Hartmann-Hirsch, C. and Ametepe, S. F. (2011). *Luxemburg's Corporatist Scandinavian Welfare System and Incorporation of Migrants* (Working Paper no. 2011–29). Luxembourg: CEPS/INSTEAD.

Jenson, J. (1998). *Mapping Social Cohesion: The State of Canadian Research* (CPRN Study No. F|03). Ottawa: Canadian Policy Research Networks.

Jones-Correa, M. (2005). Bringing outsiders in: questions of immigrant incorporation. In C. Wolbrecht and H. Rodney (eds), *The Politics of Democratic Inclusion* (pp. 75–101). Philadelphia: Temple University Press.

Larsen, L., Harlan, S. L., Bolin, B., Hackett, E. J., Hope, D., Kirby, A.,... Wolf, S. (2004). Bonding and bridging: understanding the relationship between social capital and civic action. *Journal of Planning Education and Research, 24*, 64–77.

Morales, L. and Giugni, M. (eds) (2011). *Social capital, political participation and migration in Europe*. Chippenham and Eastbourne: Palgrave Macmillan.

Pauly, M. (2010). Le phénomène migratoire: une constante de l'histoire luxembourgeoise [The migratory phenomenon: a historical constant in Luxembourg]. In M. Pauly (ed.), *30 ans de migrations – 30 ans de recherches – 30 ans d'ASTI* [30 Years of Migration – 30 Years of Research – 30 Years of ASTI] (pp. 62–73), Luxembourg: ASTI.

Paxton, P. (1999). Is social capital declining in the United States? A multiple indicator assessment. *American Journal of Sociology, 105*, 88–127.

Putnam, R. (2000). *Bowling Alone: The Collapse and Revival of American Community*, New York: Simon & Schuster.

Torres, S. (2006). Elderly immigrants in Sweden: 'otherness' under construction. *Journal of Ethnic and Migration Studies, 32*, 1341–1358.

White, P. (2006). Migrant populations approaching old age: prospects in Europe. *Journal of Ethnic and Migration Studies, 32*, 1283–1300.

Zahlen, P. (2012). *50 ans de migrations* [50 years of migration] (Série: Le Luxembourg 1960–2010 [Series: Luxembourg 1960–2010]). Luxembourg: STATEC.

4 UK's elderly care and migration regimes

Anya Ahmed

Introduction

This chapter presents the welfare and migration regimes for the UK and addresses the impact that these have on the lives of older migrants in terms of access to Long Term Care (LTC) and social exclusion. The implications of these regimes for both elderly care recipiency and elderly care provision are considered and discussed in relation to how both care giving and recipiency are related to mobility and migration decisions (Ackers and Dwyer, 2002). A central argument of this chapter is that older migrants in the UK are relatively disadvantaged vis-à-vis the host population due to their heterogeneous migration trajectories,[1] being regarded as 'Other' (Warnes *et al.*, 2004), and also in terms of how they engage with and experience social policies. The chapter considers how and why older migrants are excluded in the UK and places this in the context of both welfare and migration regimes. The issues related to accessing welfare services and navigating systems are discussed in conjunction with perceptions of older migrants shaped by increasingly 'selective' approaches to migration to the UK.

The chapter begins by discussing the socio-demographic processes behind ageing and migration, highlighting that both are shaped by macro-social forces, for example modernisation and economic growth (Warnes *et al.*, 2004). It establishes the migration regime in the UK and summarises key historical and contemporary landmarks, highlighting UK migrants profiles and settlement patterns. These issues are then considered within the current context of progressive conservatism underpinning the UK's welfare reform. The potential implications for older migrants' access to LTC are then explored further.

Socio-demographic processes behind ageing and migration

International migration has transformed the demographics and ethnicity of ageing populations worldwide and poses questions about who older migrants are, and how their care needs can be met (Torres, 2006, drawing on Castles and Miller, 1998). Additionally, international migration raises further issues regarding the complexities of ageing, welfare needs and policy responses, since older people are at risk of social exclusion (Torres, 2012). In this way, older migrants experience a 'double jeopardy' of marginalisation due to being older and migrants, or, as Torres (2012) explains, the social position of old age intersects with the social position of being a migrant.

Warnes *et al.* (2004) differentiate between those older migrants who migrate early in life and 'age in place' in the destination country, and those who migrate in retirement. Non-European Labour Migrants (NELM) and retirement migrants are the two categories of older migrants in Europe which are ageing the most rapidly (Warnes *et al.*, 2004). For the purposes of this chapter I am looking at the first group of migrants as this fits with migratory patterns and settlement in the UK. Using Warnes *et al.*'s (2004) typology the migrants discussed in this chapter are NELM. This is important in terms of the care expectations and implications for provision. Welfare and immigration policies intersect and impact on the social welfare of migrants (Warnes and Williams, 2006, drawing on Jordan and Düvell, 2002). Immigration policies determine migrants' status and this, in conjunction with labour market participation determines their welfare eligibility (Ackers and Dwyer, 2004). Dwyer and Papadimitriou, (2006) identify four interrelated factors in influencing the welfare rights available to older migrants in the EU: first, their migration history; second, their socio-legal status; third, past employment history; and finally, location within a particular member state. This is significant for NELM in a number of interrelated ways, since migration histories are shaped by a convergence of economic imperatives and freedom of global movement, both of which were short-lived. In the UK context, this meant that post-war economic expansion and labour shortages converged with the former colonies' right to settle in the UK. The socio-legal status of NELM was secured by holding a British passport and being able to settle and naturalise as British citizens. Employment in often poorly paid jobs, usually without occupational pensions, means dependence on state pensions in retirement. Finally, the potential crisis facing EU welfare states regarding LTC provision and the increasing marketisation of welfare, combined with prolonged austerity measures in the UK, shapes the experiences of older NELM in relation to securing care in later life: welfare rights for migrants range from full to none (Bolderson, 2011). In this chapter I am focusing on older migrants who are entitled to a full range of welfare and LTC rights, but acknowledge that this is not always the case. Bolderson (2011) highlights that welfare and immigration policies have become increasingly joined up and access to welfare is contingent on immigrant status. She plots the historical relationship between immigration and welfare policies in the UK and concludes that immigration policies are dominant in the 'immigration-welfare nexus' (Bolderson, 2011, p. 224).

UK migration regime: historical overview

International migration, population diversity and population ageing are high on the agenda of policy discussions in Europe and the UK (White, 2007; Lievesley, 2010). Increasing diversity is often framed in terms of a potential threat to the dominant culture, and discussions about increases in the ageing population are characterised by concerns about resources for meeting escalating demand for welfare (Khan, 2010). Migratory patterns since the 1950s mean that the UK is now home to a significant and diverse Black and Minority Ethnic (BME) or Black Asian and Minority Ethnic (BAME)[2] population which is now reaching old age and in need of welfare support (Lievesley, 2010).

At the end of the Second World War, there were severe labour shortages in Britain and the then government's solution was to recruit from countries previously ruled by the British Empire. Migrants from the ex-colonies moved to the UK to improve their life chances and to increase income (Warnes and Williams, 2006), therefore the driving force was, for them, economic. At this time, people from countries previously subjected to imperial rule had unrestricted rights to a British passport enabling migration to the 'mother country' (White, 2007). The 1950s were characterised by migration from Poland (although not a former British colony) and the West Indies, while the 1960s saw the beginnings of African and South-East Asian migration (ONS (Office for National Statistics), 2013a). Migrants from the former colonies moved to the UK to fill labour shortages in shipbuilding, metal manufacture, transport, textiles, foundry work, vehicle manufacture and manufacturing generally. They were concentrated in those occupations, which were unattractive to British workers, since pay was low, hours were long, and often involved shift work. They became geographically concentrated in major urban areas across the UK, for example Liverpool, Manchester, the West Midlands, Cardiff, Greater London and Yorkshire.

However, legislation in the form of an Immigration Act was introduced in 1971 with the aim of imposing restrictions to UK entry from the former colonies. The introduction of this legislation meant that British passport holders born overseas were now only eligible to settle in the UK if they had a work permit and a parent or grandparent who was born in the UK. By the 1980s, further restrictions were imposed and immigration controls were tightened as demand for foreign labour decreased due to the decline of the manufacturing industries (White, 2007). When migrants from the ex-colonies arrived in the UK from the 1950s, to fill gaps in the labour market, it was during the period of high economic growth. The expectation was that these migrants would eventually return 'home' when their labour was no longer required, however, this did not happen. Consequently, labour migration to the UK following the Second World War has now resulted in an immigrant population in old age (White, 2007). On census day 2011, there were 1.25 million people aged 85 or over living in England and Wales, compared to 1.01 million in 2001 (ONS, 2013b). In 2011, 13 per cent (7.5 million) of the resident population of England and Wales were born outside the UK compared to 4.3 per cent (1.9 million) in 1951, so migration has contributed to 45 per cent of the total population change over the last 60 years (ONS, 2013a).

It is now estimated that by 2051 the BME (including white ethnic minority groups) population in the UK will have reached 25 million, making it 36 per cent of the total. Projected figures for the size of the non-white population by 2051 are 20 million, or 29.7 per cent of the total population. Estimates indicate that by

2051 there will be 3.8 million BME older people aged 65 and older, and 2.8 million aged 70 and older. In terms of the BME population, projections suggest that by 2051 there will be 2.7 million people aged 65 and over, and 1.9 million aged 70 and over (Lievesley, 2010). These projected figures indicate that demand for welfare services for older people will increase and that a significant proportion of this demand will come from BME populations.

The UK current context of welfare

The welfare state is not neutral but operates within the context of wider social, cultural and ideological structures (Hudson, 2013). The UK has a mixed economy of welfare (Powell, 2007), characterised by welfare services being provided by the state, the private sector, families/communities and the voluntary/ independent sector. In the UK, although social care has always been a mixed economy of provision, the private sector role has increased dramatically (UKHCA (UK Home Care Association), 2012a). In 1993 5 per cent of the social care sector was privately funded, in 2011, this figure was 81 per cent (Lewis and West, 2014). Importantly too, the austerity measures introduced by the Coalition Government in 2010 – where cuts to spending on public services were made – have created further pressures on health and formal care services (Lewis and West, 2014). More preventative approaches to providing LTC are currently being explored. This is important in the UK context with welfare reform and reductions in public spending; however, there are significant challenges to adopting a genuinely preventative approach (Allen and Glasby, 2013), not least when there is limited knowledge about the needs of older migrants.

The implications of changing demographics for Long Term Care Provision in the UK

Changing demographic patterns and socio-economic changes have made the future of LTC an important issue for all EU membership states, with financial sustainability positioned at the core of the debate (Kraus *et al.*, 2011). Sustainability is also a consideration in terms of environmental, social and economic change, which adds further challenges for the future of LTC in the UK and the EU (Evans *et al.*, 2012). The UK is experiencing rapid changes in the structure of the population and significant change in population composition. People are living longer and getting older, and fertility rates are decreasing which means that the need for social care is increasing while the availability of informal carers to provide such care is declining (Herlofson and Hagestad, 2011; Geerts *et al.*, 2012; Ross, and Lloyd, 2012). The UK Home Care Association (UKHCA) recorded a 24 per cent increase in people needing home care between 2005 and 2010 and a reduction in the number of available informal carers, due to declining fertility rates (UKHCA, 2012b). This has implications for all aspects of public service delivery (Ipsos MORI Social Research Institute, 2011). Financing Long Term Care is an important issue since projected demographic change in the future means that costs will increase (Royal Commission on Long-Term Care, 1999).

The challenges facing LTC systems in modern welfare states are seen by many as posing the biggest threat to welfare systems (Lewis and West, 2014). The LTC system in the UK is characterised by a legacy of enduring problems, for example underfunding and lack of clarity about what constitutes 'good care' (Lewis and West, 2014). Recently, these problems have become more pressing as a result of the rapidly ageing population. The increase in demand for care by an ageing population inevitably results in an increase in the costs of providing care. Presently in the UK, there are serious concerns about the sustainability of the long term care (LTC) system since the current funding arrangements cannot meet the growing demand (Ipsos MORI Social Research Institute, 2011) and there has been much recent debate on the future of LTC (Comas-Herrera *et al.*, 2010). Debate centres on two solutions: first, to reduce people's entitlement to care (through increasing the use of means testing); and second, to reduce the cost of care by introducing efficiency and cost-effectiveness measures (Ipsos MORI Social Research Institute, 2011; Comas-Herrera *et al.*, 2010).

The organisation and delivery of LTC in the UK[3]

Kraus *et al.* (2011) developed an organisational and funding typology of EU member states based on qualitative and quantitative data in order to provide contextual information to inform the potential changes to LTC. This includes axes of financial generosity and patient friendliness. The UK is deemed to have moderate financial generosity and moderate patient friendliness (Kraus *et al.*, 2011). A further typology developed by Kraus *et al.* (2011) is the 'use and financing typology', which in simple terms categorises LTC in England as being characterised by informal care orientated with high private financing, medium state spending and high informal care use and support. The LTC system in the UK is characterised by complexity, in terms of how it is administered, and how people engage with it (Comas-Herrera *et al.*, 2010), and also regarding what the public know about it (Ross and Lloyd, 2012). Its complexity is further compounded by the lack of integration of care and health services (Comas-Herrera *et al.*, 2010). LTC is effectively a safety net and access to it is means-tested.

Older people fund LTC (including residential care) through their own money or benefit payments while the National Health Service (NHS) funds nursing care and health care elements of LTC (Comas-Herrera *et al.*, 2010). LTC refers to help with domestic tasks, personal care and nursing care. LTC can be split into formal and informal care categories. Formal services include: local authority community health services; independent/voluntary sector services; care homes; nursing homes; and home/day care services. These services, therefore, are delivered by a range of providers in a number of settings: They can be funded by the local authority, NHS, charities and older people themselves. Older people living alone are more likely to receive formal care than those living with others (Ipsos MORI Social Research Institute, 2011; Comas-Herrera *et al.*, 2010).

Informal care relies heavily on unpaid care from friends and neighbours (Pickard *et al.*, 2000; Pickard *et al.*, 2007). The voluntary and community sector is also playing an increased role in the delivery of 'public' services to older people and also relies heavily on volunteers (Ipsos MORI Social Research Institute, 2011).

It is the responsibility of each local authority (Social Services Department) to assess an individual's LTC needs, arrange care services and provide financial support for those eligible. People are classified according to needs using the eligibility bands of the Fair Access to Care Initiative (DoH, 2002) in terms of low, moderate, substantial and critical needs. A care manager may be involved in assessing LTC needs. However, although there is a national framework in place, there is evidence of variation between local authorities (Comas-Herrera *et al.*, 2010).

The NHS is funded by Central Government through taxation and national insurance contributions (NIC). Since the NHS reforms in 2013, resources are distributed through Clinical Commissioning Groups (CCGs) which are responsible for commissioning health services, while Social Service Departments (SSDs) are funded by grants from Central Government, again through taxation (Comas-Herrera *et al.*, 2010). The Care Quality Commission (CQC), established in 2008, is responsible for regulating, monitoring and improving quality in health and social care services. It is also responsible for registering and inspecting services to ensure they meet the national minimum standards (NMS). LTC services, therefore, involve a range of providers and a range of services including nursing, institutional/residential care, or care at home. To clarify, the local authority purchases care from public, private or voluntary sector organisations. Although fees for services are negotiated, charges for residential care are set by Central Government (Comas-Herrera *et al.*, 2010). New Labour introduced the 'personalisation' agenda in adult social care in 2007, with the idea that choice and control in LTC would be achieved through devolving direct payments or personal budgets to older people eligible for LTC costs. In this way, the local authority must also offer a cash equivalent to care packages. This effectively means that the care user has become the 'care purchaser' and this has led to the development of a new industry in brokering in LTC (Comas-Herrera *et al.*, 2010), since arguably negotiating systems has become more complex. The Coalition Government has continued the tradition of personalisation, evident in the publication in November 2010 of the policy document, *A vision for adult social care: capable communities and active citizens* (DoH, 2010), which emphasises the importance of personal budgets and direct payments, and choice and control over LTC decisions. The underlying assumption behind the 'personalisation agenda' is that this will increase the independence of older people (Rabiee, 2013). However, for this to work properly, practitioners need to have a 'nuanced understanding' (Rabiee, 2013, p. 87) of people's perception of independence for them to exercise their rights as citizens. This is important when considering the needs of older migrants and this is unravelled in the following section. However, in the UK, much of what used to be 'health care' has now been reconceptualised as social care so the financial burden falls on individuals rather than health service providers. Redefining health care as social care coupled with reductions in grants from Central Government mean that costs to service users have increased (Lewis and West, 2014). In this way, older people are being penalised for needing care in later life (Johnson, 2002). In England it is estimated that adult social care costs could double in the next 20 years (Allen and Glasby, 2013) and a further important challenge is how to communicate this message to older people, in particular to older migrants. The implications of the organisation and delivery of LTC for older migrants is considered in the following concluding section.

Conclusion

As has already been highlighted throughout this chapter, the intersection of old age and the migratory life course has important implications in terms of older migrants being at greater risk of social exclusion (Warnes *et al.*, 2004; Torres, 2006). This can operate in terms of exclusion from citizenship, employment, social networks, and financial inclusion and welfare since, 'the social position associated with being a migrant can heighten the risk of social exclusion in relation to production, consumption and savings activities' (Torres, 2012, p. 37). With regard to welfare, and LTC in particular, this has implications for older migrants accessing services in the UK. There are a number of key ways that this could happen which are now addressed.

First, there is a historical legacy of not catering for the needs of BME older people, and a lack of knowledge about what their needs actually are. There is evidence that social care services have not in the past effectively addressed the issues of working with BME communities in the UK (Bowes and Dar, 2000) and this can result in their needs being unaddressed, or inappropriate service provision. Some researchers (Richards *et al.* 2013; Torres, 2012) argue that policies and institutions that claim to want to reduce the deprivation of marginalised communities lack the capacity and awareness to address such exclusion. Older people are the largest group of users of Local Authority services; however, although there is much emphasis on the challenges of meeting the needs of an ageing population within the health and social care arena, little is known about the capacity of agencies – for example, Social Services – to take on new responsibilities and to respond to increasing numbers of older people with complex and fluid needs. This is particularly important for older migrants since, arguably, even less is known about them (Richards *et al.*, 2013). It is evident therefore, that there is a need for more knowledge and understanding of older migrants in order to properly address their needs.

Second, the marketisation of LTC could also have implications for older migrants. Although governments since the 1990s have argued that increasing market competition and user choice results in better quality and lower cost services, and also provides the services that people want, now there is much evidence that casts doubt over these claims. Questions are being raised about how much choice there actually is and also how far people want to exercise such choice (Lewis and West, 2014). Services have been judged as unequal, inefficient and of poor quality (EHRC (Equality and Human Rights Commission), 2011). Johnson (2002) considers social justice in relation to social care, which is important when thinking about equality and access regarding older migrants in the UK. Johnson (2002) questions whether the marketisation and commodification of care – evidenced through the personalisation agenda and move towards care users as care purchasers in the UK – is in itself 'just'. This lack of equitability centres on the fact that older people are disadvantaged in terms of the way that costs for LTC packages are calculated, since they are underpinned by a different set of values from those for care for younger people where independence is core, and cost limitations apply. In this sense, social justice refers to injustices in day-to-day practices. Social Services have become residual providers of LTC for poorer people and assessment for LTC is determined by means rather than need (Johnson, 2002).

Third, migrants' 'life course attributes' – timing of migration; age; country of origin; previous occupation; gender and geographical location in the UK – also have a particular relevance when they reach old age and impact on their needs (Burholt, 2004). It is essential that the present (and future) welfare needs of older BME migrant populations are taken into account to avoid their marginalisation and exclusion (White, 2007). Older migrants in the UK are a diverse group, in terms of their country of origin and also regarding their levels of social capital (Warnes and Williams, 2006). Limited social capital and social networks can impact on older migrants as they may not have access to informal care and support. This can also impact on their knowledge and use of benefit entitlements (Warnes and Williams, 2006). Many of these migrants came from poor rural areas and had very limited education and skills. These factors, compounded by lack of language, low income and discrimination mean that they are the most socially excluded and disadvantaged people in Europe (Warnes and Williams, 2006).

Fourth, there are further issues facing older people in institutional settings in terms of their marginalisation and exclusion from the wider community and mainstream society (Scourfield, 2007). So in this sense, 'social justice is about citizenship and social inclusion' (Johnson, 2002, p. 74).

Fifth, inequalities among older people also impact on end-of-life experiences since the social status – and inclusion – of an individual during their lifetime is reflected in the way that their death is perceived (Kinghorn, 2013). Choices and control over the end of life are easier for the wealthy (Twomey *et al.*, 2007) and again this could be an issue facing older migrants in the UK.

Finally, although it is inequitable and socially unjust not to take account of the needs of older migrants, to overplay their differences from the indigenous population and 'problematize' their needs also creates difficulties and leads to exclusion (White, 2007). In other words, not planning for the specific needs of older migrants can lead to their marginalisation but narrowly focusing on the distinctiveness of their needs can also create exclusion (White, 2007).

This chapter has reflected on the welfare and migration regimes in the UK and how these intersect, and also on how older migrants can experience a double jeopardy of being older and also being a migrant. The challenges faced by cuts to public spending in the UK, coupled with the marketisation of welfare have been highlighted with regard to how these pose challenges to older migrants in terms of accessing LTC and facing social exclusion.

Notes

1 Migrants to the UK do not constitute a homogeneous group, as is explained throughout the chapter.
2 Black and Minority Ethnic (BME) or Black, Asian and Minority Ethnic (BAME) are the terms normally used in the UK to describe people of non-white descent. I use BME as an encompassing term.
3 This refers to England and Wales as the funding arrangements differ for Scotland and Northern Ireland.

References

Ackers, L. and Dwyer, P. (2002). *Senior Citizenship? Retirement, Migration and Welfare in the European Union.* Bristol: The Policy Press.

Ackers, L. and Dwyer, P. (2004). Fixed laws, fluid lives: the citizenship status of post-retirement migrants in the European Union. *Ageing & Society, 24*, 451–475. doi:10.1017/S0144686X0300165X.

Allen, K. and Glasby, J. (2013). 'The billion dollar question': embedding prevention in older people's services – ten 'high-impact' changes. *British Journal of Social Work, 43*, 904–924. doi:10.1093/bjsw/bes024.

Bolderson, H. (2011). The ethics of welfare provision for migrants: a case for equal treatment and the repositioning of welfare. *Journal of Social Policy, 40*, 219–235. doi:10.1017/S0047279410000899.

Bowes, A. M. and Dar, N. S. (2000). Researching social care for minority ethnic older people: implications of some Scottish research. *British Journal of Social Work, 30*, 305–321. doi:10.1093/bjsw/30.3.305.

Burholt, V. (2004). The settlement patterns and residential histories of older Gujeratis, Punjabis and Sylhetis in Birmingham, England. *Ageing & Society, 24*, 383–409. doi:10.1017/S0144686X0400211.

Castles, S. and Miller, M. J. (1998). *The Age of Migration: International Population Movements in the Modern World.* London: McMillan.

Comas-Herrera, A., Pickard, L., Wittenberg, R., Malley, J. and King, D. (2010). *The Long-term Care System for the Elderly in England* (ENEPRI Research Report No. 74).

DoH (Department of Health) (2002). *Fair Access to Care.* Local Authority Circular, Department of Health, London.

DoH (Department of Health) (2010) *A Vision for Adult Social Care: Capable Communities and Active Citizens.* Department of Health, London.

Dwyer, P. and Papadimitriou, D. (2006). The social security rights of older international migrants in the European Union. *Journal of Ethnic and Migration Studies, 32*, 1301–1319. doi:10.1080/13691830600927773.

EHRC (Equality and Human Rights Commission) (2011). *Close to Home: An Inquiry into Older People and Human Rights in Home Care.* London: EHRC. Retrieved from www.equalityhumanrights.com/sites/default/files/publication_pdf/Close%20to%20home.pdf.

Evans, S., Hills, S. and Orme, J. (2012). Doing more for less? Developing sustainable systems of social care in the context of climate change and public spending cuts. *British Journal of Social Work, 42*, 744–764. doi:10.1093/bjsw/bcr108.

Geerts, J., Willeme, P., Pickard, L., King, D., Comas-Herrera, A., Wittwer, J., Goltz, Mot, E. A., Schultz, E., Sowa, A. and Vegas, R. (2012). *Projections of Use and Supply of Long-term Care in Europe: Policy Implications* (ENEPRI Policy Brief No. 12). Retrieved from www.ceps.eu/book/projections-use-and-supply-long-term-care-europe-policy-implications.

Herlofson, K. and Hagestad, G. O. (2011). Challenges in moving from macro to micro: population and family structures in ageing societies. *Demographic Research, 25*, 337–370. doi:10.4054/DemRes.2011.25.10.

Hudson, J. (2013). Welfare. In P. Dwyer and S. Shaw (eds), *An Introduction to Social Policy* (pp. 3–13). London: Sage.

Ipsos MORI Social Research Institute (2011). *The Future Funding of Social Care: Qualitative research for Age UK. Report (final).* Retrieved from www.ageuk.org.uk/Documents/EN-GB/For-professionals/Research/The_future_of_social_care_funding. pdf?dtrk=true.

Johnson, J. (2002). Taking care of later life: a matter of justice? *British Journal of Social Work, 32*, 739–750. doi:10.1093/bjsw/32.6.739.

Jordan, B. and Düvell, F. (2002). *Irregular Migration: The Dilemmas of Transnational Mobility.* Cheltenham: Edward Elgar.

Khan, O. (2010). Foreword. In N. Lievesley, *Older BME people and financial inclusion report: The Future Ageing of the Ethnic Minority Population of England and Wales.* London: Runnymede Trust and Centre for Policy on Ageing. Retrieved from http/www.runnymedetrust.org.

Kinghorn, K. (2013). Death and the end of life. In P. Dwyer and S. Shaw (eds), *An Introduction to Social Policy* (pp. 113–127). London: Sage.

Kraus, M., Czypionka, T., Riedel, M., Mot, E. and Willeme, P. (2011). *How European Nations Care for Their Elderly: A New Typology of Long-Term Care Systems* (ENEPRI Policy Brief No. 7). Retrieved from www.ceps.eu/book/how-european-nations-care-their-elderly-new-typology-long-term-care-systems.

Lewis, J. and West, A. (2014). Re-shaping social care services for older people in England: policy development and the problem of achieving 'good care'. *Journal of Social Policy, 43*, 1–18. doi:10.1017.S004727941300561.

Lievesley, N. (2010). *Older BME People and Financial Inclusion Report: The future ageing of the ethnic minority population of England and Wales.* London: Runnymede Trust and Centre for Policy on Ageing. Retrieved from http/www.runnymedetrust.org.

ONS (Office for National Statistics) (2013a). *What does the 2011 census tell us about the 'oldest old' living in England and Wales?* London: Home Office. Retrieved from www. ons.gov.uk/ons/dcp171776_342117.pdf.

ONS (Office for National Statistics) (2013b). *Immigration patterns of non-UK born populations in England and Wales in 2011.* London: Home Office. Retrieved from http/www.statistics.gov.uk.

Pickard, L., Wittenberg, R., Comas-Herrera, A., Davies, B. and Darton, R. (2000). Relying on informal care in the new century? Informal care for elderly people in England to 2031. *Ageing & Society, 20*, 745–772.

Pickard, L., Wittenberg, R., Comas-Herrera, A., King, D. and Malley, J. (2007). Care by spouses, care by children: projections of informal care for older people in England to 2031. *Social Policy and Society, 6*, 353–366. doi:http://dx.doi.org/10.1017/S1474746407003685.

Powell, M. A. (2007). *Understanding the Mixed Economy of Welfare.* Bristol: The Policy Press.

Rabiee, P. (2013). Exploring the relationships between choice and independence: experiences of disabled and older people. *British Journal of Social Work, 43*, 872–888. doi:10.1093/bjsw/bcs022.

Richards, S., Sullivan, M. P., Tanner, D., Beech, C., Milne, A., Phillips, J.,... Lloyd, L. (2013). On the edge of a new frontier: is gerontological social work in the UK ready to meet twenty-first-century challenges? *British Journal of Social Work, 44*, 2307–2324. doi:10.1093/bjsw/bct082.

Ross, A. and Lloyd, J. (2012). *Who Uses Telecare?* London: The Strategic Society Centre.

Royal Commission on Long-Term Care (1999). *With Respect to Old Age* (Cm 4192). London: The Stationery Office.

Scourfield, P. (2007). Helping older people in residential care remain full citizens. *British Journal of Social Work, 37*, 1135–1152. doi:10.1093/bjsw/bcl086.

Torres, S. (2006). Culture, migration, inequality and 'periphery' in a globalized world: challenges for ethno- and anthropogerontology. In J. Baars, D. Dannefer, C. Phillipson and A. Walker (eds), *Ageing, Globalization and Inequality: The New Critical Gerontology* (pp. 231–251). Amityville, NY: Baywood Publishing.

Torres, S. (2012). International migration: patterns and implications for exclusion in old age. In T. Scharf and N. C. Keating (eds), *From Exclusion to Inclusion in Old Age: A Global Challenge* (pp. 33–50). Bristol: Policy Press.

Twomey, F., McDowell, D. and Corcoran, G. D. (2007). End-of-life care for older patients dying in an acute general hospital: can we do better? *Age and Ageing, 36*, 462–464. doi:10.1093/ageing/afm031.

UKHCA (UK Home Care Association) (2012a*). An Overview of the UK Domiciliary Care Sector*. London: UKHCA. Retrieved from www.ukhca.co.uk/pdfs/domiciliary-caresectoroverview.pdf.

UKHCA (UK Home Care Association) (2012b). *Care Is Not a Commodity*, Commissioning Survey. London: UKHCA. Retrieved from www.ukhca.co.uk/pdfs/UKHCACommissioningSurvey2012.pdf.

Warnes, A. M. and Williams, A. (2006). Older migrants in Europe: a new focus for migration studies. *Journal of Ethnic and Migration Studies, 32*, 1257–1281. doi:10.1080/13691830600927617.

Warnes, A. M., Friedrich, K., Kellaher, L. and Torres, S. (2004). The diversity and welfare of older migrants in Europe. *Ageing & Society, 24*, 307–326. doi:http://dx.doi.org/10.1017/S0144686X04002296.

White, P. (2007). Migrant populations approaching old age: prospects in Europe. *Journal of Ethnic and Migration Studies, 32*, 1283–1300. doi:10:1080/13691830600927708.

5 Troublesome movements

Migration and ageing regimes in Germany

Hans-Joachim von Kondratowitz

Introduction

Welfare states are nowadays being challenged in numerous ways. Population ageing, for example, places new demands on the welfare institutions that cater to the needs of a growing number of older people. The global phenomenon that is migration also challenges, for example, the social fabric and the nation-based logic that lies at the very core of welfare state's self-justification. Although the migration of young, single job-seeking males from the South to the North still prevails, we now also have international migration of female domestic helpers as well as transnational migration of whole uprooted families. The developed welfare states of the northern hemisphere are therefore nowadays faced not only with transcontinental movements of groups of impoverished job seekers, political refugees, victims of natural disasters, but also with ambitious professionals from different fields of specialisation, trying to find favourable conditions for a decent life.

That migration of any kind will constitute a serious challenge to reconceptualising European welfare states was an observation made by traditional North American immigration countries. Economists have argued that these welfare states will be unable to deal with migration because it will jeopardise the consensual expectations of its respective national memberships.[1] Such objections have instigated debates about citizenship entitlements, cultural rights and identity management. The emergence of cosmopolitan norms and the development of deterritorialised law stand in contradiction to the reality of nation-state criteria as well as to the strengths of local democratic procedures (Benhabib, 2007; Bloemrad *et al.*, 2008). However, building institutional networks that are conducive to a country's acceptance of immigrants is seen as an appropriate way to deal with negotiating possibly problematic diversity consequences and to help general consensus-building (Crepaz, 2008). This theme of advocating a lasting establishment of consensus in these divergent migrant societies has been a moot point. The concept of multiculturalism (Banting and Kymlicka, 2006) – as a commitment to structure and influence processes of recognition – has met with increasing criticism, mainly by politicians, but also by some scientists (Alesina and La Ferrara, 2005; Goodhart, 2013; Putnam 2007). Recent research evidence presented by Koopmans using cross-national data-sets for eight European countries (Germany, France, UK, Netherlands, Switzerland, Sweden, Austria and Belgium), notes clear differences in integration outcomes (Koopmans, 2010; Ersanilli and Koopmans, 2010).[2]

In order to address the intersection of migration and welfare regimes, it seems interesting to shed light on the case of Germany. Since Germany is, in Esping-Andersen's terms, a typical example of a conservative, employment-centred and bureaucratic type of European welfare state, it will be instructive to follow its controversies on migration policy and ageing.

The migration regime in Germany: bygone fictions of homogeneity

After a unified German Empire had been established in 1871, the public debate on migration in Germany concentrated on the aspect of new arrivals. Preventing immigration and hence possible intruders into this new, economically flourishing Empire was a central objective for governmental activity. Here, the vision of 'homogeneity' of the *Volksstaat* became a central unifying ideology for a society that was in reality characterised by a mixture of regional and religious lifestyles, neighbouring language families and different ethnic backgrounds (Brubaker, 1992; Dohse, 1985). The only exceptions made were for the necessary mobilisation of informal work and of low-priced labour for the heaviest physical work in certain branches of industry and for seasonal work in the still predominantly rural economy by allowing a contingent of immigration on a temporary basis. Since 1914, the legal regulation of citizenship entitlements has been based on the concept of *ius sanguinis* in order to distinguish 'foreigners' (not from 'our blood' or lineage) from 'pure' German citizens. The construction of homogeneity that lays behind *ius sanguinis* survived in legislation right up into the Federal Republic of Germany. It was finally abolished in 2000 by re-introducing legal *ius solis* conceptions.[3]

In reality, Germany has a long history of migration (Oltmer, 2013). Internal migration streams were already pronounced in nineteenth century Germany (Bade, 1984). Another wave of massive migration was a consequence of World War II and later of the crisis of communist rule in East Germany until 1961.[4] Following this, supranational cooperation on the European level changed the reference for migration in Germany profoundly. It was a political decision to opt for opening Germany to the introduction of foreign labour, the aim being to relieve some Southern European governments of unemployment pressures and to use this as a gesture to reintegrate Germany into the circle of respectable countries (from 1955 to 1973, when recruitment stopped). The term 'guestworker' clarified the conditions: a formal employment permit with social insurance entitlements (hence with long-term benefit obligations from the welfare state) and the inclusion of the national employment agency on the basis of recruitment agreements with several Southern European countries (Italy, Greece, Spain, Portugal, Turkey among them). The work permit, valid initially only for a limited time span, was a part of a job rotation chain which never materialised

(Chin, 2007; Knortz, 2008). The interest of employers in a stable workforce favoured contracts being consolidated and up into the 1980s, the first outlines became apparent in Germany of a policy that allowed a 'well-organised' but limited immigration (Hunn, 2011; Schönwälder, 2001, especially pp. 298–338). The official institutions for job placement had the possibility to examine labour market priorities before granting entry. From 1973 on, a further influx of foreigners occurred in the form of follow-up immigration of migrants' *family members*, mostly from Turkey and former Yugoslavia.

Finally, with the demise of the Eastern socialist bloc and the war in Yugoslavia, new groups of immigrants arrived.[5] Among them, we find: (1) Jewish refugees from Russia and Ukraine entering Germany with certain special entitlements; (2) the new group of *Spätaussiedler* (late repatriates of German descent) from several East and South European countries and, because of the *ius sanguinis* rule, endowed with special privileges and (3) as a consequence of the ongoing civil war, ex-Yugoslav citizens from Croatia, Serbia, Bosnia and Herzegowina, Montenegro and, up to 1999, refugees from Kosovo. The main legal divide nowadays is, however, formed by the 'internal' migration of labour inside the EU, the 'external' migration from outside the EU and by asylum seekers and refugees. The asylum seeking issue has brought contradictory developments in its wake. As a consequence of the dissolution of Eastern Europe and of the civil war in Yugoslavia, the years 1991–1993 saw a strong increase in the number of asylum seekers per month. Granting asylum became a hotly debated topic and resulted in 1993 in the almost total abolition of the once quite generous asylum provisions of the German constitution (Weinzierl, 2009). The focus of such a decision also reflected the long-term negotiations at the EU level to put the extremely restrictive Dublin II regulations into effect in 2003 (Herbert, 2001). The Roma, as European citizens or as asylum seekers, have experienced an extreme entanglement in legal terms which has meant that they have had a particularly precarious situation.

Public controversy has undoubtedly influenced the societal climate on how migration is perceived, so that a populist vein has prevailed, where migration is seen essentially as a strain on society rather than a potentially valuable influence. This rejection took a dramatic form when several arson attacks on housing quarters of Turkish migrants (i.e. November 1992 in Mölln, May 1993 in Solingen), carried out by extreme right-wing youths, later escalating even into a series of murders of Turkish migrants by a small Neo-Nazi group, took place in 2000–2006. The attitudes of the German population to migration have been highly ambivalent over the years: while migration in the 1980s was regarded with reserved benevolence, in the second half of the 1990s the focus has been more on the requirement of integration into German lifestyles (Dietrich, 2007 on ALLBUS data; Kühnel *et al.*, 2013). In this regard it seems worth noting that research shows that where there are negative attitudes towards immigrants, these are often correlated with anti-Semitism and with other worldview dimensions, such as the notion of authoritarian models of society and darwinistic visions of human competition (Alba *et al.*, 2004; Engels *et al.*, 2011). Data on xenophobic attacks from the yearly reports of Federal Office for the Protection of the Constitution show a considerable number of incidents, mostly physical assaults, and it is suspected that there may be a number of undetected cases.[6]

Recent developments show also that the rise of anti-Islamic sentiments after 9/11 has affected attitudes toward migration in Germany. The publication of a notorious book claiming a lack of hereditary intelligence in Turks and an alleged rejection of integration among Muslim immigrants (Sarrazin, 2010) caused a heated debate, for example, and resulted in numerous, quite aggressive local meetings with a surprising degree of competing standpoints from the middle class (MiGAZIN, 2012; critic: Foroutan et al., 2011; Haller and Niggeschmidt, 2012). This generally dormant rejection at the local level, directed particularly at Turkish-Muslim migrants, contrasts with the absence of powerful right-wing political parties in Germany. The official policy has tried to balance this adverse situation by advancing a National Integration Plan, particularly for the local level (Nationaler Integrationsplan, 2007), and by convening the National Islam Conference. The latter is a highly conflict-laden forum for dialogue between the German welfare state and representatives of Muslim associations which aimed at encouraging new cooperation forms with the Muslim community, preventing societal polarisation and securing consensus (Mushaben, 2008; Yurdakul, 2006). In effect, these societal practices of migration management contain few incentives for the recognition of migrants. However, the way leading to an immigration country has now been irretrievably opened.

Social parameters and the impact of ageing

At present, for the cohorts of foreigners living in Germany, ageing is considered to be a topic relevant for the future (see Table 5.1). At the end of 2010, Turkish citizens were the largest group of all foreign citizens living in Germany (24.1 per cent), followed by 7.7 per cent Italians, 6.2 per cent Polish citizens and 4 per cent Greeks and Serbs (Schimany et al., 2012, p. 87). Of those foreigners aged over 65 in 2010, the largest group by far were the Turks with 29.5 per cent, all other foreign citizens accounted for less than 10 per cent (Schimany et al., 2012, p. 89). For the first generation of migrants (offspring of Turkish and Yugoslav

Table 5.1 Germany: Cohorts of foreigners (%)

Year	Age group		
	20–65	65–80	Over 80
2007	73.6	6.9	1.5
2008	73.8	7.3	1.6
2009	74.1	7.7	1.6
2010	74.1	7.7	1.7
2011	74.4	8.0	1.8

Source: Statistisches Bundesamt, 2013.

migrants compared in the TIES-study: a study on the integration of second gen-eration migrants in Europe), several social characteristics should be mentioned since they have shaped migrants' life-courses and could consequently affect their positions in old age as well as their experiences. Thus, when speaking of the situation of first-generation migrants in Germany it is important to keep in mind the following:

- low unemployment rate signalling a relatively successful economic integra-tion (at least until the late 1970s);
- Yugoslav workers were more qualified than Turkish workers;
- the number of Turkish women migrating were fairly low, only the subse-quent immigration of spouses and family relatives after 1973 changed this;
- traditional gender roles were strong in both groups, but more intrinsic with Turkish workers;
- female educational background showed differences between and inside both migrant groups;
- competences in speaking German were more developed among mostly male Yugoslav migrants than among male Turkish migrants (Sürig and Wilmes, 2011).

According to the TIES-study (in which second generation migrants were inter-viewed about the year of arrival of their parents) the fathers (67.6 per cent) and mothers (49.9 per cent) of Turkish participants arrived in Germany in the years 1961–1973; between 1974 and 1999 (during subsequent immigration) fathers amounted to 31.6 per cent and mothers 49.6 per cent. In contrast, the ex-Yugoslav participants exhibited for the time segment 1964–1973 a more gender-balanced migration pattern: fathers 36.3 per cent and mothers 31.8 per cent, then for 1974–1999 38.4 per cent and 44.4 per cent (Sürig and Wilmes 2011, p. 23, Table 1.12).

For the first generation, life circumstances were not inflexible from the outset – the return option after some time in Germany was still an alternative for some. Up to the present day, the importance for ageing migrants of going back and forth between the two countries has been confirmed as a new dimension in trans-national movements in several studies (Strumpen, 2012; Laubenthal and Pries 2012). When the economic situation is highlighted, contrasts between several groups of foreign immigrants in comparison to German households show ongoing income inequalities to the disadvantage of the Turks in particular as well as poverty (Engels *et al.*, 2011; Sürig and Wilmes, 2011; Tucci and Yildiz, 2012; Fuhr, 2012).[7] Such imbalances show also in the general educational level of migrant pension receivers in 2007 (see Table 5.2).

This imbalance has also implications for migrants' health in old age. The life situation for the *first generation* of migrants was characterised by highly disad-vantageous conditions in the economic standing of households and in educa-tional attainment levels. Exposures to health risks are more likely for migrants than for ageing people in general (cf. report on indicators: Engels *et al.*, 2011).

Table 5.2 Germany: Educational level of migrant pension receivers according to descent and status (%)

Educational level and educational course	Persons without migration background	Persons with migration background				
	Total	Spätaussiedler (late repatriates)	Turkey and former Yugoslavia	EU-recruitment countries	Western countries	Non-Western countries
School education in foreign country	2.7	61.1	76.7	73.9	52.5	30.9
Vocational training in foreign country	1.6	24.1	26.3	33.3	29.1	9.9
Type of graduation						
Without graduation	0.8	12.0	32.6	21.2	1.3	0.5
Primary school without vocational training	20.1	30.5	27.2	29.0	6.3	31.8
Primary school and vocational training	43.4	35.2	31.4	35.3	16.9	29.2
Secondary school	15.0	7.4	4.7	5.8	11.7	8.1
College qualification	4.6	1.4	1.4	0.2	4.0	8.3
College qualification with certificate	5.6	4.7	1.4	0.0	26.5	16.0
University certificate	10.5	8.8	1.4	8.6	33.4	6.2

Source: Schimany *et al.*, 2012, Tab. 6.11, p. 189; reduced table.

There are similarities between migrants and native Germans, but an age group comparison reveals that people in middle and old age coming from a migration background show a higher illness rate depending on the degree of exposure in their former work situation (Bundesministerium für Gesundheit, 2011; Kohls, 2012). The presence of chronic diseases is in certain age groups of migrants more apparent than in the rest of the population (Migration und Gesundheit, 2008, Figure 5.4.1).

Migration and care: setting future directions

According to the Statistical Office estimates for 2011, 8 per cent of older migrants living in private households are in need of care, 7 per cent are cared for by health services and 9 per cent in nursing homes (Kohls 2012, pp. 61–63). In total that would amount to approximately 201,000 older people with a migration background. The proportion of older migrants of all persons in need of care would be around 8.6 per cent, which is somewhat similar to their ratio to the overall population (Kohls, 2012, section 3.1). Older migrants' use of benefits of the Long Term Care Insurance (LTCI) is clear: there is a preference for cash benefits which can be added to the generally lower household budget. This situation also reflects insecurity about the practical conditions of service delivery, but even more a lack of general trust in the social and medical service programmes of the community and private agencies (Bundesministerium für Gesundheit, 2011; Kohls, 2012). In the Turkish community, care is still considered to be a family affair and it is often the case that people unfamiliar with a family's dynamics are assumed to have no role in replacing the informal care that is often given by female members of the family (Zielke-Nadkarni, 1999; Raven and Huismann, 2000; Tüsün, 2002). Thus, when relatives are not available, older migrant families tend to use programmes that cater to their religious and cultural preferences (Kohls, 2012, 72). In some metropolitan areas in Germany there are new service options that deliver care in some of the languages that older migrants speak and/or in a culturally sensitive way. These services are often organised by professionals who have a migration background themselves. In order to further develop care arrangements that cater to older migrants, several working groups now exist which favour 'culturally sensitive old age care' (Arbeitskreis Charta, 2002; Memorandum, 2009). The existing structures of service delivery and its main agent in Germany, the LTCI, are not yet flexible enough to make such an enhancement of perspectives productive. Rigidities have to be confronted, but at present new provisions for dementia care have indirectly helped to bring forward such new cultural sensitivity streams. Therefore, the debate about the services that should or can be provided for older migrants has prompted a discussion about the ways in which mainstream service delivery can be further developed. Several suggestions are discussed today:

- improving care-related information and its distribution to older migrants, especially to older women in the households (Olbermann, 2012);

- an urgent stepping up of the promotion of primary preventive measures;
- increasing older migrants' access to the professional field of care;
- the low participation rate of younger migrants in the social and health care system has to be improved and final recognition of foreign diplomas and graduations has to be accomplished (cf. Brussig *et al.*, 2013; Friebe, 2006; for data: Engels *et al.*, 2011);
- development of different curricula for further education and training.

Finally, the long suppressed activity of *migrant carers* in many German households is now a public matter so it is expected that every household in Germany that needs to plan for ageing parents and relatives is very much aware of the migration issue.

Conclusion

It is obvious that Germany has now embarked on a course leading to its becoming an 'immigration country'. In the wide political arena, there are no advocates for going back (except for the very small extreme right). However, up to now the steps undertaken have often faltered because of central and local state's controlling interests. The most recent example of this ambivalence was the introduction of *double citizenship*, but only under several concomitant conditions. Nevertheless, public discourse has undergone an important change in perspective: from a situation marked by years of complaint about poorer migrants trying to get their hands on social benefits to a search for educated migrants from middle-class backgrounds and with technologically advanced knowledge as a way to balance the shortage of qualified personnel caused by demographic change in Germany. The ageing of migrants themselves still has to find its place in the media and in communication channels – it seems to be almost absent in the perception of large segments of the population. Moreover, while following an economy-driven motivation in migration policy, the time for the other aspect of intensive control and blockage is not over, as the political reactions to the recent increase in asylum-seekers have demonstrated. Such control-intensive orientations seem to have the approval of some sections of the population, but are also met with criticism from other groups. Germany has, in other words, a lot to do still in following *recognition* strategies for migrants of all ages.

Notes

1 To quote Freeman:

> "immigration has tended to erode the more general normative consensus on which the welfare state is built. Welfare state benefits are now for the first time associated in the public mind with a visible and subordinate minority.... When the welfare state is seen as something for 'them' paid for by 'us', its days as a consensual solution to societal problems are numbered"
>
> (Freeman, 1986, pp. 62–63)

2 Worth noting is the fact that multiculturalist policies (with no incentives for host-country language acquisition and inter-ethnic contact as well as easy access to equal rights) in combination with generous welfare state benefits have resulted in low levels of labour market participation and high levels of segregation and incarceration in various countries (Koopmans 2010, p. 5, Table 1). Immigrants in Sweden, Belgium and Netherlands – which are examples of this combination – display relatively poor integration outcomes, while immigrants in Germany, Austria, Switzerland and France show better integration results. These countries follow more restrictive integration policies in combination with favourable welfare benefits and can be contrasted with the UK which is a country with equivalent limitations, but with markedly less welfare security (Koopmans, 2010, p. 13, Table 3; 19, Table 5; see Schiffauer, 2008 for a critical perspective).

3 In German, 'foreigner' translates not so much as *Fremde*, but as *Ausländer*, which signals the fact that one comes from 'outside', from the other side of a boundary, and draws attention to the country of origin – *Land* – as a separate entity. Usually, in colloquial German it is a word used by *Inländer* to signify differences or even deficiencies with those 'outside'. This implicitly discriminatory use of language has been widely disseminated and even adopted by several local institutions and legal frameworks in Germany. In legal use, *Ausländer* means to have the place of residence outside of Germany and to have a non-German citizenship. Thus, the actual locality in which a person was born used to be of minor importance until the changes of 2000 (*ius soli*). This is also when additional criteria with legal implications came into effect: EU or non-EU membership of country of residence (Asbrock *et al.*, 2014). Using this category in statistical terms has created permanent problems of attribution in research. Therefore, the term 'with migration background' was introduced for the first time into the microcensus of 2005. It means all immigrants coming to Germany after 1949 as well as all foreign citizens born in Germany and all born as Germans in Germany with at least one immigrant parent or born as a child of a foreign citizen in Germany. The term includes offspring of migrants with no migration experience of their own, which can also be used as an additional mark of distinction. This term is now widely used in official communications, often in connection with the term *Zuwanderer* (*Zuwanderer in Deutschland*, 2013). See more recent data in Frick *et al.*, 2009; Schimany *et al.*, 2012; Statistisches Bundesamt, 2013. Worth noting also is that 13.1 per cent of Germany's total population have a migration background.

4 What migration effects and forced integration even among 'insiders' could mean, has been an experience in both Germanys after World War II. This is when millions of Germans who were expelled from former parts of Germany or German-populated areas in Eastern and South-eastern Europe were forced to settle in the two remaining halves of Germany. At least in the Western part material compensation and the benefits of general economic well-being helped an altogether successful integration process (Hughes, 1999; Schwartz, 2008).

5 If one looks at different age groups in the percentages of first application for asylum over time (i.e. 2001–2010), it is clear that seeking asylum has been a concern for those aged under 25 (average age 59.7 per cent) and to a lesser degree for those aged 25–49 (37.5 per cent) (Baykara-Krumme *et al.*, 2012, 52, Table 4). Unlike asylum-seekers, in the group of Jewish immigrants, higher age groups are strongly represented. For instance, the proportion of three age groups among all Jewish migrants for 2008 was: under 20 – 15.9 per cent; 20–64 – 62.1 per cent; over 65 – 22 per cent, with a stronger representation of women in higher age groups (Schimany and Baykara-Krumme, 2012, p. 51).

6 Xenophobic acts are differentiated between a. direct violence and b. other criminal acts. 2008: a. 1042, b. 19,894; 2009: a. 891, b. 18,750; 2010: a. 762, b. 15,905; 2011: a. 755, b. 16,142; 2012: a. 802, b. 17,134 (Verfassungsberichte 2008–2012: cf. yearly reports of Bundesamt für Verfassungsschutz in Köln. They are edited by Bundesminister des Inneren, Berlin).

7 Differentiating values for equivalent income of households per month of Germans and immigrants in *West Germany* (considering number and age of persons in household, average values in €) for 1996 and 2004. *Germans*: 1996 – 1,140 to 2004 – 1,360; *SW European migrants*: 870 to 1,110; *Yugoslav migrants*: 750 to 870; *Turkish migrants*: 630 to 850; *Spätaussiedler:* 810 to 940 (*Migration und Gesundheit*, 2008, 22, Table 2.3.5.1; Statistisches Bundesamt, 2006.). Actual SocioEconomicPanel data-based analyses for differently skilled immigrant groups show that discrepancies in wages between natives and migrants still remain (Zibrowius, 2012).

References

Alba, R., Schmidt, P. and Wasmer, M. (eds) (2004). *Germans or Foreigners? Attitudes toward Ethnic Minorities in Post-Reunification Germany*. London: Palgrave Macmillan.

Alesina, A. and La Ferrara, E. (2005). Ethnic Diversity and Economic Performance. *Journal of Economic Literature, 43*, 762–800. doi:10.1257/002205105774431243.

Arbeitskreis Charta (2002). *Arbeitskreis Charta für eine kultursensible Altenpflege, Kuratorium Deutsche Altershilfe* [Working Group Charta for a Culturally Sensitive Provision for Old Age]. Eine Handreichung. KDA: Köln. Retrieved from www.bagso.de/fileadmin/Aktuell/Themen/Pflege/handreichung.pdf.

Asbrock, F., Lemmer, G., Becker, J. C., Koller, J. and Wagner, U. (2014). 'Who are These Foreigners Anyway?' The Content of the Term 'Foreigner' and its Impact on Prejudice. *SAGE Open, 4(2)*, 1–8. doi:10.1177/2158244014532819.

Bade, K. J. (ed.) (1984). *Auswanderer, Wanderarbeiter, Gastarbeiter. Bevölkerung, Arbeitsmarkt und Wanderung in Deutschland seit der Mitte des 19. Jahrhunderts.* [Immigrants, Migrant Workers, Guestworkers: Population, Labour Market and Migration in Germany from Mid-19th Century] (Volume 2). Ostfildern: Thorbecke.

Banting, K. and Kymlicka, W. (eds) (2006). *Multiculturalism and the Welfare State: Recognition and Redistribution in Contemporary Democracies*. Oxford: Oxford University Press.

Baykara-Krumme, H., Motel-Klingebiel, A. and Schimany, P. (eds) (2012). *Viele Welten des Alterns. Ältere Migranten im alternden Deutschland* [Many Worlds of Ageing: Ageing Migrants in an Ageing Germany]. Wiesbaden: Springer VS.

Benhabib, S. (2007). Twilight of Sovereignty or the Emergence of Cosmopolitan Norms? Rethinking Citizenship in Volatile Time. *Citizenship Studies, 11*, 19–36. doi:10.1080/1362102060109980.

Bloemraad, I., Korteweg, A. and Yurdakul, G. (2008). Citizenship and Immigration: Multiculturalism, Assimilation, and Challenges to the Nation-State. *Annual Review of Sociology, 34*, 153–179. doi:10.1146/annurev.soc.34.040507.134608.

Brubaker, R. (1992). *Citizenship and Nationhood in France and Germany*. Cambridge: Harvard University Press.

Brussig, M., Mill, U. and Zink, L. (2013). *Wege zur Anerkennung – Wege zur Integration? Inanspruchnahme und Ergebnisse von Beratung zur Anerkennung von im Ausland erworbenen Berufsabschlüssen.* [Ways for Recognition – Ways for Integration? Utilisation and Results of Counseling to Recognize Foreign Vocational Qualifications] (IAQ-Report 2013–05). Retrieved from www.iaq.uni-due.de/iaq-report/2013/report2013-05.php.

Bundesministerium für Gesundheit (2011). *Abschlussbericht zur Studie 'Wirkungen des Pflege-Weiterentwicklungsgesetzes'* [Final Report about the Study 'Effects of the Law for Further Developing Long Term Care Insurance']. Berlin. Retrieved from www.tns-infratest.com/SoFo/_pdf/2011_Abschlussbericht_Wirkungen_des_Pflege-Weiterentwicklungsgesetzes.pdf.

Chin, R. (2007). *The Guest Worker Question in Postwar Germany*. Cambridge, New York: Cambridge University Press.

Crepaz, M. M. L. (2008). *Trust beyond Borders: Immigration, the Welfare State, and Identity in Modern Societies*. Ann Arbor, MI: University of Michigan Press.

Dietrich, B. (2007). Einstellungen der deutschen Bevölkerung zu 'Ausländern' anhand von ALLBUS-Daten [Attitudes of the German population toward 'foreigners' based on ALLBUS data]. In H. Flam (ed.), *Migranten in Deutschland. Statistiken-Fakten-Diskurse* (pp. 235–257). Konstanz: UVK Verlagsgesellschaft.

Dohse, K. (1985). *Ausländische Arbeiter und bürgerlicher Staat. Genese und Funktion von staatlicher Ausländerpolitik und Ausländerrecht: vom Kaiserreich bis zur Bundesrepublik Deutschland* [Foreigen Workers and the Bourgeois State. Genesis and Function of State Policies and Law on Foreigners: From the German Empire to the Federal Repubic of Germany] (2nd edn). Berlin: Express.

Engels, D., Köller, R., Koopmans, R. and Höhne, J. (2011). *Zweiter Integrationsindikatorenbericht, erstellt für die Beauftragte der Bundesregierung für Migration, Flüchtlinge und Integration* [Second Report on Indicators of Integration]. Köln, Berlin: Beauftragte der Bundesregierung. Retrieved from www.bundesregierung.de/Content/DE/Publikation/IB/2012-01-12-zweiter-indikatorenbericht.pdf.

Ersanilli, E. and Koopmans, R. (2010). Rewarding integration? Citizenship regulations and the socio-cultural integration of immigrants in the Netherlands, France and Germany. *Journal of Ethnic and Migration Studies, 36*, 773–791. doi:10.1080/13691831003764318.

Foroutan, N., Schäfer, K., Canan, C. and Schwarze, B. (2011). *Sarrazins Thesen auf dem Prüfstand – Ein empirischer Gegenentwurf zu Thilo Sarrazins Thesen zu Muslimen in Deutschland* [Sarrazins Theses under Scrutiny – An Empirical Counter-Concept to Sarrazins Theses about Muslims in Germany]. Berlin: Humboldt University. Retrieved from www.heymat.hu-berlin.de/sarrazin2010.

Freeman, G. F. (1986). Migration and the political economy of the welfare state. *Annals of the American Academy of Political and Social Science, 485*, 51–63. Retrieved from www.sum.uio.no/english/research/doctoral-degree/doctoral-courses/2012/the-political-determinants-of-health/syllabus/freeman_1986_migration-and-the-political-economy-of-the-welfare-state.pdf.

Frick, J. R., Grabka, M. M., Groh-Samberg, O., Hertel, F. R. and Tucci, I. (2009). *Alterssicherung von Personen mit Migrationshintergrund* [Provision in Old Age of People with Migration Background]. Forschungsstudie im Auftrag des BMAS. Berlin: DIW. Retrieved from www.bmas.de/SharedDocs/Downloads/DE/PDF-Publikationen/forschungsbericht-f398.pdf.

Friebe, J. (2006). *Migrantinnen und Migranten in der Altenpflege: Bestandsaufnahme, Personalgewinnung und Qualifizierungen in Nordrhein-Westfalen* [Male and Female Migrants in Old Age Care: Inventory, Personnel Recruitment and Qualifications in Nordrhein-Westphalia]. Bonn: Deutsches Institut für Erwachsenenbildung.

Fuhr, G. (2012). Armutsgefährdung von Menschen mit Migrationshintergrund – Ergebnisse des Mikrozensus 2012 [The poverty risk of people with migration background: results from the micro-census 2012]. *Statistisches Bundesamt, Wirtschaft und Statistik*, 549–562. Retrieved from https://www.destatis.de/DE/Publikationen/WirtschaftStatistik/Bevoelkerung/ArmutsgefaehrdungMigrationshintergrund_72012.pdf.

Goodhart, D. (2013). *The British Dream: Successes and Failures of Postwar Immigration*. London: Atlantic Books.

Haller, M. and Niggeschmidt, M. (eds) (2012). *Der Mythos vom Niedergang der Intelligenz. Von Galton zu Sarrazin: Die Denkmuster und Denkfehler der Eugenik* [The Myth of the Decline of Intelligence. From Galton to Sarrazin: Patterns and Errors of Eugenics]. Wiesbaden: VS Verlag für Sozialwissenschaften.

Herbert, U. (2001). *Geschichte der Ausländerpolitik in Deutschland. Saisonarbeiter, Zwangsarbeiter, Gastarbeiter, Flüchtlinge* [History of German Policies on Foreigners: Seasonal Workers, Forced Labourer, Guest Workers, Refugees]. München: C. H. Beck.

Hughes, M. L. (1999). *Shouldering the Burdens of Defeat: West Germany and the Reconstruction of Social Justice*. Chapel Hill: University of North Carolina Press.

Hunn, K. (2011). *Arbeitsplatz Deutschland, Heimat Türkei? Die Anwerbung von Arbeitskräften aus der Türkei im Kontext der bundesdeutschen Ausländerbeschäftigungspolitik* [Workplace Germany, Home Country Turkey? Recruiting Labor Force from Turkey in the Context of West-German Employment Policy of Foreigners]. Gütersloh: Bertelsmann Stiftung. Retrieved from www.bertelsmann-stiftung.de/en/publications/publication/did/arbeitsplatz-deutschland-heimat-tuerkei.

Knortz, H. (2008). *Diplomatische Tauschgeschäfte: 'Gastarbeiter' in der westdeutschen Diplomatie und Beschäftigungspolitik 1953–1973* [Diplomatic Barter Business: 'Guestworkers' in West-German Diplomacy and Employment Policy 1953–1973]. Köln: Böhlau.

Kohls, M. (2012). *Pflegebedürftigkeit und Nachfrage nach Pflegeleistungen von Migrantinnen und Migranten im demographischen Wandel* [Being in Need of Care and Demand for Care Benefits of Migrants within the Demographic Change]. (Abschlussbericht zur Studie 'Wirkungen des Pflegeweiterentwicklungsgesetzes'-Kurzfassung). Nürnberg: Bundesamt für Migration und Flüchtlinge. Retrieved from www.bamf.de/SharedDocs/Anlagen/DE/Publikationen/Forschungsberichte/fb12-pflegebeduerftigkeit-pflegeleistungen.pdf.

Koopmans, R. (2010). Trade-Offs between equality and difference: immigrant integration, multiculturalism and the welfare state in cross-national perspective. *Journal of Ethnic and Migration Studies, 36*, 1–26. doi:10.1080/1369183090325088.

Kühnel, S., Leibold, J. and Mays, A. (2013). Die gegenseitigen Wahrnehmungen und Einstellungen von Einheimischen und Migrantinnen. Ergebnisse aus der Umfrageforschung im Zeitverlauf bis 2011 [Mutual perceptions and attitudes of inborn und migrants: results from survey research up to 2011]. In H. U. Brinkmann and H. H. Uslucan (eds), *Dabeisein und Dazugehören – Integration in Deutschland* (pp. 203–226). Wiesbaden: Springer VS.

Laubenthal, B. and Pries, L. (2012). Alter und Migration: Eine transnationale Perspektive [Ageing and migration: a transnational perspective]. In H. Baykara-Krumme, A. Motel-Klingebiel and P. Schimany (eds), *Viele Welten des Alterns. Ältere Migranten im alternden Deutschland* (pp. 385–410). Wiesbaden: Springer VS.

Memorandum (2009). *Memorandum für eine kultursensible Altenpflege* [Memorandum for a culturally sensitive provision of old age care]. Ein Beitrag zur Interkulturellen Öffnung am Beispiel der Altenpflege. Forum für eine kultursensible Altenpflege, gefördert durch die Beauftragte der Bundesrepublik für Migration, Flüchtlinge und Integration. Retrieved from www.bagso.de/fileadmin/Aktuell/Themen/Pflege/memorandum2002.pdf.

MiGAZIN (2012). *Sarrazin, NSU, NPD, Terror, Türkei, PKK, Frankreich, Integration.* Retrieved from www.migazin.de/2012/03/22/22-03-2012-sarrazin-nsu-npd-turkei-pkk-frankreich-terror-integration.

Migration und Gesundheit (2008). *Schwerpunktbericht der Gesundheitsberichterstattung des Bundes* [Migration and Health – Federal Health Report (Authors: O. Razum, H. Zeeb, U. Meesmann, L. Schenk *et al.*]. Berlin: Robert Koch Institut. Retrieved from www.gbe-bund.de/gbe10/owards.prc_show_pdf.

Mushaben, J. M. (2008). *The Changing Faces of Citizenship. Integration and Mobilization among Ethnic Minorities in Germany.* New York, Oxford: Berghahn Books.

Nationaler Integrationsplan (2007). *Der Nationale Integrationsplan – Neue Wege – Neue Chancen* [National Integrationplan – New Ways – New Opportunities]. Berlin: Presse- und Informationsamt der Bundesregierung. Retrieved from www.bundesregierung.de/Content/DE/_Anlagen/IB/nip-broschuere-best-practise.pdf.

Olbermann, E. (2012). Gesundheitliche Situation und soziale Netzwerke älterer MigrantInnen [Health situation and social networks of ageing migrants]. *Dossier Altern in der Migrationsgesellschaft* (ed. by Heinrich Böll Stiftung), 33–37.

Oltmer, J. (2013). *Migration im 19. und 20. Jahrhundert* [Migration in the 19th and 20th century]. München: Oldenbourg.

Putnam, R. D. (2007). E Pluribus Unum: Diversity and Community in the Twenty-first Century – The 2006 Johan Skytte Prize Lecture. *Scandinavian Political Studies, 30*, 137–174. doi:10.1111/j.1467–9477.2007.00176.x.

Raven, U. and Huismann, A. (2000). Zur Situation ausländischer Demenzkranker und deren Pflege durch Familienangehörige in der Bundesrepublik Deutschland [On the situation of foreign dementia sufferers and their care by family members in Germany]. *Pflege, 13*, 187–196.

Sarrazin, T. (2010). *Deutschland schafft sich ab. Wie wir unser Land aufs Spiel setzen* [Germany abolishes itself: How we gambled with our country]. München: DVA.

Schiffauer, W. (2008). *Parallelgesellschaften. Wieviel Wertekonsens braucht unsere Gesellschaft? Für eine kluge Politik der Differenz* [Parallel Societies. How Much Consensus in Values does Our Society Need? For a Shrewd Policy of Difference]. Bielefeld: transcript.

Schimany, P. and Baykara-Krumme, H. (2012). Zur Geschichte und demografischen Bedeutung älterer Migrantinnen und Migranten in Deutschland [History and demographical relevance of older migrants in Germany]. In H. Baykara-Krumme, A. Motel-Klingebiel and P. Schimany (eds), *Viele Welten des Alterns. Ältere Migranten im alternden Deutschland* (pp. 43–73). Wiesbaden: Springer VS.

Schimany, P., Rühl, S. and Kohls, M. (2012) *Ältere Migrantinnen und Migranten. Entwicklung, Lebenslagen, Perspektiven* [Older Female and Male Migrants. Development, Life Situations, Perspectives] (Forschungsbericht 18). Nürnberg: Bundesamt für Migration und Flüchtlinge. Retrieved from: www.bamf.de/SharedDocs/Anlagen/DE/Publikationen/Forschungsberichte/fb18-aeltere-migranten.pdf.

Schönwälder, K. (2001). *Einwanderung und ethnische Pluralität: Politische Entscheidungen und öffentliche Debatten in Großbritannien und der Bundesrepublik von den 1950er bis zu den 1970er Jahren* [Immigration and Ethnic Plurality: Political Decisions and Public Debates in the United Kingdom and the Federal Republic from 1950 until 1970]. Essen: Klartext.

Schwartz, M. (2008). Vertriebene im doppelten Deutschland. Integrations- und Erinnerungspolitik in der DDR und in der Bundesrepublik [Displaced people in a double Germany. Integration and remembrance policies in the GDR and FRG]. *Vierteljahrshefte für Zeitgeschichte, 56(1)*, 101–151. Retrieved from www.ifz-muenchen.de/heftarchiv/2008_1_4_schwartz.pdf

Statistisches Bundesamt (2006). *Strukturdaten zur Migration in Deutschland 2004* [Migration Demographics in Germany 2004]. Wiesbaden: Statistisches Bundesamt.

Statistisches Bundesamt (2013). *Bevölkerung und Erwerbstätigkeit*, Fachserie 1 Reihe 2.2: Bevölkerung mit Migrationshintergrund – Ergebnisse des Mikrozensus 2012 [Population and Employment. Population with Migration Background in the Microcensus 2012]. Wiesbaden. Retrieved from https://www.destatis.de/DE/Publikationen/Thematisch/Bevoelkerung/MigrationIntegration/Migrationshintergrund2010220127004.pdf.

Strumpen, S. (2012). Altern in fortwährender Migration bei älteren Türkeistämmigen [Ageing in continuous migration of older Turks]. In H. Baykara-Krumme, A. Motel-Klingebiel and P. Schimany (eds), *Viele Welten des Alterns. Ältere Migranten im alternden Deutschland* (pp. 411–433). Wiesbaden: Springer VS.

Sürig, I. and Wilmes, M. (2011). *Die Integration der zweiten Generation in Deutschland: Ergebnisse der TIES-Studie zur türkischen und jugoslawischen Einwanderung* [The Integration of the Second Generation in Germany] (IMIS-Beiträge 39). Retrieved from www.imis.uni-osnabrueck.de/fileadmin/4_Publikationen/PDFs/imis39.pdf.

Tucci, I. and Yildiz, S. (2012). Das Alterseinkommen von Migrantinnen und Migranten: zur Erklärungskraft von Bildungs- und Erwerbsbiografien [Income of migrants in old age: explanatory power of educational and employment biographies]. In H. Baykara-Krumme, A. Motel-Klingebiel and P. Schimany (eds), *Viele Welten des Alterns. Ältere Migranten im alternden Deutschland* (pp. 101–126). Wiesbaden: Springer VS.

Tüsün, S. (2002). Wenn türkische Frauen pflegen [When Turkish women care]. In W. Schnepp (ed.), *Angehörige Pflegen* (pp. 90–111). Huber: Bern.

Weinzierl, R. (2009). *Der Asylkompromiss 1993 auf dem Prüfstand. Gutachten zur Vereinbarkeit der deutschen Regelungen über sichere EU-Staaten und sichere Drittstaaten mit der Europäischen Menschenrechtskonvention, dem EU-Recht und dem Deutschen Grundgesetz.* [The Compromise on Granting Asylum 1993 under Scrutiny]. Berlin: Deutsches Institut für Menschenrechte. Retrieved from www.institut-fuer-menschenrechte.de/uploads/tx_commerce/studie_der_asylkompromiss_1993_auf__dem_pruefstand.pdf.

Yurdakul, G. (2006). State, political parties and immigrant elites: Turkish immigrant associations in Berlin. *Journal of Ethnic and Migration Studies, 32*, 435–453. doi:10.1080/13691830600555244.

Zibrowius, M. (2012). *Convergence or Divergence? Immigrant Wage Assimilation Patterns in Germany* (SOEP papers 479). Berlin: DIW.

Zielke-Nadkarni, A. (1999). Krankheits-, Gesundheits- und Pflegeverständnis türkischer Migrantinnen. Eine empirische Studie [Illness, health and care conceptions of Turkish female migrants. An emprical study]. *Pflege, 12*, 283–288.

Zuwanderer in Deutschland (2013). *Ergebnisse einer repräsentativen Befragung von Menschen mit Migrationshintergrund* [Immigrants in Germany – Results of a Representative Survey of People with Migration Background]. Durchgeführt durch das Institut in Allensbach im Auftrag der Bertelsmann Stiftung. Gütersloh: Bertelsmann. www.ifd-allensbach.de/uploads/tx_studies/7405_Zuwanderer.pdf

Part II

Ageing in the context of migration

A multifaceted phenomenon

6 Older migrants' ageing and dying

An intergenerational perspective

Claudine Attias-Donfut[1]

Introduction

Migration experience is a long-term and multi-faceted phenomenon that continuously evolves over time and shapes the life course of not only those who migrate but also their future generations. An intergenerational perspective seems relevant in migration studies, since migration experiences are continually evolving throughout the life course and they tend to be very different from one generation to the next. This is why it is often noted that migration can exacerbate generational differences. Therefore, it is necessary to develop studies that identify changes from one generation to the next within migrant families and that focus on determining how generational dynamics intersect with the construction (and change) of different realms of belonging (Silverstein and Attias-Donfut, 2010). This is notably illustrated by the enduring debate around what is known as 'Hansen's law'. In his 1938 essay, Marcus Lee Hansen developed 'the principle of third generation interest', a principle captured in his often quoted phrase 'what the son wishes to forget the grandson wishes to remember'. Although this principle has been highly criticised for simplifying the complexity of drivers and contextual factors which produce variable effects on generational behaviour, the strength of Hansen's work is that he raised some interesting questions (such as the question of time and the passage of one generation to another, the process of transmission of norms, cultural values, identity, the interplay between state, family and community and the impact on the process of immigrant integration).

Our hypothesis, drawn from a comparative study (Attias-Donfut *et al.*, 2012), is that the most radical shift in sense of belonging is likely to be with the first generation; the second generation tends to be eager to assimilate fully, irrespective of the type of reception they receive from the host country. This eagerness may conflict with the reluctance of the host society to embrace these migrants fully as equal fellow citizens. This may make migrants prone to develop multiple identities that both acknowledge their present citizen status and the background of their family. Irrespective of whether 'Hansen's law' holds well between the first and the second generation, it appears not to do so with the third generation (although it must be noted that the latter is less easy to observe and has been less frequently investigated). While there may be some symbolic association made by this generation with ancestral roots (e.g. through food, music and art) this cannot be understood as a reversion to the cultural and religious norms of grandparents.

This chapter focuses on some of these processes of transmission and integration in migrants who are retired, or in transition to retirement in the context of the French society. Since the eighteenth century, France has been viewed as 'a country of immigrants in a continent of emigrants' (Blanc-Chaléard, 2001). The history of immigration in France merges with the history of the constitution of its population, i.e. the 'French melting pot' (*le creuset français*) to quote Gérard Noiriel (1988, 1992), who likens France to 'Europe's America'. Those waves of migration have been occurring over a very long period of time. Contemporary history focuses on a last decisive period, which began in the nineteenth century with mass migration stemming from the Industrial Revolution. The population of ageing immigrants has increased as immigrants who arrived in the 1960s – the largest wave in France's migration history – reach retirement age and many choose to stay on in France. When the crisis of 1973 halted labour migration, family migration took over and has considerably expanded since (Blanc-Chaléard, 2001). Migration has become a family-based project, whether it involves the migration of the whole family, the formation of family post-migration or the financial support of family in the country of origin (CoO). The growing tendency of migrants to settle permanently rather than to practice circular migration raises new challenges, not only for migration policy but also for integration patterns and for family policy and practices.

Migrants arriving in this largest wave have been progressively reaching retirement age at the end of the twentieth century. Therefore, it is not surprising that France's concern about the process of retirement of immigrants appeared earlier than in other European countries, and it explains why France initiated the first large, representative survey on ageing of immigrants at the beginning of the twenty-first century, supported by various public institutions and the main providers of retirement pension funds. The topics addressed in this chapter are mainly based on the results of this ground-breaking survey, entitled *Passage à la Retraite des Immigrés* (PRI) (results from this survey are published in Attias-Donfut, 2006 and in Attias-Donfut and Wolff, 2009). Following a description of the survey, this chapter first examines the main changes in generational relationships due to migration, including generational transfers. Second, several aspects of the transition to retirement such as life course perception, transnational practices, desire to return and burial place preferences, whether in home or host country (which appeared to represent a strong indicator of sense of identity and belonging) are described. Finally, the main concluding statement is presented which clarifies that a strong process of enrooting in the host country is at work with the ageing of first generation, driven by the second generation, thus starting a new generational line, in the host country.

Description of the PRI survey

The cross-sectional data set that is used in this chapter derives from a survey conducted in France from December 2002 to March 2003 within the framework of the CNAV (*Caisse Nationale d'Assurance Vieillesse* – National Fund for Retirement Pensions), in collaboration with the INSEE (*Institut National de la Statistique et des Etudes Economiques*). It has been followed by statistical data-sets by INSEE on 2008 and 2012, which confirmed the main trends shown in the 2003 PRI survey (INSEE 2012). The primary focus of this survey is to provide an accurate description of the lives of migrants currently living in France, especially with respect to retirement, and including their migration history and location expectations. Migrants included in the survey must have been born abroad and of foreign nationality at birth (some of them became French citizens at a later point in life). As one of the main aims of the survey is to better understand the retirement decisions of migrants, the sample consists of 6,211 individuals who are aged between 45 and 70 years. The sample, representative of this cohort of immigrants, comprises 51 per cent of respondents who originate from Europe, 38 per cent from Africa and 11 per cent from other countries. Also, the different subsamples at the country level are rather concentrated since only six nationalities represent approximately 70 per cent of the sample. These countries are Portugal, Italy and Spain for the European countries, and Algeria, Morocco and Tunisia for African countries.

As they grow older, it is of utmost importance to know whether migrants intend to stay in France or whether they intend to return to their CoO. It is important for both home and host countries' coordination in managing retirement pensions and in planning health and social services for the elderly. One of the main – and surprising – findings is that only a very small percentage of migrants still actively employed have expressed the desire to go back to their CoO when they retire. Specifically, about 7 per cent of migrants in France, on average, want to return to their CoO, with values of about 2 per cent among Algerians and 10 per cent among Portuguese. The sub-Saharan African group of migrants express a greater desire to return to their home countries, with 17 per cent of these respondents expressing such an intention (Attias-Donfut, 2006).

Each respondent is asked not only about his or her own situation with respect to migration, but also about the characteristics of other family members (i.e. father, mother, siblings, children). The survey is especially well-suited for investigating generational transfers because of the evidence it provides on extended family composition and intra-household distribution. Given the life-cycle position of the respondents, they generally tend to have most often adult children who are beginning their adult life and thus are characterised by substantial financial needs. However, it should be noted that the sample is a rather unusual one. On the one hand, some significant cultural differences exist among migrants coming from different continents. On the other hand, as we consider a sample of migrants, some families may still have children who live (along with other family members) in the CoO. This has specific consequences for the forms of family solidarity that can be observed and for the financial transfers that are made.

Intergenerational relations and transfers within migrant families

Migration has a strong impact on family relations. Two main, opposing propositions have been offered to describe family changes following migration (Baykara-Krumme, 2008). On the one hand, family cohesion is assumed to be higher in immigrant families as compared to non-migrant families in the receiving countries (Nauck, 1988; Baldassar *et al.*, 2007). On the other hand, the second proposition suggests greater family disintegration and alienation or conflict due to the contradiction between traditional family values and individualisation as proposed by modernisation theory, primarily developed by Durkheim (Durkheim 1921; see Lagrange, 2010, among others). In fact, neither of these propositions has been really validated so far. According to several studies, there is no evidence of significant differences between migrants and non-migrants in the level of solidarity or conflict (see, for example, Attias-Donfut and Wolff, 2009; Baykara-Krumme, 2008; Bolzman *et al.*, 2006).

As a family project, migration involves all family generations linked by a complex set of gifts, debts and reciprocity. Help given to parents, including financial assistance, as well as other forms of help, is part of a gift contract. In addition, conflicts and solidarity are not incompatible with each other, and the notion of ambivalent relationships, advanced by Lüscher and Lettke (2002), is applicable both to migrant and non-migrant families. Thus, rather than a fracturing of intergenerational relations, post-migration research has revealed complex processes of renegotiation that take place in migrant families that involve restructuring, contestation, compromise and, in some circumstances, conflict (Creese *et al.*, 1999; Foner, 1997; Kofman, 2004). These approaches reveal the fluid nature of migrant families and the complex renegotiations that take place across generations to ensure the successful settlement of the family in a new land. This process is not specific to migration but it is part of the processes involved in the framework of extensive changes within family life.

Inevitably migration brings specific changes in the structure and functioning of families following migration. These include namely: the contraction around nuclear family relations, limited to the two parents and their children; the central positions taken by the children; and changes in gender relations, in intergenerational social mobility and in transfer behaviours of migrants (Foner, 1997; Yuval-Davis, 1997; Kofman, 2004; Itzigsohn and Giorguli-Saucedo, 2005; Attias-Donfut and Cook, forthcoming). The contraction around nuclear family relations, common to many migrants coming from traditional families from different countries, is reinforced by the political and legal difficulties that family members encounter when joining their families in the new country. In the context of migration, women mainly suffer from the loss of extended family networks in everyday practices and in bringing up children. The latter used to be a 'shared project' in many CoOs, especially for those from African and Arab countries. However, the importance of the larger family group remained and is upheld through the transmission of the bonds between the generations which often continues to operate transnationally, as shown by the frequent comings and goings between the two countries.

The family project (in the sense of the main goals and aspirations for the future that family members share) is reconstructed mainly around the central positions taken by the children, who have the moral obligation to socially succeed in the host country, and as a return gift, to repay their parents' and grandparents' 'sacrifices', and to contribute to taking care of family members. Furthermore, children in migrant families often play an important role, as helpers at a younger age than children in non-migrant families tend to do. Since they tend to be more knowledgeable than their parents about the host country's language and social codes, they are able to serve as mediators between them and the social environment. This can result in a kind of inversion of the respective positions of parents and children in family responsibilities. In a comparative study of African migrants living in France, the UK and South Africa (Attias-Donfut *et al.*, 2012), high educational values and a drive for the success of the children's generation were prominent in all the African families across the three countries. Education was seen as the key route to social mobility for the family as a whole (which, however, does not protect them from some cases of painful failure).

Changes in gender relations are closely linked to changes in intergenerational relations, both resulting in a decrease in traditional familial patriarchal norms. Women may experience a process of 'liberation' in the host country since they benefit from the relaxation of gender divisions (in most of the immigration countries in this study, women's status was, at the time of migration, less favourable than in France, including European countries such as Portugal). In addition, more and more women are playing an increasingly important role in financially supporting their families post-migration. Female migration can be seen in some cases as a process of migrant women empowerment (Foner, 1997; Hansen, 2008; Itzigsohn and Giorguli-Saucedo, 2005). The PRI results show that at the time of retirement, women are less willing than men to return to the country of origin. Some of them might be reluctant to go back to the traditional female role they once had in their home country (Attias-Donfut, 2006).

With the circulation of people, there is an increasing circulation of financial capital. Money transfers undertaken by migrants represent a considerable amount of capital that changes hands. The economic stakes involved in these international flows are huge, both at the macro- and micro-level functioning of the families involved. Money sent by migrants may, to a great extent, improve the standard of living of the family left behind. This also has an impact on the receiving countries, as migrants reduce their standard of living and consume less in the host country because they devote a part of their revenue to their families in the CoO. At the macroeconomic level, remittances affect the economic growth of CoO as well as the brain drain from those countries (Beine *et al.*, 2008).

Despite the importance of this phenomenon, the money transfer behaviours of migrants living in Europe have not been sufficiently studied. We lack data on this topic as we do on many other questions related to migration. We hypothesise that migrants' attitudes and decisions regarding financial transfers are different from those of the general population, based on four reasons (Attias-Donfut and Wolff, 2008). First, family structures vary according to the CoO. Fertility rates are still high in some developing countries, resulting in large extended families, including many siblings. The family solidarity network size is essential for the functioning of transfers, large families providing multiple opportunities and obligations to help and get support. Second, migrants often belong to a 'transnational family', with part of it located in the CoO and part of it in the country of residence. This particularly concerns the first generation of immigrants. Consequently, they are submitted to two distinct pressures: from the family in the country of residence and from the family left behind. Some migrants have children both in the host country and in the country of origin. In other cases, parents and siblings are still in the home country, while spouse and children live in their new place of residence. In such a configuration we can expect the existence of a double channel of transfers, one directly linked to migration through the return of money to the CoO and another one circulating between family members living in the new country. Third, the level of responsibilities towards either parents or children is strongly shaped by the social benefits available to family members in the country where they live. Consequently, they are expected to vary greatly according to migratory waves and the origins of the migrants. The level of social welfare in the CoO directly impacts the financial transfer behaviour of migrants. Therefore, we do not expect to find the same transfer decisions among them as in the general population of the host country. Lastly, these differences in transfer behaviours are not only due to economic and political factors, but also to cultural ones (Antonucci and Jackson, 2003; Wolff *et al.*, 2007).

Migrants are largely involved in money exchanges and they are mainly givers in this respect. They give much more money and do so more frequently than they receive. The proportion of respondents in the PRI survey claiming to have made cash gifts or loans during the last five years amounts to 38.6 per cent, but only 6.2 per cent of them report having received money during this time (Attias-Donfut and Wolff, 2008). This difference may be due to the fact that migrants have higher wages in the host country as compared to the other family members. They may also have received money from the family at an earlier date before the migration, and now have to honour their outstanding debt. The structure of their solidarity network is less exclusively focused on the intergenerational line compared to what we already know about the general population in France (Attias-Donfut and Arber, 2007). There are also significant exchanges with siblings (8.5 per cent) and to a lesser extent with non-family members (4.8 per cent).[2] When considering the direction of money given, we find that parents are more frequently receivers than children. The frequency of gifts to children is 14.4 per cent, while it is 17.7 per cent for gifts to parents. In comparison to family transfers among natives in France, the importance of ascending transfers is the main characteristic of migrants' behaviour.

Those who give to their elderly parents mainly come from developing countries where retirement systems are scarce or absent. While approximately 2 or 3 per cent of the respondents send money to their parents in Italy or Spain, this proportion amounts to 30.5 per cent for migrants born in Morocco and to 29 per cent for migrants born in Tunisia. Many financial transfers made by migrants are sent to the CoO, not only to the parents living there (and children left behind), but also to a bank account belonging to the respondent. The purpose of these savings accounts is related to expenses that will be incurred during short stays in the CoO or in expectation of future investments when returning there, among others. The magnitude of these remittances is very important among the migrant population (Attias-Donfut and Wolff, 2008). Monetary transfers to children represent a human capital investment. It is motivated not only by a desire to help those in need but also to promote children's social success in the future. Parents belonging to richer families face a higher probability of receiving financial help from their own parents and of giving help to their children, while migrants from poor families not only do not receive economic support of any kind, they also have to send financial transfers (remittances) to their parents, as is evident from the findings of the PRI survey. This diminishes their ability to invest in their own well-being in the host country as well as in their children's education.

The social background of immigrants in the CoO has a strong impact on their accomplishments in the host country and this is captured by the indicator of subjective standard of living which characterises the social status of the family in the CoO. This is true across different ethnicities and nationalities of immigrants. This important result supports the hypothesis of *dominance de milieu* (Boudon, 1973) and challenges the standardised images of groups of migrants coming from specific countries of origin (Attias-Donfut and Dimova, 2010). It emphasises the fact that the social heterogeneity of migrants coming from the same CoO, but having different life and family histories, is a major determinant of their own life course. Socio-economic status transmission takes place across borders through monetary, cultural, social and symbolic capital transfers. What economists call 'human capital', or one's level of education, has an important influence on achievements in the destination country. However, even after controlling for the level of education and other crucial variables that are typically used in analyses on migration, the PRI data show that social status has an important impact on socio-economic mobility, and this impact holds irrespective of the ethnic and national origin of migrants. This observation could be explained by the social and symbolic dimensions of the socio-economic position of individuals. One is the feeling of 'social legitimacy', given by the social status of the family, which is called *habitus* by Bourdieu (1981). The other is the help, of any kind, available to the migrant from transnational and family networks due to the family 'social capital'. Although most research generalises the influence of transnational networks for people coming from the same countries, it is reasonable to assume that people from wealthier and more powerful families would have stronger networks in the higher socio-economic strata of the host country (Michel *et al.*, 2011).

The perception of inter-generational social mobility is one important indicator for the feeling of having achieved and succeeded in their migration project (the family project being at the origin of migration, which means the project of giving better life chances to family members and to children). In this respect it is worth noting that the largest majority of immigrants feel that they have been more socially successful than their parents. This perception is even stronger among retirees (75.6 per cent) than among working-age people (68.9 per cent). This difference is verified within the different ethnic groups and is particularly obvious among immigrants from North Africa. While upward mobility is felt strongly (73.9 per cent) by working-age people, this feeling is extremely widespread among retirees from North Africa (82.3 per cent). This difference probably cannot be solely attributed to selection effects between the employed and retired; it is likely that the state of retirement in itself contributes to the feeling of social advancement.

Transition to retirement, life choices and preferences for the place of burial

As people age and approach retirement, the migration experience balance sheet becomes closely linked to life satisfaction, as shown by the PRI results and the comparative data (Cook *et al.*, forthcoming). When the time for retirement arrives, and when there is no longer the constraint of work to stay in the same place, what are the perceptions and desires of migrants regarding where they should live after retirement? Is retirement in the host country *illegitimate* on behalf of those who migrated to seek work? Does retirement then signify the end of the 'imagined return'? That is the thesis developed by Abdelmalek Sayad, a famous pioneer of migration studies in France. Sayad interprets non-return as a double disconnection, from the community of origin and from the community of those who 'emigrated' and have returned home. Immigrants who retire in France might feel their isolation, their double exclusion (Sayad, 1986, 1999). By its 'permanence', retirement removes the contradictions of immigration, no longer justified by 'the alibi of work'. Does such a doubly excluding perception of immigrants' retirement stand up to the facts? The question of legitimacy fails to see retirement as deferred income, as an entitlement earned through a life of work. It also overlooks the strong integrating power of pensions, as reflected in their history and the development of the welfare state.

The results of the PRI study show that many immigrants in France, despite inequalities and the increasing health difficulties associated with ageing, enjoy a sense of accomplishment as they reach retirement – diametrically opposed to Sayad's thesis of an 'illegitimate old age' – with benefits reception fostering integration into the nation. As emphasized by Noiriel (1992), receiving social benefits gives the feeling of being part of the nation. This is in line with the history of the German unity constitution, which brings attention to how the founder of the German Unity, Bismarck, promoted Social Security in the nineteenth century in order to create a national identity and to prevent riots from the working class. According to the same dynamics, receiving retirement benefits is assumed to increase migrants' sense of belonging to the host country. Data on the situation of retired immigrants in France shows that they are both attached to France and to their home countries. Also, when they express strong attachment to their CoO, they rarely transmit this attachment to their children who belong more to the new country, which is generally their country of birth. When children visit their parents' CoO, some do not feel closely attached to it and may feel like foreigners. Very few would like to live there, as has been shown in all countries included in the comparative study (Attias-Donfut *et al.*, 2012). Both the PRI survey and the comparative study reveal a generational discontinuity between first and second generation in most domains including socio-economic milieu, sense of belonging, citizenship, language, ways of life, women's roles and values. Thus, the generational chain has been interrupted; there is no more reproduction from one generation to the next, but rather an unchaining process which favours membership in the new society.

Many of the parents appear to be torn between two places. Comings and goings, difficult choices about where to live after retirement, where to be buried, multiple identities, home place nostalgia, competitive belonging and attachments – these considerations constitute a large part of the ageing of many immigrants. The evidence reveals that most of them choose to stay in the host country despite the fact that they could enjoy a better living standard in the home country since their retirement pension is of more value in a less developed country. Irrespective of this, they find many reasons to stay in France, not only to receive better health care but mainly to remain close to their children and grandchildren. Thus, it is clear that their intergenerational bonds are powerful enough to make them want to stay in the host country.

Among the first generation migrants, another important choice remains to be made regarding the final resting place after they are deceased (Attias-Donfut and Wolff, 2005, see also Francis *et al.*, 2001). Migrants express a diversity of preferences regarding place of burial, between those who opt to be buried in France, those who wish their body to be returned to their CoO, and those who do not indicate a choice, either because they do not care or are undecided. These preferences have multiple determinants, among which CoO and religion have significant influence. France is the first choice for Europeans when taking an extensive definition of Europe including Eastern Europe and Russia. More than half of the migrants born in Europe express this preference (55 per cent). Less than one European in five wants their remains returned to their CoO, whereas 25 per cent do not care or are undecided. The only real contrast is found among the Portuguese with a third desiring a burial in their CoO, a third in France, and the remaining third without a clear idea about place of burial, which confirms 'the Portuguese exception'. The results are practically reversed among migrants from North and sub-Saharan Africa: 56.4 per cent want to be buried in their home country, and less than a quarter in France. These sharp differences reflect a strong attachment to the CoO among North and sub-Saharan Africans. The same pattern is found among migrants from the Middle East and Turkey, more than half of whom want to be buried in their home country. Conversely, people born in Asia show a very strong preference for burial in France (32.4 per cent) whereas burial in the home country is desired by fewer than 12 per cent. Lastly, migrants from the Americas, who are grouped together for reasons of numbers, are located between these two positions, but a high proportion of them have no preference (40 per cent). The results of an INED (National Institute for Demographic Studies in France) survey conducted in 1992 among a large sample of adult migrants, living in France, less than 60 years old (Tribalat, 1996), shows very similar rates for the countries and regions studied, which indicates stable trends in this respect. These preferences involve religious affiliation, territorial attachments (level of affective and social attachments to the home country and to France) and, above all, kinship ties, mainly to family left behind and towards ancestors.

Whatever the feeling of attachment or loyalty to a place, to individuals or to a lineage, the choice of where one wants be buried is not simple. Migration is expected to introduce spatial discontinuity between the place where family members and ancestors are buried (in the home country) and the place where they live (now elsewhere), thereby breaking the territorial link in the chain of generations. Filiation and memory of the deceased both have the same eschato-logical purpose, i.e. warding off annihilation (complete disappearance through death). According to Déchaux (1997, p. 281), 'memory of ancestors provides a sense of belonging to a natural order, that of the perpetuation of life as testified by the succession of family generations'.[3] Thus, the only two options are either to break with the dead (and be buried in the host country) or to break with the living (and be buried in the home country). Burial in the country of adoption consecrates the break with the past and with the dead, forcing those who make this choice to abandon any hope of joining the chain of generations, though it preserves their chance of being remembered by the living and, hence, their sur-vival by proxy. Conversely, being laid to rest with one's ancestors as a mark of loyalty to family history may cut individuals off from the living generations, those of the future, and compromise their chances of survival by proxy, since their graves are likely to be abandoned by the living. In this case, the migrants whose offspring have settled in France may thus face a dilemma which was expressed in a very evident way in the interviews of ageing migrants. The ceme-tery consecrates filiation and family continuity; memory of the deceased is an integral component of all kinship ties. The timescale of kinship transcends that of individual lives and provides a means to escape the finite nature of existence. The results also show that the choice to be buried in France is always made by those whose parents are buried in France. The cemetery has a strong integrative power. Its importance is revealed by the Muslim migrants' demands for Muslim burial sections in cemeteries. Time of retirement and death rituals reveal the complexity of processes of integration and of generational transmission among migrant families. Our results confirm the great difficulty in the transmission of personal and social identities in migrant families, with each generation recon-structing its own identity in new ways across generations, while at the same time generally maintaining family solidarity.

Notes

1 I wish to thank Ute Karl and Sandra Torres for their remarks and suggestions on the first version of this chapter; I am also very grateful to Lisa Trierweiler for having corrected and improved the English of the chapter.
2 We note that non-family members are more frequently involved in money lending than in money giving.
3 Quotation translated by Catriona Dutreuil, who was the article translator for the English version of the journal *Population*.

References

Antonucci, T. C. and Jackson, J. S. (2003). Ethnic and cultural differences in intergenerational social support. In V. L. Bengtson and A. Lowenstein (eds), *Global Ageing and Challenge to Families* (pp. 355–370). New York: de Gruyter.

Attias-Donfut, C. (ed.) (2006). *L'Enracinement: Enquête sur le vieillissement des immigrés en France* [The Rootedness: A Survey on Immigrants' Ageing in France]. Paris: Armand Colin.

Attias-Donfut, C. and Arber, S. (2007). Equity and solidarity across the generations. In S. Arber and C. Attias-Donfut (eds), *The Myth of Generational Conflict: The Family and State in Ageing Societies* (2nd edn) (pp. 1–21). New York: Routledge.

Attias-Donfut, C. and Cook, J. (forthcoming). Intergenerational relationships in migrant families. In C. Bolzman, L. Bernardi and J.-M. LeGoff (eds), *Second Generation Transition to Adulthood and Intergenerational Relations: Exploring Methodological Issues and Innovations*. Wiesbaden: Springer.

Attias-Donfut, C. and Dimova, R. (2010). Social mobility 'sans frontières'? Results from a survey on immigrants in France. *European Societies, 13*, 51–68. doi:10.1080/146166 96.2010.483000.

Attias-Donfut, C. and Wolff, F.-C. (2005). The preferred burial location of persons born outside France. *Population (English edition), 60*, 699–720. doi:10.3917/popu.505. 0813.

Attias-Donfut, C. and Wolff, F.-C. (2008). Patterns of intergenerational transfers among immigrants in France: a comparative perspective. In C. Saraceno (ed.), *Families, Ageing and Social Policy: Intergenerational Solidarity in European Welfare States (Globalization and Welfare)* (pp. 259–284). Cheltenham: Edward Elgar.

Attias-Donfut, C., and Wolff, F.-C. (2009). *Le Destin des enfants d'immigrés: Un désenchaînement des générations* [The Destiny of Children of Immigrants: A Generation Unchaining]. Paris: Stock.

Attias-Donfut, C., Cook, J., Hoffman, J. and Waite, L. (eds) (2012). *Citizenship, Belonging and Intergenerational Relations in African Migration*. London: Palgrave.

Baldassar, L., Vellekoop Baldock, C. and Wilding, R. (2007). *Families Caring across Borders: Migration, Ageing and Transnational Caregiving*. London: Palgrave Macmillan.

Baykara-Krumme, H. (2008). *Immigrant Families in Germany: Intergenerational Solidarity in Later Life*. Berlin: Weißensee.

Beine, M., Docquier, F. and Rapoport, H. (2008). Brain drain and human capital formation in developing countries: winners and losers. *Economic Journal, 118*, 631–652. doi:10.1111/j.1468–0297.2008.02135.x.

Blanc-Chaléard, M.-C. (2001). *Histoire de l'immigration* [History of Immigration]. Paris: La Découverte.

Bolzman, C., Fibbi, R. and Vial, M. (2006). What to do after retirement? Elderly migrants and the question of return. *Journal of Ethnic and Migration Studies, 32(8)*, 1359–1375. doi:10.1080/13691830600928748.

Boudon, R. (1973). *L'Inégalité des chances* [Life Chances Inequality]. Paris: Armand Colin.

Bourdieu, P. (1981). *Questions de sociologie* [Questions of Sociology]. Paris: Les Editions de Minuit.

Cook, J., Attias-Donfut, C. and Hoffman, J. (forthcoming). 'We always had our bags packed…': the desire to engage in return migration among African families in Britain, France and South Africa.

Creese, G., Dyck, I. and McLaren, A. (1999). *Reconstituting the Family: Negotiating Immigration and Settlement* (RIIM (Research on Immigration and Integration in the Metropolis) Working Paper Series 99–1). Retrieved from http://mbc.metropolis.net/assets/uploads/files/wp/1999/WP99-10.pdf.

Déchaux, J.-H. (1997). *Le Souvenir des morts: Essai sur le lien de filiation* [The Memory of the Deceased: An Essay on the Filiation Bond]. Paris: Puf.

Durkheim, E. (1921). La Famille conjugale [The conjugal family]. *Revue Philosophique, 46(9)*, pp. 1–14.

Foner, N. (1997). The immigrant family: cultural legacies and cultural changes. *International Migration Review, 31(4)*. 961–974. Retrieved from www.jstor.org/stable/2547420.

Francis, D., Kellaher, L. and Neophytou, G. (2001). The cemetery: evidence of continuing bonds. In J. Hockey, J. Katz and N. Small (eds), *Grief, Mourning and Death Ritual* (pp. 226–236). Buckingham: Open University Press.

Hansen, M. L. (1938). *The Problem of the Third Generation Immigrant.* Rock Island, IL: Augustana Historical Society.

Hansen, P. (2008). Circumcising migration: gendering return migration among Somalilanders. *Journal of Ethnic and Migration Studies, 34*, 1109–1125. doi:10.1080/13691830802230422.

INSEE (Institut National de la Statistique et des Etudes Economiques) (2012). *Immigrés et descendants d'immigrés en France* [Immigrants and Descendants of Immigrants in France]. Paris: INSEE References.

Itzigsohn, J. and Giorguli-Saucedo, S. (2005). Incorporation, transnationalism, and gender: immigrant incorporation and transnational participation as gendered processes. *International Migration Review, 39(4)*, 895–920. doi:10.1111/j.1747-7379.2005.tb00293.x.

Kofman, E. (2004). Family-related migration: a critical review of European studies. *Journal of Ethnic and Migration Studies, 30*, 243–262. doi:10.1080/1369183042000200687.

Lagrange, H. (2010). *Le déni des cultures* [The Denial of Cultures]. Paris: Seuil.

Lüscher, K. and Lettke, F. (2002). L'Ambivalence, une clé pour l'analyse des relations intergénérationnelles [Ambivalence: a key for intergenerational analysis]. *Retraite et Société, 35*, 142–169.

Michel, A., Prunier, D. and Faret, L. (2011). Familles migrantes et ancrages locaux au Mexique: Trajectoires et patrimoines migratoires dans la region de Tehuantepec [Migrant families and local rooting (foothold) in Mexico: trajectories and patrimony in the land of Tehuantepec]. *Autrepart, 57–58*, 77–94.

Nauck, B. (1988). Migration and change in parent-child relationships: the case of Turkish migrants in Germany. *International Migration, 26(1)*, pp. 33–55.

Noiriel, G. (1988). *Le Creuset français: Histoire de l'immigration* [The French Melting Pot. History of Immigration]. Paris: Seuil.

Noiriel, G. (1992). *Population, immigration et identité nationale en France: XIXe-XXe siècle* [Population, Immigration and National Identity in France: 19th–20th Centuries]. Paris: Hachette.

Sayad, A. (1986). La 'Vacance' comme pathologie de la contradiction d'immigré: le cas de la retraite et de la préretraite ['Vacancy', as a pathology of the contradiction of the immigrant: the case of retirement and pre-retirement]. *Gérontologie, 60*, 37–55.

Sayad, A. (1999). *La double Absence: Des illusions de l'émigré aux souffrances de l'immigré* [The Double Absence: From the Illusions of the Emigrant to the Suffering of the Immigrant]. Paris: Le Seuil.

Silverstein, M. and Attias-Donfut, C. (2010). Intergenerational relationships of international migrants in developed Western nations: United States and France. In D. Dannefer and C. Phillipson (eds), *The Sage Handbook of Social Gerontology* (pp. 177–189). London: Sage.

Tribalat, M. (1996). *De l'Immigration à l'intégration: Enquête sur les populations d'origine étrangère en France* [From Immigration to Integration: A Survey on Populations from Foreign Origin in France]. Paris: La Découverte/Ined.

Yuval-Davis, N. (1997). *Gender and Nation*. London: Sage.

Wolff, F.-C., Spilerman, S. and Attias-Donfut, C. (2007). Transfers from migrants to their children: evidence that altruism and cultural factors matter. *Review of Income and Wealth, 53*, 619–644. doi:10.1111/j.1475–4991.2007.00248.x.

7 Is there a way back?

A state-of-the-art review of the literature on retirement return migration

Ruxandra Oana Ciobanu and Anne Carolina Ramos

Introduction

International labour migration after World War II (WWII) was thought to be a transient period (Bolzman *et al.*, 2006; Témime, 2001; White, 2006); manpower would come to Western and Northern Europe, work for a few years, 'set aside some capital and then return to their country where they [would] invest it' (Ganga, 2006, p. 1395). Return was anticipated both by the countries of destination and the migrants themselves. Nonetheless, they have often ended up staying longer. Employment, the dream of saving to buy a property and the opportunity to provide a better future for their children are important factors when deciding whether or not to return to the country of origin. With the ever-increasing incidence of return not taking place, countries have had to change the focus in migration policies from admission to integration (Bolzman *et al.*, 2006). For many migrants, return to the country of origin became a 'myth' – an 'unfulfilled expectation or desire' (Leavey *et al.*, 2004, p. 764).

Subsequently, a sedentariness of migration (Machado and Roldão, 2010) has occurred, and many guest workers have grown older in the destination country. Once they retired, the question of whether to stay or return re-emerged (De Coulon and Wolff, 2010; Hunter, 2011). They ceased to be 'foreign labourers' or 'guest workers' and assumed a new social status that allows them to make new plans for the future (Bolzman *et al.*, 2006). Such plans include the decision to stay in the host country, to return to the country of origin, or even to go 'back and forth' between the two (De Coulon and Wolff, 2006). The decision to 'put down roots' in the host country or keep open the possibility of a return depends on the lifestyle of older people and the way they combine personal resources and cultural identity when reaching 'the critical milestone of retirement' (Bolzman *et al.*, 2006, p. 1360). The literature shows that retirement is different for natives and migrants as 'most immigrants accepted that their presence in the [host] society was provisional', and that the main 'justification of their presence was the work that they performed' (Bolzman *et al.*, 2006, p. 1360). However, this group of migrants who are ageing in place is a highly selected one, since many of their compatriots have already returned 'home' (Böcker and Balkır, 2012).

Klinthäll (2006) has shown that there is a clear 'retirement effect' impacting the propensity to return: many of those who return had made a conscious plan to spend retirement in their home country. This decision may bring new challenges to public policies, impacting the planning of social and health services in both home and destination countries. Despite its relevance, the study of retirement return migration among pensioner labour migrants has received little attention in the literature (Warnes and Williams, 2006). The aim of this chapter is to present an overview of the existing research in this area focusing on the aspects playing a key role in older migrants' decisions to remain in the host country or return to the country of origin after retirement.

This literature review is carried out based on a pool of 60 publications in English, French, German and Portuguese from different continents, with a majority from Europe. We started building this database following three selection principles corresponding to three themes: return migration, ageing migrants' return and ageing migrants. Based on our review of the references of each publication, our database was expanded consequently allowing for a thorough review of the European literature. The database contains 24 publications on return migration in general, three on ageing migrants and 33 on retirement return migration. For the purpose of this chapter we reference 37 of these publications. The journals surveyed deal largely with ageing and migration studies.

The chapter is structured in two main parts. The first part looks at the factors influencing return and the 'back and forth' choice in retired guest workers. In the second part, the existing research is summarised, gaps in the literature identified, and the themes and topics needing more attention are delineated.

Explaining return

Return migration depends on the combination of a large number of factors that may constrain or favour it. Economic, social, cultural and health related aspects appear to play an important role in older migrants' decision to return to the country of origin or to stay in the host country after retirement. In the following part we will discuss the main factors influencing return migration according to our literature review.

Age and gender

'Age is an important predictor of return migration' (Yahirun, 2014, p. 4). Return intentions may vary depending on *when* people are asked about it, since their circumstances of life may change over time (Klinthäll, 2006). Bessy and Riche (1993) highlight that the return desire is more representative among 'young-old', since active migrants do not (yet) think about retirement, and the oldest have already made 'definitive' plans. Age, together with one's health, care needs and the medical system, can influence the decision to return to the home country (Böcker and Balkır, 2012; Bolzman *et al.*, 2006; Leavey *et al.*, 2004; Yahirun, 2014). De Coulon and Wolff (2006, 2010) and Klinthäll (2006) observed that older migrants are more likely to intend to stay in the host country.

Regarding gender, the question is if men and women aspire in a similar way to return to the home country. One needs to take into account the difference in life expectancy between men and women, the migration history, participation in the labour market (Attias-Donfut *et al.*, 2005), and presence in the public sphere (Buffel, forthcoming). The literature shows clear differences between men and women migrants.

Empirical studies emphasise the return preferences of Turkish, Portuguese, Italian and Spanish men, and a reluctance among women to return (Böcker and Balkır, 2012; Bolzman *et al.*, 2006). Similar results exist for a variety of migrants in France (Attias-Donfut and Wolff, 2005; De Coulon and Wolff, 2006) and in Sweden (Klinthäll, 2006). Women while abroad have acquired a certain independence and are afraid of losing it when returning to the country of origin (De Haas and Fokkema, 2010). They, however, do not always have a say in the return decision (De Bree *et al.*, 2010; De Haas and Fokkema, 2010). Another gender-mediated difference is the financial situation upon return, with women being more often in a dependent situation (Gualda and Escriva, 2014).

Culture and integration: education, language and naturalisation

Studies show that the propensity to return to one's home country diminishes as older migrants become more integrated in the host country (Bolzman *et al.*, 2006; Klinthäll, 2006). However, Hunter (2011) also shows an opposite situation where spatially segregated 'faux célibataire or "geographically single" men' (p. 180) from North and West Africa end up far from their families, spending their old age in migrant worker hostels in France. Variables such as time spent in the host country, citizenship acquisition, years of schooling and language acquisition reduce the return likelihood (Bessy and Riche, 1993; De Bree *et al.*, 2010; De Coulon and Wolff, 2010; Dos Santos and Wolff, 2010; Klinthäll, 2006; Yahirun, 2014), while cultural differences such as education system, traditions and moral values can boost return (Razum *et al.*, 2005). Holding the host country passport may 'enhance a person's local sense of belonging' (De Bree *et al.*, 2010, p. 500), providing social status and the option to circulate between the host and home countries. Dos Santos and Wolff (2010) also suggest that migrants' prior return intentions may influence the degree of investment in learning the language of the host country.

Economic situation: pension, occupation and home ownership

The propensity to return is greater when remittances are sent, and the migrant has economic ties with the country of origin. Being able to receive pensions and benefits (e.g. disability) in the country of origin are strong motives for return, since income acquired abroad is worth more in the home country due to purchasing power differentials between home and host countries, giving migrants a socio-economic advantage (Cerase, 1974; De Bree *et al.*, 2010; Dos Santos and Wolff, 2010; Hunter, 2011; Langers, 2008; Leavey *et al.*, 2004). A more comfortable economic situation also allows old migrants to go 'back and forth' after retirement (Bolzman *et al.*, 2006; De Haas and Fokkema, 2010). The return intentions are also influenced by the profession and by homeownership: Individuals who are owners and those that have a valued profession are less likely to return than renters and migrants with more modest professions and weaker attachments to the labour force (Bessy and Riche, 1993; Yahirun, 2014). Likewise, house or land ownership in the country of origin can potentially boost return (Falkingham *et al.*, 2012; Langers, 2008).

Norms, values and infrastructure of the villages

As De Bree *et al.* (2010) point out, 'return migration is not simply a matter of "going home", as feelings of belonging need to be renegotiated upon return' (p. 489). In fact, living conditions in the country of origin may be idealised and this, in combination with long periods away from home, may generate difficulties with reintegration (Gualda and Escriva, 2014). The everyday reality may be different from the one imagined while abroad or during the short visits on holidays (Ganga, 2006). Studies show that older people tend to prefer to live in the countryside or by the seaside, especially those who grew up in more rural areas or who are looking for a better climate and amenity-rich locations (De Coulon and Wolff, 2010; Langers, 2008; Lundholm, 2012; Rodríguez *et al.*, 2002). However, this may have a significant impact not only on moving from one country to another, but also from large cities to small ones, or from the city to the countryside. Furthermore, migrants might feel like outsiders when going back to their birthplace, since their different life course means that they no longer have much in common with members of their origin community (Falkingham *et al.*, 2012). A perception of rapidly changing values and behaviour also contributes to the rejection of return or difficulties with reintegration among older migrants (De Haas and Fokkema, 2010; Hunter, 2011; Leavey *et al.*, 2004). Long decades of living abroad may have brought economic and social changes that they 'do not always understand properly' (Rodríguez *et al.*, 2002, p. 251), preventing them for instance, from opening new businesses since they may be disconnected from the local market and have difficulties to find suppliers and customers (Schaeffer, 2001).

Neighbours, friends and social isolation

Advanced age and many years living abroad may cause the weakening or even loss of ties with neighbours and friends in the country of origin. Return migrants are thus twice more likely than non-migrants to have other return migrants as closest friends (Barrett and Mosca, 2013). Consequently, many migrants may also experience social isolation and loneliness, particularly those who are returning to their homeland in old age (Barrett and Mosca, 2013; Schaeffer, 2001).

The lack of contact with old friends and neighbours may represent a significant deterrent to return. However, other studies also show that ties to the place of origin may be sustained through regular visits during which migrants maintain their visibility and presence in the community of origin (De Bree *et al.*, 2010; Falkingham *et al.*, 2012). In fact, maintaining positive contacts with friends and family left behind in the country of origin appears to be a key element in ensuring a successful return (Leavey *et al.*, 2004). Rodríguez and Egea (2006) and Gualda and Escriva (2014) show that many older people may even have the support of relatives, friends and acquaintances from their home country with whom they have never lost contact.

The location of the family: spouse, children and grandchildren

The decision to return is strongly related to the place of residence of family members, especially spouses, children and grandchildren (Bolzman *et al.*, 2006; De Coulon and Wolff, 2006; Gualda and Escriva, 2014; Razum *et al.*, 2005), whereas the location of collaterals and ascendants only slightly modifies the return intention (Bolzman *et al.*, 2006). Having a spouse who is a native of the host country reduces one's return likelihood; while being in an endogamous marriage or having the spouse at the origin increases the return propensity (Bessy and Riche, 1993; De Haas and Fokkema, 2010). The presence of children and grandchildren also contributes very strongly to immigrants' settlement at the destination (Bessy and Riche, 1993; Ganga, 2006; Razum *et al.*, 2005). Having at least one child in the country of origin increases the likelihood of returning, while having all children in the host country reduces it (De Coulon and Wolff, 2010). However, this does not necessarily mean there is a preference for living full time in the host country, and migrants might go 'back and forth' between the two countries (Bolzman *et al.*, 2006; Krumme, 2003, 2004). Spending part of the year in each country allows immigrants to maintain contacts with children wherever they live (De Coulon and Wolff, 2006). Still, older parents may opt to settle closer to their daughters for caregiving purposes (De Coulon and Wolff, 2010). This choice may be stronger for the widowed than for those with another marital status (Liaw and Frey, 2003). Those without children tend to opt more often for staying in the host country (Bessy and Riche, 1993).

Health services and social rights

Ageing labour migrants have experienced a life of hard work, usually in tough conditions (Beirão, 2010; Bolzman *et al.*, 2006; Hunter, 2011; Schaeffer, 2001). Therefore, the range of diseases affecting them is broad, adding weight to their return decision. Medical treatments can be accessed in the health systems at both the origin and destination countries, especially when they maintained transnational family relations, social and legal ties (Gualda and Escriva, 2014). However, the welfare system from the country of origin is often less reliable, and certain treatments and drugs may not be available, which means that many stay in or return frequently to the host country to renew prescriptions or to receive specialised treatment (Hunter, 2011; Schaeffer, 2001). When, for medical or economic reasons, they are not able to go 'back and forth', many choose to stay at the destination to benefit from the health and social security system in the host country and their children's company (Böcker and Balkır, 2012; Bolzman *et al.*, 2006; Leavey *et al.*, 2004; Schaeffer, 2001). However, some also have the wish to 'die at home' (Hunter, 2012) or return in case of terminal illness, opting to return at the end of life (Razum *et al.*, 2005).

Formal policy constraints

Older migrants may also have to face formal policy constraints regarding their decision to return. In France, the Netherlands and Switzerland, there is a limited number of months foreigners can stay away without risking the loss of their residence permits and entitlements to social rights, and this reduces their mobility (Böcker and Balkır, 2012; Bolzman *et al.*, 2006; Hunter, 2011). Similarly, in Sweden retired immigrants can receive their pension abroad if there are agreements with their home country (Klinthäll, 2006). De Haas and Fokkema (2010) highlight that 'the restrictive European immigration policies imply that migrants have little incentive to give up their residency rights' (p. 555). In this sense, acquiring dual citizenship is perceived as a means of ensuring their residency and their permanent option to return to the host country, as well as a way of obtaining social benefits (De Bree *et al.*, 2010).

The third option: going 'back and forth'

The literature review shows that the opposition between 'staying' or 'returning' does not reflect the complexity of influences and life strategies that connects migrants to their host and origin countries (Bolzman *et al.*, 1999, 2006; De Coulon and Wolff, 2006; Rodríguez and Egea, 2006). Those who decide to stay often continue to cultivate relations with their home country, and those who decide to return do not necessarily lose contact with their former host country. There seems to be a circulatory model that 'allows migrants to preserve their origins and to keep in touch with both realities that are significant to them' (Bolzman *et al.*, 2006, p. 1373), whether they 'reside' in their origin or host country. This 'transnational lifestyle' enables many older people to 'maintain and continue to develop residential opportunities, social networks and welfare entitlements in more than one country' (Warnes and Williams, 2006, p. 1265). However, the extent of such circulation varies depending on the symbolic ties migrants have with their destination and country of origin, the quality of their family relations, friendships, their state of health and economic circumstances, as pensions shrink and extreme old age puts considerable restraints on mobility. Analysing older Turks in Germany, Krumme (2004) identified three different patterns of pendulum migration: bilocal circular migration (pensioners spend the summer in Turkey and the winter in Germany), circular migration after returning to one's country of origin (older migrants live mostly in Turkey but come to Germany for business or personal relations) and circular migration with primary residency in the country of former employment (pensioners live mainly in Germany but still spend some time in the home country).

Böcker and Balkır (2012) found a similar behaviour among Turkish migrants in the Netherlands. De Bree *et al.* (2010), De Haas and Fokkema (2010) and Schaeffer (2001) also found this residential mobility among older Moroccans who immigrated to Belgium, France and the Netherlands. Older Italians in England also circulate between two countries doing a kind of 'seasonal migration' in order to take advantage of milder weather throughout the year and meet other migrants who might spend the summer in their origin villages (Ganga, 2006). Several studies identified circular migration in the intentions of migrants approaching retirement (Attias-Donfut *et al.*, 2005; Bolzman *et al.*, 1993, 1999, 2006; De Coulon and Wolff, 2006, 2010; Dos Santos and Wolff, 2010; Klinthäll, 2006). Adopting pendulum migratory strategies, older migrants can visit family and friends left behind, do business, use the welfare system of both countries while satisfying the legal requirements in order not to lose their social assistance benefits and residence rights (Böcker and Balkır, 2012; De Haas and Fokkema, 2010; Krumme, 2003, 2004). As De Haas and Fokkema (2010) point out, '[t]his emerging form of transnational mobility defies conventional migration categories since these migrants can be classified neither as permanent settlers nor as returnees, and are usually ignored by official migration statistics' (p. 557), making it difficult to accurately conduct quantitative research on actual return as opposed to intentions.

Conclusion

The results of this literature review reveal some methodological conclusions, and point out limitations and gaps to address in future research. First, defining return is increasingly difficult given the rise in mobile and fluid lives, and the decrease in those who are sedentary at the destination or return permanently to the home country. Second, measuring return poses also formal problems because many persons 'do not complete the arrival and departure forms, which are the main documentary source' (Rodríguez *et al.*, 2002, p. 235). Consequently, it is difficult to capture the characteristics of older migrants who choose to return and provide updated information on migration flows between origin and destination (Rodríguez *et al.*, 2002). Furthermore, this lack of research may also be related to the cost involved in finding individuals after their move to another country (De Coulon and Wolff, 2006); or to the fact that return migrants mix with the native population and become indistinguishable from the older population as a whole (Barrett and Mosca, 2013).

Another problematic element is the location of data collection: in the country of destination, the country of origin or in both. Accordingly, studies on return migration among older migrants need to be interpreted with caution depending on where the data was collected. Attias-Donfut *et al.* (2005) found that only 7.4

per cent of the retired immigrants miss their country of origin 'very often'. There might be a selection effect behind these differences, since at the end of the active period, some of the most nostalgic migrants might have already returned to the country of birth. As a consequence, research conducted solely in the destination country overlooks the actual return population. There seems to be a gap between the perspectives of the destination country and the home country, since 'little has been done to analyse actual rates of retirement return migration from a host country perspective' (Klinthäll, 2006, p. 155).

Most of the existing studies present older migrants by nationality (Attias-Donfut *et al.*, 2005; Bolzman *et al.*, 1993, 1999, 2006), e.g. Algerians or Portuguese in France, Italians or Spaniards in Switzerland. This can lead to the impression that national groups are homogeneous, a rather erroneous conclusion. Within these groups there are differences. In order to better analyse their return intentions it would be important to consider their migration history, age at migration, labour market integration, legal, economic and health status.

The present review of the literature has allowed us also to uncover a series of gaps in the existing research. As Warnes and Williams (2006) have underlined, 'many of the issues at the intersection of ageing, retirement and migration have been neglected' (p. 1266). Because immigrants' presence in the destination country is mainly connected to their work activity (Témime, 2001), much of the research on return is mainly dedicated to economically active persons (De Coulon and Wolff, 2010), focusing predominantly on return intentions (Attias-Donfut *et al.*, 2005; Bolzman *et al.*, 2006; Razum *et al.*, 2005) rather than on real *decisions* made by immigrants. Another aspect that needs more attention concerns the impact of living in migrant neighbourhoods on the return propensity (Yahirun, 2014). Little is known about the lives of older migrants upon return and the process of reintegration in the countries of origin. Linked to this, there are few studies on friends and social isolation after return migration (Barrett and Mosca, 2013). Their transnational lives and continuous mobility at an advanced age are also often overlooked (Hunter, 2011; Klinthäll, 2006). There is limited research on return migration to the place of birth (and not just home country); this constitutes an important underplayed aspect (Rodríguez *et al.*, 2002).

The exploration of whether one's growing frailty can lead to return to the country of origin is also little researched. However, this could be the case for migrants who do not have the economic or formal means to access care in the destination country and aim to take advantage of the facilities and lower costs of informal care in their country of origin. Furthermore, De Coulon and Wolff (2010) underline the significance of longitudinal studies to understand return decision making and its consequences, by following respondents in time and space. Due to cost limitations, however, most studies on return migration explore only intentions. Often intentions and behaviour are discrepant (Bolzman *et al.*, 2006), which brings challenges to the study of return. Until now there has been only one longitudinal study (Yahirun, 2014).

Looking back at the existing work, we notice differences and discrepancies between different groups of older migrants, and between host and home countries.

Most labour migrants who brought their families with them or had children while abroad are motivated to stay in the host countries by the presence of adult children and grandchildren. Nevertheless, they travel frequently and spend periods of time every year in their home countries (Bolzman *et al.*, 2006; Ganga, 2006), taking advantage of 'free movement' agreements for EU citizens (in the case of migrants from Southern Europe). At the same time, there are migrants from West and North Africa who, in spite of having family in the home country, have lower return intentions and tend to prefer engaging in back-and-forth trips (Hunter, 2011).

Noteworthy is the lack of comparative research between settlers and returnees, between older migrants in different destinations and between older migrants from different regions within the same country of origin. At this point, there is much left unknown because the current state of research has not uncovered, for example, if Italians in Australia, France, Switzerland and the UK behave differently or similarly, and which variables influence their return migration or mobility choice. It is not known if older emigrants from rural or urban areas opt differently for return. In addition, we do not yet know the return behaviour of those individuals who arrived as asylum seeker in various destination countries, received refugee status, and later on aged as refugees or received a more permanent status, and even took on citizenship. The return intentions of European migrants who left for North or South America are also another topic that has not been explored, and likewise the return behaviour of highly skilled retired migrants, since most studies focus on lower skilled former labour immigrants after WWII. Thus, if we want to build on the former research while simultaneously moving forward, we need more systematic comparative studies on return migration.

Acknowledgements

The research by Ruxandra Oana Ciobanu leading to this publication has received funding from the People Programme (Marie Curie Actions) of the European Union's Seventh Framework Programme (FP7/2007–2013) under REA grant agreement no. 328518. We would like to thank Alistair Hunter, Sandra Torres and Ute Karl for their valuable comments and the editors for inviting us to be part of this important discussion about ageing and migration.

References

Attias-Donfut, C. and Wolff, F.-C. (2005). Transmigration et choix de vie à la retraite [Transmigration and life choices at retirement]. *Retraite et société, 44(1)*, 79–105. Retrieved from www.cairn.info/revue-retraite-et-societe-2005-1-page-79.htm.

Attias-Donfut, C., Tessier, P. and Wolff, F.-C. (2005). Les Immigrés au temps de la retraite [Immigrants at the time of retirement]. *Retraite et société, 44(1)*, 11–47. Retrieved from www.cairn.info/revue-retraite-et-societe-2005-1-page-11.htm.

Barrett, A. and Mosca, I. (2013). Social isolation, loneliness and return migration: evidence from older Irish adults. *Journal of Ethnic and Migration Studies, 39*, 1659–1677. doi:10.1080/1369183X.2013.833694.

Beirão, D. (2010). La Parole aux retraités portugais! Vieillir entre deux patries [The word to the Portuguese retirees! Ageing between two countries]. In M. Pauly (ed.), *ASTI 30+: 30 ans de migrations, 30 ans de recherches, 30 ans d'engagements* [30 Years of Migration, 30 Years of Research, 30 Years of Engagement] (pp. 190–197). Luxembourg: ASTI.

Bessy, P. and Riche, C. (1993). Le Retour au pays pour la retraite des personnes nées dans les DOM: Une enquête sur les intentions [People born in the DOM returning home after retirement: a survey of intentions]. *Economie et statistique*, *270(10)*, 51–61. doi:10.3406/estat.1993.5825.

Böcker, A. and Balkır, C. (2012). *Migration in Later Life: Residence, Social Security and Citizenship Strategies of Turkish Return Migrants and Dutch Retirement Migrants in Turkey* [Adobe Digital Editions version]. Retrieved from http://repository.ubn.ru.nl/bitstream/handle/2066/99154/99154.pdf?sequence=1.

Bolzman, C., Fibbi, R. and Vial, M. (1993). Les Immigrés face à la retraite: Rester ou retourner? [Immigrants approaching retirement: to stay or to go back?]. *Swiss Journal of Economics and Statistics*, *129(3)*, 371–384. Retrieved from www.sjes.ch/papers/1993-III-8.pdf.

Bolzman, C., Fibbi, R. and Vial, M. (1999). Les Italiens et les Espagnols proches de la retraite en Suisse: Situation et projets d'avenir [Italians and Spaniards close to retirement in Switzerland: situation and future plans]. *Gérontologie et société, 91*, 137–151.

Bolzman, C., Fibbi, R. and Vial, M. (2006). What to do after retirement? Elderly migrants and the question of return. *Journal of Ethnic and Migration Studies, 32*, 1359–1375. doi:10.1080/13691830600928748.

Buffel, T. (forthcoming). Experiences of home, mobility and belonging: ageing migrants in inner-city Brussels. *Population, Space and Place*.

Cerase, F. P. (1974). Expectations and reality: a case study of return migration from the United States to Southern Italy. *International Migration Review, 8(26)*, 245–262. doi:10.2307/3002783.

De Bree, J., Davids, T. and De Haas, H. (2010). Post-return experiences and transnational belonging of return migrants: a Dutch-Moroccan case study. *Global Networks, 10*, 489–509. doi:10.1111/j.1471–0374.2010.00299.x.

De Coulon A. and Wolff, F.-C. (2006). *The Location of Immigrants at Retirement: Stay/Return or 'va-et-vient'?* (IZA Discussion Paper No. 2224). Retrieved from http://ssrn.com/abstract=921393.

De Coulon, A. and Wolff, F.-C. (2010). Location intentions of immigrants at retirement: stay/return or go 'back and forth'? *Applied Economics, 42*, 3319–3333. doi:10.1080/00036846.2010.482518.

De Haas, H. and Fokkema, T. (2010). Intra-household conflicts in migration decision-making: return and pendulum migration in Morocco. *Population and Development Review, 36*, 541–561. doi:10.1111/j.1728–4457.2010.00345.x.

Dos Santos, M. D. and Wolff, F.-C. (2010). *Pourquoi les immigrés portugais veulent-ils tant retourner au pays?* [Why do Portuguese Immigrants Want So Much to Return to Their Country?] (Lemna Working paper). Retrieved from http://hal.archives-ouvertes.fr/docs/00/44/96/30/PDF/LEMNA_WP_201005.pdf.

Falkingham, J., Chepngeno-Langat, G. and Evandrou, M. (2012). Outward migration from large cities: are older migrants in Nairobi 'returning'? *Population, Space and Place, 18*, 327–343. doi:10.1002/psp. 678.

Ganga, D. (2006). From potential returnees into settlers: Nottingham's older Italians. *Journal of Ethnic and Migration Studies, 32*, 1395–1413. doi:10.1080/13691830600928789.

Gualda, E. and Escriva, A. (2014). Diversity in return migration and its impact on old age: the expectations and experiences of returnees in Huelva (Spain). *International Migration, 52*(5), 178–190. doi:10.1111/j.1468-2435.2011.00728.x.

Hunter, A. (2011). Theory and practice of return migration at retirement: the case of migrant worker hostel residents in France. *Population, Space and Place, 17*, 179–192. doi:10.1002/psp. 610.

Hunter, A. (2012). *Retirement home? France's migrant worker hostels and the dilemma of late-in-life return* (Unpublished doctoral dissertation). University of Edinburgh, Edinburgh.

Klinthäll, M. (2006). Retirement return migration from Sweden. *International Migration, 44(2)*, 153–180. doi:10.1111/j.1468-2435.2006.00367.x.

Krumme, H. (2003). 'Halbe hier, halbe da': Pendelmigration türkischer Arbeitsmigranten im Ruhestand ['Half here, half there': Circular migration of Turkish migrant workers after retirement]. *Informationsdienst Altersfragen, 30(1)*, 6–8. Retrieved from www. dza.de/fileadmin/dza/pdf/Heft_01_2003_Januar_Februar_2003_gesamt.pdf.

Krumme, H. (2004). Fortwährende Remigration: Das transnationale Pendeln Türkischer Arbeitsmigrantinnen und Arbeitsmigranten im Ruhestand [Continual return: transnational circular migration of Turkish migrant workers in retirement]. *Zeitschrift für Soziologie, 33*, 138–153. Retrieved from www.zfs-online.org/index.php/zfs/article/viewFile/1160/697.

Langers, J. (2008). *Immigrés retraités: Resteront-ils au Luxembourg?* [Retired immigrants: will they stay in Luxembourg?] (STATEC Working paper No. 24). Retrieved from www. statistiques.public.lu/catalogue-publications/economie-statistiques/2008/24-2008.pdf.

Leavey, G., Sembhi, S. and Livingston, G. (2004). Older Irish migrants living in London: identity, loss and return. *Journal of Ethnic and Migration Studies, 30*, 763–779. doi:10. 1080/13691830410001699603.

Liaw, K.-L. and Frey, W. H. (2003). Location of adult children as an attraction for black and white elderly return and onward migrants in the United States: application of a three-level nested logit model with census data. *Mathematical Population Studies, 10*, 75–98. doi:10.1080/08898480306713.

Lundholm, E. (2012). Returning home? Migration to birthplace among migrants after age 55. *Population, Space and Place, 18*, 74–84. doi:10.1002/psp. 645.

Machado, F. L. and Roldão, C. (2010). *Imigrantes idosos: uma nova face da imigração em Portugal* [Elderly Ageing Immigrants: A New Face of Immigration in Portugal]. Lisboa: Alto-comissariado para a imigração e diálogo intercultural.

Razum, O., Sahin-Hodoglugil, N. N. and Polit, K. (2005). Health, wealth or family ties? Why Turkish work migrants return from Germany. *Journal of Ethnic and Migration Studies, 31*, 719–739. doi:10.1080/13691830500109894.

Rodríguez, V. and Egea, C. (2006). Return and the social environment of Andalusian emigrants in Europe. *Journal of Ethnic and Migration Studies, 32*, 1377–1393. doi:10.1080/13691830600928771.

Rodríguez, V., Egea, C. and Nieto, J. A. (2002). Return migration in Andalusia, Spain. *International Journal of Population Geography, 8*, 233–254. doi:10.1002/ijpg.258.

Schaeffer, F. (2001). Mythe du retour et réalité de l'entre-deux: La retraite en France, ou au Maroc ? [Myth of return and reality of the in-between: Retirement in France or Morocco?]. *Revue européenne de migrations internationales, 17(1)*, 165–176. doi:10.3406/remi.2001.1768.

Témime, E. (2001). Vieillir en immigration [Ageing in the context of immigration]. *Revue Européenne des Migrations Internationales, 17(1)*, 37–54. doi:10.3406/remi.2001.1761.

Warnes, A. M. and Williams, A. (2006). Older migrants in Europe: a new focus for migration studies. *Journal of Ethnic and Migration Studies, 32*, 1257–1281. doi:10.1080/13691830600927617.

White, P. (2006). Migrant populations approaching old age: prospects in Europe. *Journal of Ethnic and Migration Studies, 32*, 1283–1300. doi:10.1080/13691830600927708.

Yahirun, J. J. (2014). Take me 'home': return migration among Germany's older immigrants. *International Migration, 52(4)*, 231–254. doi:10.1111/imig.12009.

8 Expectations of care and support in old age by Bangladeshi and Pakistani elders

Christina Victor and Maria Zubair

Introduction

It is well established that the populations of developed countries are 'ageing' in terms of both the absolute and relative number of older people present within the population. What is much less well recognised is the increasing diversity of this segment of the population. Within Britain it is now well recognised that gender (Shah, 2014) and class (Formosa and Higgs, 2013; St John *et al.*, 2013) are important differentiators of the experience of ageing and later life. There is also a literature emerging about the distinctive experiences of the 'oldest old' (Freeman *et al.*, 2013) and the 'baby boomer' cohort (Buckley *et al.*, 2013). Lowton (2014) has drawn our attention to the term 'new ageing populations', which includes those ageing with disabilities such as Down's Syndrome or long-term transplant survivors. Within the British context, which mirrors the European experience, we can include the ageing of the migrant groups who came to find work in the decades from 1950 to 1970 in this category since most of these migrants never intended to 'grow old' in Britain (Herbert, 2008; Victor *et al.*, 2012). We begin this chapter by first presenting a brief summary of the demography of ethnic diversity of our older population in Britain. We then move to focus upon elders (aged 50+) from the Pakistani and Bangladeshi community, who demonstrate the highest levels of long-term illness and consider their expectations of their family in responding to care needs in old age using data from our project 'Families and Caring in South Asian Communities'.

The ageing of minority populations in Britain

In Britain, ethnicity is administratively defined on the basis of self-identification from a standard list of 18 categories. Data from the decennial censuses demonstrate that the older (aged 65+) population of Britain is becoming more ethnically diverse (Jivraj, 2012). In 2011, 12.2 per cent of the population aged 65+ defined themselves as 'non-white', compared with 6.5 per cent in 1991, with 5.3 per cent defining themselves as Indian, Pakistani and Bangladeshi. Overall, 18 per cent of the total population are aged 65+ compared with 14 per cent for the Caribbean group; 8 per cent for Indians and 4 per cent each for both the Pakistani and Bangladeshi populations. The relative youth of the minority communities in Britain is illustrated by the median ages which are 42 years for White British; 40 for the Caribbean group; 32 for Indians; and 25 for Pakistani and Bangladeshi communities.

The experience of ageing and later life for minority elders is not homogenous, varying between and within groups as well as with gender and social class. Ethnic minority elders in Britain experience significant levels of deprivation and, in particular, high levels of physical and mental health problems. Census data from 2011 report rates of long-term limiting illness: a measure of chronic health problems (i.e. ones that limit daily activities and which have lasted for at least 12 months). Overall, 53 per cent of the population aged 65+ reports the presence of long-term limiting illness. This compares with 56 per cent for the Caribbean population; 60 per cent for the Indians, 70 per cent for Pakistani elders; and 75 per cent for the Bangladeshi group (Bécares, 2013). The Bangladeshi and Pakistani communities, the focus of our research, are especially vulnerable, being characterised by profound material and social exclusion when compared with both the general population and other minority groups (Botsford *et al.*, 2011; Brice, 2008).

Who provides care for older people?

Most care for older people in Britain with long-term conditions and disabilities, regardless of ethnicity, is provided by their family, friends or neighbours (Giuntoli and Cattan, 2012). Approximately 75 per cent of care to this group is provided by the 'informal sector'; 10 per cent by formal services; and a further 10 per cent by a combination of both formal and informal services (Pickard *et al.*, 2012). Typically, the vast majority of 'informal care' for older people is provided either by a spouse (intra-generational caring) or by adult children (inter-generational caring). The 2011 census includes a question about the provision of care to family, friends or neighbours, with 11 per cent of the adult white population self-defining as carers compared with 10 per cent for the Caribbean and Indian groups and 9 per cent for both the Pakistani and Bangladeshi populations (Office of National Statistics, 2013). These data raise some interesting issues. Given the very much higher levels of chronic illness amongst our minority communities, these data suggest that some older people are not in receipt of family-based care. Family carers may not define what they do as 'caring' but rather conceptualise these activities as part of normal 'family' relationships. These prevalence type data do not provide insights into why families care, how patterns of family-based care vary across and between populations, how such patterns may vary across generations or older peoples' expectations of receipt of care and support from their family.

Using data from our project 'Families and Caring in South Asian Communities' we explore the expectations of older people from Bangladeshi and Pakistani communities regarding care and support in old age. In eliciting responses, we did not provide them with a definition of care and support but rather focussed upon their own definitions and understandings. As such they could interpret both the terms 'care' and 'support' as they wished. Neither did we define for them the types of care – financial, emotional, personal or practical – that their expectations may be linked to. Our intention was to focus upon participants identifying their 'normative' expectations of who they expected to provide care and support should the need arise. Our data consists of 109 interviews with people aged 50+ from Bangladeshi ($n=50$) and Pakistani ($n=59$) populations. Almost half of our samples, 57, were female, the mean ages were 57 years for the Bangladeshi group and 62 years for the Pakistani group and mean length of residence in the UK was 20 and 29 years respectively. In this chapter all participants are referred to by their pseudonyms and words underlined are English words used by participants in interviews conducted in Punjabi, Urdu or Sylheti and subsequently translated ($N=104$). Further details of our study design and issues of recruitment can be found in some of our earlier work (Zubair *et al.*, 2012a, 2012b). Ethical approval was given by the University of Reading and all participants gave written informed consent.

Expectations of care and support

Empirical evidence demonstrates that care and support for the general population of older people is provided predominantly by spouses (intra-generational support) and adult children (inter-generational support) and we use this empirically derived distinction to discuss the expectations for care and support articulated by our participants.

Expectations of intra-generational care and gender

Within the general population of older people, intra-generational care is almost exclusively provided by spouses rather than by siblings or friends. There is a strong basis for this deriving from notions of reciprocity, marital bonds of love and affection and the creation of a common household and co-residence, often over many decades. For the general population of older people in Britain there is little difference in the gender balance of spouse carers (Dahlberg *et al.*, 2007). Our data contained comparatively few references to the expectations of receiving care from a spouse and this was exclusively articulated by men. In contrast, women predominantly described how they cared for their husbands. We observed clear expectations from our older male participants that their wives would (or currently did) provide care for them as illustrated by Haaris, a 73-year-old Pakistani male, thus: 'If I need any care and support of course I receive it from my wife.' Similarly, Nasir, a 61-year-old Pakistani male observed: 'My wife is very supportive. Every time I go out somewhere, she cooperates with me a lot. Cooking and everything else, there is no problem at all for me. She helps me with everything'; a view echoed by Aalim, a 54-year-old Pakistani male: 'My look after in my family – only one person does it – my wife.' In contrast, women described how they had cared for their husbands and the important religious element of providing such care:

I provided care for my husband for nearly ten years. He died two years ago after a stroke. He could not move without help. I looked after him, lifting him, changing clothes, bathing him, and helping him to the toilet. I enjoyed it because he was my husband. Allah said if you take care of your husband you earn God's reward [...] lifting him over a period has given me a bad back. He did not want a nurse looking after him [...] he only wanted me to do everything, also I did not want another woman to look after my husband, so I did what made him happy. When he died we were all close to him. That is my peace.

(Kashifa, a 57-year-old Bangladeshi female)

She also described the effect that caring for her husband had had upon her own health: 'I feel weak and lonely and also I have back ache. I think caring for my husband has made me older', whilst others such as Laila, a 52-year-old Bangladeshi female, worried about their ability to care for their husband because of their own ill-health: 'I worry about how I will look after my husband when he is ill, as I am ill too.'

There were few instances of wives receiving (or expecting to receive) care from their spouse. Where such care was provided it was predominantly practical and 'administrative' types of activities such as providing transport or attending doctor's appointments as described by Aisha, a Bangladeshi female aged 53: 'I have my husband, too, he will drop me off if I want to go anywhere. He will say "I will call you and pick you up".' There were no examples of men providing personal care for their wives. Occasionally husbands were mentioned along with children as (potential) sources of care: 'My children and my husband will look after me. Even now, the day I do not feel good my children look after me, cook meal, housework they do everything' (Daniya, a 46-year-old Bangladeshi female). Iffat, a 60-year-old Bangladeshi female, was unusual in suggesting that she would prefer care from her husband rather than her children:

I am scared to think about my future in case I will not be able to walk as I get old. I do not want to be dependent on my children. They have their own families to look after and they have very busy lives. I think my husband will take care of me.

However, her narrative serves both to challenge the stereotypical assumptions relating to gendered caring in South Asian communities and reveals the actual heterogeneity and diversity of experiences and expectations that exist within them.

Expectations of inter-generational caring

Muslim societies in general and families are stereotypically presented as 'gerontocractic' in nature. 'Elders' are afforded respect by the community by virtue of their age which also brings expectations of elders to behave and dress in age-appropriate fashion (Victor *et al.*, 2012). Parents are entitled to care from their children as an Islamic duty and as a way of repaying the care provided for them by their parents. This suggests a rather monolithic set of expectations from participants about care from their children in response to the vicissitudes of old age. However our participants provided a broad and nuanced range of expectations of care and support from their children and in this section we provide examples of the different types of expectations of care and support participants had of their children. These illustrate the cultural diversity and dynamism within these ageing minority communities with respect to inter-generational expectations of care and support from adult children in a newer social context but are much more complex than that. In line with their own perceived, dominant, cultural norms participants described their children as being the key resource they would look towards in the future for care and support. These narratives exemplified the 'traditional model' of expectations that many of our participants aspired towards linked to what they perceived as a generalised and appropriate expectation that all parents should have of their children. Faatih, a 47-year-old Bangladeshi man exemplifies the 'traditional' expectations of care from children articulated by many of the participants when asked about his expectations of care from his children: 'Of course such expectation is there. I think not only myself, but others also should have such expectations.' Similarly, Aisha, a 53-year-old Bangladeshi female, stated clearly her expectation of her children: 'My plan (for old age) is that I have my children; my children will look after me, I can see the way they are, their nature, they <u>will look after</u> me.' Some participants had made an explicit transfer of assets to their children as 'security' for the provision of care in old age:

> When we got them married then I gave it [the house] to them as a <u>gift</u>. That was all the saving that I had – that, I gave to them. So now, they have given us the <u>guarantee</u> that 'you will live only with us'. For this reason, they have built a room downstairs for me; and toilet, bath, everything – they have given me the <u>facility</u>. Our children are good. Right now, they are good.

Others such as Laila, a 52-year-old Bangladeshi woman, linked their narratives of care expectations with a direct act of reciprocity from their children:

> I keep faith in Allah, that my sons will look after me and my daughters may look after me if their husbands are happy to do so. I like my sons-in-law as they do look after me too. I have finished my duty of looking after my children and now my children have a duty towards me.

Others offered a more nuanced set of expectations linked both to normative ideas about expectations of care resultant from the roles, responsibilities and obligations of parents and children as well as the affective aspects of the parent-child relationship which they deemed as making it a lasting and reliable care and support relationship for the future. Batool, a 57-year-old Pakistani woman, had expectations of her children that were focused around spending time together rather than more direct forms of care. She observed: 'I expect that when I age a lot and I want that my children and their children come and spend time with me.' Participants, who perceived old-age in Bangladesh and Pakistan in more positive terms than in the UK, described their children who lived here as being an important reason for their decision against return migration. For those who had a part of their extended family still residing in the country of origin, their plans for the future included dividing their time between their children in the UK and the extended family and social networks in the countries of origin. For Batool, the nature of the relationship with her children means that although she would like to spend more time in Pakistan with her extended family it is not at the expense of her expected contact with her children living in the UK. She described her future plans to spend time in Pakistan, emphasising her greater social resources there and the positive response that she receives from her extended family living in Pakistan. These plans, however, did not mean for her a return-migration but actually involved her 'stay[ing] there for some months and come[ing] back; spend[ing] time with the children'. Similarly, Fakhir, a 58-year-old Bangladeshi man observed:

> I go back home to visit, I have gone back home for some work [i.e. wed-dings; to see family; etc.]. I have gone to see everyone back home, that is how I will spend my time, a few days there and a few days here, how long do I have left?

Our participants' expectations of their children to maintain social contact and to carry on spending time together as they aged, revealed the particular significance attached to supportive social relationships with their children. For some, these links were based on the desire to be able to continue to fulfil the parental caring role until the end of life and was part of their perceptions of a fulfilled old age. Fakhir describes his concerns for his old age and his desire to spend time with his children in order to provide them with all the love he can:

> How long will I remain on this earth! That is what I think about, I am getting older, I was like this before and now I am like this. Some of the people that I knew have gone from this world; I have to go one day, too. That is what I think about, I want to be happy, spend time with the family for the rest of my life. Death will happen to everyone sooner or later, everyone has to leave one day. Mother, father, everybody is going, my granddad has gone; I will have to go one day. When the time comes you cannot tie anyone up and keep them. The day it is time to go, you will have to go! We are getting older, we will say that 'when will Allah take us!' Give all the love we can to the children, grandchildren within that time we have left, and spend the rest of the days like this.

Expectations from their children for future care and support were, however, far more wide-ranging than spending time together or providing emotional support.

Ghazi, a 62-year-old recent migrant from Pakistan, who worked long and difficult shift-hours to support himself financially, despite being in poor health, illustrates these broader expectations. His poor economic and social resources, as well as poor health, meant that he envisaged an old age of dependency for himself, requiring far greater types of care and support from his children than many of the other participants: 'see […]. If [one] doesn't work, then he is looked after – like – so […] they will look [after my] every need; they will serve [me]; they will sit you down and feed you.' The different forms of care and support that he expects from his children in the future after he has retired include not only financial support and physical caring on a day-to-day basis which may be needed because of retirement and old age respectively, but also provision for his needs for emotional support and self-esteem as an ageing parent through being 'serve[d] and cared for respectfully by his children'. In contrast to the all-encompassing forms of future care and support expected by Ghazi from his children, some of the other participants described their expectations as being of a more ordinary nature – not requiring their children to make any substantive adjustments to their own daily lives and routines. Ghaffaar, a 72-year-old Pakistani man, when asked what he expected from his children, responded:

> Nothing especial – [just] everyday life. My daughter comes in the evening and says salaam [hello] to me I get happy. If she doesn't then I don't mind. If I want tea she will make it for me then if not it doesn't matter and I can make it myself. Life goes on.

Deference to parental authority was expected as an important aspect of care and support from one's children. It was also deemed to be an important quality of the parent-child relationship which was likely to ensure the provision of other forms of care and support by children in the future. Participants revealed their concerns about maintaining parental authority as their children had grown up in the UK. Barkat, a 75-year-old Pakistani male, for example, in talking about his frequent trips to Pakistan after his retirement which are all paid for by his adult children, emphasises his own maintenance of parental authority within the UK context:

> Well first, I used to go after five, six, four – four, five years, but since I retired, any time I feel like going I have no problem. I just [er] I ask any of my son 'Well, I'm feeling like –'. They just buy me a ticket and say 'Well, if you need something, let – let us know' and pop on the plane, because [er] as far as the children are concerned, although they are – the eldest one is fifty two or fifty – still they don't confront me. They – they don't dare to confront me, I'll tell you something, because sometime I'm very – I'm very hostile, [er] if I get upset they know that I'll, but they never try to upset me, and they don't confront me, and don't answer me back, whatever I do. But [er] one thing I made certain, I realise in this country that if I need family united or if I want respect from my children, it's better to let them live on their own.

For Barkat, the specific nature of his current parental relationship with his children – particularly the maintenance of parental authority – allowed him considerable confidence with respect to his children being compliant to all his wishes and demands for care and support in the future also: 'Well, actually I haven't come across that one but if I come across, I tell you something if I ask any of my children "I need this", they'll [er] do their best to provide me.'

While many of the participants perceived their children as an important resource for their old age, they were also conscious of the generational changes in parent-child care and support relationships resultant from their children's British upbringing. Barkat confronts such generational changes and maintaining his parental authority and respect by allowing his adult children to live separately to him, thus avoiding any day-to-day conflicts with his children and the resultant upfront challenges to his parental authority. He observes: 'They said to me "We want to live with you, you're old." I said "No son, you live your own place. I live my place. That way we will be better off and have good relation then".' Ghazi, on the other hand, describes sending his children back to Pakistan at a young age because of his fears of the potential Western cultural influences on the latter. At the same time as Ghazi expresses his confidence that his children will provide him with care and support in his old age, this confidence is based on his particular cultural notions of the parent-child relationship and the related perceptions of the children's roles and responsibilities vis-à-vis their parents.

Concluding comments

Expectations for care and support in old age were rooted in the family not the wider community. As Mahfooz, a 57-year-old Pakistani male, observed now: 'Only your own people [meaning close family] do anything for you [...] only person that person will really help you who is your blood; any other person won't do.' Intra-generational caring expectations were clearly gendered. For men, there were clear expectations of receiving care and support from their wives which was not echoed by their wives. However this differential may reflect gendered ways of talking about care with women reluctant to reveal personal care from their husbands and husbands unwilling to talk about providing such care. Children were expected to provide care and support as a consequence of established cultural values, a response to parental authority and from affection-based relationships. Participants made favourable comparisons between their own attitudes towards the care of older people and 'English'. Fakhir, a Bangladeshi male aged 58 observes:

> You know we have a tradition that we should respect our murrubbi [elder], but here they do not show much respect to the elderly [...] English people here, the children leave when they are <u>over</u> 17, 18 years; they do not look after their parents or their grandparents. We have been looking after our families like our forefathers, <u>take caring</u>, <u>and looking after</u>.

The Bangladeshi and Pakistani populations are, however, not set in stone and we see evidence from our participants as to how expectations and care for older people is changing. We also see from some respondents a concern that their expectations will not be met.

> I have this expectation, that if I get sick, or something happens, I hope God wills that they will help me. With my daughters, I hope that I don't go to this 'Old People's House', I don't want to go there. I just want this that my own children just look after me, and that I stay at home.

Mafhooz, a 57-year-old Pakistani male, gives a more extreme example of older people being abandoned by their children and put into care homes:

> It is really happening a lot. And there are so many men that I have seen myself [pause] those who used to work with me, I have seen them – they did so much for their children – so much – they sometimes get <u>surprised</u> – I tell them that I am living with my children – they start crying – they start crying. It is so <u>bad</u>, what is happening in our <u>community</u>. When they find out – the men who used to work with me – when they find out that I live with my sons, then <u>sometimes</u> they say to me that you are a very <u>lucky</u> man as you have been living with your sons for such a long time now, and your daughter-in-laws or your sons are looking after you. They start crying. Like, I saw a man who, for his son, did so much <u>overtime</u> – so much <u>overtime</u> – work – so that he could get a house for his son – do this; do that. Then when he got old – so now he lives with the <u>old people</u>. His son doesn't go to see him. His <u>wife</u> [i.e. the son's wife] said, 'I won't <u>look after</u> him – take him away from here'. So then they left the father with the <u>old people</u>. It is very much the case in our <u>community</u> now.

Torres (2006) cautions against the (over)simplification of many aspects of the life and experiences of minority elders and this comment is very apposite when considering expectations of care and caring within Pakistani and Bangladeshi groups. Whilst for the current generation expectations of care and support from their children are rooted in a strong set of normative values, we can see evidence as to how these expectations and values may change for future generations of elders.

Acknowledgements

This study was funded by ESRC grant reference RES-352–25–0009 as part of the *New Dynamics of Ageing Programme.* Dr. Wendy Martin was the co-investigator. We wish to formally acknowledge Dr. Subrata Saha for her work on the project between 2007–2009.

References

Bécares, L. (2013). *Which Ethnic Groups Have the Poorest Health? Ethnic Health Inequalities 1991 to 2011* (Briefing of October 2013 in the 'Dynamics of Diversity: Evidence from the 2011 Census' series). Retrieved from www.ethnicity.ac.uk/medialibrary/briefings/dynamicsofdiversity/which-ethnic-groups-have-the-poorest-health.pdf.

Botsford, J., Clarke, C. L. and Gibb, C. E. (2011). Research and dementia, caring and ethnicity: a review of the literature. *Journal of Research in Nursing, 16*, 437–449. doi:10.1177/1744987111414531.

Brice, J. (2008). Migrants and the second generation: health inequalities in Bristol's Bangladeshi community. *Durham Anthropology Journal, 15*, 59–105.

Buckley, J., O'Dwyer, L., Tucker, G., Adams, R., Wittert, G. and Hugo, G. (2013). Are baby-boomers healthy enough to keep working? Health as a mediator of extended labour force participation. *Australian Journal of Social Issues, 48*, 197–221.

Dahlberg, L., Demack, S. and Bambra, C. (2007). Age and gender of informal carers: a population-based study in the UK. *Health and Social Care in the Community, 15*, 439–445. doi:10.1111/j.1365–2524.2007.00702.x.

Formosa, M. and Higgs, P. (2013). *Social Class in Later Life: Power, Identity and Lifestyle*. Bristol: Policy Press.

Freeman, S., Garcia, J. and Marston, H. (2013). Centenarians self-perceptions of factors responsible for attainment of extended health and longevity. *Educational Gerontology, 39*, 717–728. doi:10.1080/03601277.2012.750981.

Giuntoli, G. and Cattan, M. (2012). The experiences and expectations of care and support among older migrants in the UK. *European Journal of Social Work, 15*, 131–147. doi: 10.1080/13691457.2011.562055.

Herbert, J. (2008). *Negotiating Boundaries in the City: Migration, Ethnicity and Gender in Britain*. Aldershot: Ashgate.

Jivraj, S. (2012). *How Has Ethnic Diversity Grown 1991–2001–2011?* (Briefing of December 2012 in the 'Dynamics of Diversity: Evidence from the 2011 Census' series). Retrieved from www.ethnicity.ac.uk/medialibrary/briefings/dynamicsofdiversity/how-has-ethnic-diversity-grown-1991-2001-2011.pdf.

Lowton, K. (2014). *Stories of a 'New' Ageing Population Gathered for the First Time* (News of the King's College London). Retrieved from www.kcl.ac.uk/newsevents/news/newsrecords/2014/January/Stories-of-a-new-ageing-population-gathered-for-the-first-time.aspx.

Office of National Statistics (2013). *Ethnic Variations in General Health and Unpaid Care Provision, 2011*. Retrieved from www.ons.gov.uk/ons/rel/census/2011-census-analysis/ethnic-variations-in-general-health-and-unpaid-care-provision/rpt-ethnic-variations-in-general-health-and-unpaid-care-provision.html.

Pickard, L., Wittenberg, R., Comas-Herrera, A., King, D. and Malley, J. (2012). Mapping the Future of Family Care: Receipt of Informal Care by Older People with Disabilities in England to 2032. *Social Policy and Society, 11*, 533–545. doi:10.1017/S147474 6412000346.

Shah, T. (2014). Learning to be old: gender, culture and aging. (Review of the book *Learning to Be Old: Gender, Culture, and Aging*, by M. Cruikshank). *Journal of Women and Aging, 26*, 203–204. doi:10.1080/08952841.2014.854144.

St John, P., Montgomery, P. and Tyas, S. (2013). Social position and frailty. *Canadian Journal on Aging, 32*, 250–259. doi:10.1017/S0714980813000329.

Torres, S. (2006). Different ways of understanding the construct of successful aging: Iranian immigrants speak about what aging well means to them. *Journal of Cross-Cultural Gerontology, 21*, 1–23. doi:10.1007/s10823–006–9017-z.

Victor, C., Martin, W. and Zubair, M. (2012). Families and caring amongst older people in South Asian communities in the UK: a pilot study. *European Journal of Social Work, 15*, 81–96. doi:10.1080/13691457.2011.573913.

Zubair, M., Martin, W. and Victor, C. (2012a). Embodying gender, age, ethnicity and power in 'the field': reflections on dress and the presentation of the self in research with older Pakistani Muslims. *Sociological Research Online, 17(3)*. Retrieved from www.socresonline.org.uk/17/3/21.html.

Zubair, M., Martin, W. and Victor, C. (2012b). Doing Pakistani ethnicity the female way: issues of identity, trust and recruitment when researching older Pakistani Muslims in the UK. In M. Leontowitsch (ed.), *Researching Later Life and Ageing: Expanding Qualitative Research Agendas and Methods* (pp. 63–83). Basingstoke: Palgrave Macmillan.

9 Migrants' post-retirement practices

A migratory life-course approach to the study of work

Ute Karl and Anne Carolina Ramos

> That's the problem. I am retired but I'm never still. I never have time to go out. I never have time to do anything.
>
> (Aurora, Portuguese, F, [66–70]-years-old)

Since the 1990s, policy strategies like the ones adopted by the European Commission and the World Health Organisation (WHO) have aimed at fostering active and productive ageing (for a critical perspective, see Karl, 2009). Both of these concepts are strongly linked with different dimensions of paid and unpaid work, although they are not always designated in this way. For example, when speaking about solidarity between generations, one seldom discusses the fact that the practice of solidarity entails work.

The productivity (and activity) of older people has been extensively analysed on an international level. The most frequently considered variables include gender, age, level of education, employment status (Wahrendorf and Siegrist, 2011), volunteering during the life course and health (Erlinghagen and Hank, 2005; Hank, 2011). If 'migration' is even considered as a category of interest, it is often reduced to a variable such as 'foreign citizenship' or 'migration background', both including at the same time people with and without migration experience, and using standardised instruments that cannot grasp the diversity of work involvement in old age (for a critical perspective see Alisch and May, 2013).

From a biographical perspective, this chapter investigates the differing *practices* and *meanings* of paid and unpaid work of people aged 65 and over, who migrated to Luxembourg in their early adulthood from Portugal, Germany and Italy and who now have reached retirement. This is especially relevant for two reasons: as life-course research has shown, first, both migration and retirement are major transition processes; and, second, different forms of work change during the life course and are interdependent. Moreover, work practices are not only situated in historical and economic contexts, policy circumstances, biographical paths, and organisational and occupational environments, but they are also related to social positioning and social ties (Moen, 2004).

What is work? – an extended understanding of work and its relation to a migratory life-course approach

A life-course perspective on older migrants' work practices should not be reduced to the question of what happens after they have left the *paid* workforce. Rather, taking into consideration 'the instability of secondary labor force participation characteristic of women, minorities, [and] some members of the working class' (Calasanti and Slevin, 2001, p. 121), different forms of work should be analysed. Therefore, our analysis is theoretically based on the sociology of work inspired by feminist debates (e.g. Eichler and Albanese, 2007; Eichler and Matthews, 2004) and a sociology of work that takes into consideration different spheres of work and their interrelations (e.g. Pettinger *et al.*, 2005). From these perspectives it is evident that different forms of work are connected with social positions, especially when looking at the intersections between gender, class (understood here as education, employment and income), migration background, migration status and ethnicity. The fact that different contexts of migration are often intertwined with participation in different labour market segments is often overlooked, as are the implications for social relationships, life course and old age.

To grasp the different spheres of work, we suggest a pragmatic structure of work that takes into consideration the fluid boundaries of paid and unpaid work, of volunteering and care work (Taylor, 2004), the multiple faces of household work, and the interconnectedness of work activities (Glucksmann, 2005) and work and leisure (Dorfman, 2013), e.g. in formal and informal volunteering (see Table 9.1). It is important to highlight that the concept of work used here may count as work some practices that our interviewees do not, such as activities they enjoy doing or that they do for the sake of love (Dorfman, 2013; Finch and Groves, 1983; Miranda, 2011).

Eichler and Albanese (2007) suggest the broader term 'household work' that includes 'care work' and 'housework' as two sides of the same coin: 'care work' emphasises the relational aspect of household work (as conflict resolution, crisis management and planning), while 'housework' focuses on the activity aspect. Thus, household work has a physical, emotional, mental and spiritual dimension. Moreover, it can be part of paid work (when performed as an employee), unpaid work (when done by the family) or informal volunteering (when provided to non-relatives), which demonstrates the complexity of this concept.

We define 'informal volunteering' as the work done in the community without any type of formal administration (e.g. organising a neighbourhood party) and 'formal volunteering' as an activity formally organised, for instance, within the framework of a club or a group. Both volunteering practices, undertaken by willing individuals, are unpaid or minimally compensated to offset costs, and they might overlap (Nesteruk and Price, 2011).

Table 9.1 Not country specific: Multiple facets of work

Unpaid work			Paid work			
Household work		*Volunteering*		*Household work*		*Other forms of paid/professional work*
Housework	Care work	Informal	Formal	Housework	Care work	Employment Freelance Irregular work

Data and methods

The data presented here were collected within the framework of the ongoing research project 'Biographies and Transnational Social Support Networks of Older Migrants in Luxembourg' (BiSoNetMig; funded by the University of Luxembourg 2013–2015).[1] This project brings attention to older migrants from different backgrounds (German, Portuguese, Italian, Belgian, French). In this chapter we use the interviews that have been collected and analysed already. This means that this chapter is based on a sample of interviews with 20 immigrants from Portugal (ten), Italy (five) and Germany (five) that were conducted in their mother tongue. The data was collected using biographical and qualitative standardised network interviews (Hollstein, 2002) that took place at two different points in time.

These three migrant groups consist of people with different linguistic knowledge of the three official languages in Luxembourg (i.e. French, German and Luxembourgish) and socio-economic background. On average, Germans understand Luxembourgish, have higher levels of education than the Italians and the Portuguese, with a significant number of them working in international institutions or the finance sector (Fehlen and Pigeron-Piroth, 2009). Older Portuguese and Italian immigrants are mainly employed at the lower end of the income scale (Pauly, 2010), tend to acquire only French (Dickes and Berzosa, 2010), and often have a relatively early retirement due to arduous working conditions and workplace accidents (see Zahlen's Chapter 3 on 'Elderly migrants in Luxembourg' in this book). Table 9.2 gives an overview of the sample.[2]

Table 9.2 Luxembourg: Overview of the sample

	Pseudonym	*Gender*	*Age group*	*Main occupation before retirement*
Germany	Mr Ahrendt	M	[66–70]	Highly qualified, EU institution
	Mrs Kessler	F	[66–70]	Administrative staff, EU institution
	Mrs Sand	F	[81–85]	Housewife (now living in a care home)
	Mr Schack	M	[61–65]	Administrative employee
	Mr Schubert	M	[71–75]	Highly qualified, EU institution
Italy	Mr Bevilacqua	M	[81–85]	Highly qualified, EU institution
	Francesca	F	[71–75]	Cleaner/Housewife
	Marcella	F	[66–70]	Cleaner
	Serena	F	[61–65]	Administrative employee
	Mrs. Rossi	F	[91–95]	Housewife (now living in a care home)
Portugal	Arthur	M	[66–70]	Worker
	Aurora	F	[66–70]	Cleaner
	Benjamin	M	[71–75]	Worker
	Cândida	F	[81–85]	Cleaner (now living in a care home)
	Carla	F	[61–65]	Tailor
	Catarina	F	[61–65]	Nanny
	Francisco	M	[61–65]	Worker
	Glória	F	[61–65]	Cleaner
	João	M	[66–70]	Worker
	Lúcia	F	[76–80]	Cleaner

Our sample comprises eight men and twelve women who were broadly distributed across the labour market segments. The reason why we chose not to focus exclusively on 'guest-workers' (i.e. those who work mainly in the construction and cleaning sectors in Luxembourg) is that we wanted to shed light on the fact that work biographies can contrast broadly among migrants.

In the following we will discuss different forms of paid and unpaid work performed by older retirees, drawing attention to their practices of: (1) unpaid household work; (2) formal and informal volunteering; and (3) professional paid work after retirement.

Performing unpaid household work: practices of housework and care work among migrant retirees in Luxembourg

Gender, class and household work from a migratory life-course perspective

In general, our data substantiates the well-known phenomenon that women are more involved in cleaning, cooking and caring, and men are more responsible for gardening, pet care and repairs (Miranda, 2011), a feature found in all three nationality groups interviewed. Women employed at the lower end of the income scale – i.e. the Portuguese in our sample and two Italians – mainly worked as cleaners, nannies or tailors, a typical labour market segment for Italian and Portuguese female immigrants in Luxembourg. After retirement, most of them just shifted from paid to unpaid work by providing household work for family members. At times, the daily lives of these women can be quite intense, as is exemplified by Aurora:

> Aurora [whose husband was in hospital at the time of the interview] – I organise my time according to the time I have. If I need to get up at six or five in the morning, I get up at this time. To prepare the meals! I go to the hospital, I bring lunch to my husband and then I bring lunch for me and my two grandchildren to [City X, Luxembourg, between 16–50 km] and I eat with them at noon. Afterwards, I put them on the bus to school from her place and then I come back to the hospital to stay with my husband. However, before that I had already prepared lunch for my grandson and my other two grandchildren here [in my house]! [...] Last week, my daughter went on holidays, and I went to her house to take all the clothes she had in the laundry. [...] I washed and ironed three laundry baskets full. [...] And for the younger daughter I do the same. I go to her place and I cannot stay still. I always see work to do, always. [...] However, this is no longer work, I mean, it is already part of the family, it is for the children, that's it. I think it is a duty. I get there and I cannot stay still.
>
> (Portuguese, F, [66–70])

Although she is retired, Aurora describes a full working day that starts very early in the morning: she wakes up at around 5.00–6.00 a.m. to help her family and throughout the day she never 'stays still'. As a former cleaning lady, Aurora 'always sees work to do'. Nonetheless, she corrects herself by saying that it cannot be considered work, but rather a familial duty: 'However, this is no longer work, I mean, it is already part of the family.' In this sense, Aurora transforms the 'work' she performed before retirement into 'non-work', once it becomes unpaid and done for her own family.

At the same time, retirement can increase men's participation in household work, especially when their professional commitments ended before those of their wives. As male guest-workers were usually unable to enjoy their fatherhood due to long shifts of work, taking care of the grandchildren may compensate for this lack. In the example below, Arthur (Portuguese, M, [66–70]) explains that retirement gave him the opportunity to devote himself to his '(grand)children', and to explore new, dormant or previously restricted activities (Byles *et al.*, 2013, p. 38).

> Arthur – With my grandchildren? The time I dedicate to them is the time I could not dedicate to my children because of work. Now I am retired and my grandchildren are my children [...]. I used to change my grandson's diapers for a long time when he was a baby. However, I never had time to change my own children's diapers. Can you imagine that? It is fantastic, isn't it? [...] My wife was still working, and I was the one who stayed with him.
>
> (Portuguese, M, [66–70])

Our analysis of household work shows the relevance of former occupation – which is, at the same time, associated with the educational level, ethnic/migratory background and gender – for the continuity and change of household work and its significance. The case of Aurora illustrates the continuity of former work, in which a change in its meaning is observed: it shifts from 'work' to 'non-work' when it becomes unpaid and given to the family. In the case of Arthur, there is the development of new practices to perhaps compensate for what he missed in his life course, due to his social positioning as a 'guest-worker'. Although it could be argued that these features are mostly connected to class and gender, one should take into consideration that the specific migratory and ethnic background of the interviewees is very much linked with the mentioned labour market segments, as these jobs were mostly performed by immigrants. From a life-course perspective, these examples reconstruct how the practices of household work acquire a specific meaning against the backdrop that is work before retirement.

The migrancy of housework and care work

In our study, most of the Portuguese interviewees – this is not the case for the Italians and Germans – maintain houses in their home country, where they spend part of the year. Housework and care work are embedded in these transnational ways of living as the own household becomes transnational: 'When we go to

Portugal, instead of staying two or three weeks, we stay a month, a month and a half. That's what we do to have time to clean the house', explains Catarina (Portuguese, F, [61–65]). João (Portuguese, M, [66–70]) takes care of his garden in Portugal, planning his travel according to the time of sowing and harvesting, while Lúcia (Portuguese, F, [76–80]) states that she will 'spend a week being busy with cleaning' before enjoying the summer.

In their pendulum migration to Portugal, older migrants also become 'mobile grandparents' (Nedelcu, 2014), bringing their (mobile) grandchildren to their home country, thereby giving a special meaning to child care: 'Every year we go to Portugal for two months and I always take them with me!', explains Arthur (Portuguese, M, [66–70]). There, the grandchildren can enjoy the coast, visit relatives and build relationships in which they use the Portuguese language:

> Carla – They go with us to Portugal for two months and they speak Portuguese with the other children because there the children don't speak French, do they? There they have to get along with the other children in Portuguese.
> (Portuguese, F, [61–65])

However, grandparents and grandchildren may face some challenges when, in the context of care, they do not master a common language. In the compulsory pre-school, children learn Luxembourgish, a language very rarely spoken by older Portuguese and Italians. Carla (Portuguese, F, [61–65]) explains that when her granddaughter speaks Luxembourgish to her, she 'understands only half of it'. For Aurora (Portuguese, F, [66–70]), the only sad thing is to know that between her and her grandchildren 'there is not the same continuous conversation as they have with their Luxembourgish grandmother'.

Even when language is a barrier in their relationship, older migrants try to transmit to their grandchildren the history and the culture of their home country in the frame of their housework: 'I speak a lot about Portugal to my grandchildren to give them an idea about my country', says Aurora (Portuguese, F, [66–70]). She also fries sardines with '*broa* bread' or bakes '*folares de Páscoa*', a traditional Portuguese Easter cake. This is quite similar to Mrs Rossi [Italian, F, [91–95], now living in a care home), who used to cook Italian specialities like 'the sauce, pasta, and *tortellini*' for her grandchildren.

Thus, to the discussions on the transnational ways of caring (Baldassar *et al.*, 2007; Merla, 2013), our analysis adds three important considerations: (1) care activities for the third generation are embedded into the transnational ways of living of the first generation; (2) the transmission of the culture takes place while caring; and (3) the possibilities of care and the quality of the caring relations are influenced by the language capacities of the different generations.

Formal volunteering

Findings from the Survey on Health, Ageing and Retirement in Europe (SHARE) have revealed that adults' formal volunteer activity rates drop around the age of

75 and above, and that they increase with the level of education and higher occupational status (Wahrendorf and Siegrist, 2011) and decrease with the level of perceived health. Furthermore, participation as a volunteer before retirement seems to be a good predictor for participation after retirement (Erlinghagen and Hank, 2005; Hank, 2011), as is being a first generation immigrant (Alisch and May, 2013).

Our data show similarities with these findings: the Portuguese in our sample are rarely involved in formal volunteering while the Germans, who have higher occupational status, are quite active. At the same time, we observe a strong involvement for their own ethnic group across all interviewees: Mrs Kessler (German, F, [66–70]) has a role of responsibility in a German-speaking group; Mrs Rossi (Italian, F, [91–95], now living in a care home) volunteered at the Italian catholic church; Mr Ahrendt (German, M, [66–70]) is an administrative officer in a German club; Mr Bevilacqua (Italian, M, [81–85]) volunteers at an Italian institute; and Mr Schack (German, M, [61–65]) volunteers for a German group at an annual international festival. A case in-between is the participation of Francisco (Portuguese, M, [61–65]) who, although not occupying a formal position, actively organises a group of Portuguese retirees. He voluntarily assumed this role thus achieving continuity with his previous occupations as head of different teams and associations. In the 1980s, he championed the guest-workers' rights to learn the host country language: 'As workers, we fought hard to have a few hours to learn Luxembourgish. We went to the parliament to strike, to protest', he says. Currently, he still represents an important voice inside the Portuguese community, struggling for the rights of older migrants who, as him, did not have the chance to learn Luxembourgish. Francisco's volunteering activity clearly depicts how his personal biography is connected with his former professional activities and political commitments over time (Taylor, 2004).

Although most (formally) volunteer with respect to their own ethnic communities, some participate in initiatives that are connected to their (international) interests and to the local needs: Mr Bevilacqua (Italian, M, [81–85]), who was involved in social issues during his former work, volunteered in an international association to help people with special health needs; Mrs Sand (German, F, [81–85], now living in a care home), who has always been oriented towards the local community, was actively involved in a Luxembourgish non-profit women's organisation; and Mr Schack (German, M, [61–65]), who always actively participated in sports, started volunteering at two Luxembourgish sport clubs after his retirement.

A possible explanation for the fact that most of the Portuguese and some of the Italians do not report any formal volunteering activities could be the language barrier, because these groups of migrants rarely speak Luxembourgish or German, and they even rate their proficiency in French as elementary. In our sample, only the Germans are involved in formal volunteering in Luxembourgish associations. However, there might be other barriers to participation that are more class specific (e.g. the formal organisation in associations) and connected to different ways of how people volunteer (formally and informally) or support each other (Alisch and May, 2013). Several studies underline the problematic division between formal and informal volunteering that often ignores the informal volunteering of specific groups and the different ways in which people volunteer (for a critique, see, for example, Martinez *et al.*, 2011; Petriwskyj *et al.*, 2012).

Informal volunteering

As decribed above, this form of work includes household work for non-relatives and volunteer work provided for the community without any type of formal organisation. The latter could be provided, for example, in support of a project-like initiative brought into being by a political or administrative entity as, for example, when Mr Arendt (German, M, [66–70]) occasionally participates in a working group in his town; when Catarina (Portuguese, F, [61–65]) helps to organise 'the feast of the village to keep the neighbourhood together'; or when Cândida (Portuguese, F, [81–85]) 'hems the towels and [sews] the aprons for the workers in the kitchen' in the care home where she lives.

The informal volunteering related to households of non-relatives includes practical support such as 'going grocery shopping' (Carla, Portuguese, for a Latin-American neighbour), 'giving a lift' (Francesca, Italian, to neighbours of different nationalities), 'bringing six packs of bottled water' (Arthur, Portuguese, for an Italian neighbour), 'repairing and hemming clothing' (Lúcia, Portuguese, for a Brazilian friend), 'watering the plants' (Francisco, Portuguese, for a Luxembourgish neighbour), 'cleaning the sidewalk' (Mr Schack, German), 'collecting the mail' (João, Portuguese, for a Luxembourgish neighbour), 'feeding the cat' (Catarina, Portuguese, for a Luxembourgish neighbour), and 'repairing the heating system [or] fixing the satellite dish' (Francisco, Portuguese, for a Portuguese friend). It also includes the informal volunteer work done for the local neighbourhood such as 'replacing the light bulbs in the building's garage' (João, Portuguese).

Furthermore, they provide care for children and for weak and sick people. Lúcia (Portuguese, F, [76–80]) 'fed and took care of the Belgian neighbour's daughter'; Carla (Portuguese, F, [61–65]) accompanied a Portuguese former colleague to the doctor because 'she was very sick and could not speak French'; and Catarina (Portuguese, F, [61–65]) took care of a Portuguese friend: 'She could not do anything and I went to her place to do everything she needed done.' This is the same for Arthur (Portuguese, M, [66–70]), who helps an older Italian neighbour: 'He is not much older than me, but he is at death's door and I feel sorry for him. […] I help this old man, poor person. He is also alone.'

The support that older people provide can also be in the emotional dimension. Catarina (Portuguese, F, [61–65]) 'listens to the problems and difficulties' of her Luxembourgish neighbour; Francisco (Portuguese, M, [61–65]) 'gives advice to [his] Portuguese friends'; Carla (Portuguese, F, [61–65]) is attentive to her Latin-American neighbour because 'she doesn't have any family in Luxembourg'; and Lúcia (Portuguese, F, [76–80]) 'always [spends] a little time with [her] Brazilian neighbour because she feels lonely'.

As can be seen, older migrants carry out different types of uncompensated, informal voluntary work for friends and neighbours of different ethnic backgrounds. This fact is especially relevant to the Portuguese interviewees, who report several informal but only few formal volunteering activities. Alisch and May (2013) have proposed that people with lower educational levels and who are more experienced in physically demanding jobs are less attracted by formalised procedures of formal volunteering and thus practise more self-help oriented forms of care and volunteering. This may be an explanation for our findings as well.

Professional paid work after retirement

As Carr and Kail (2012) point out, 'older adults are remaining engaged in the work force later in life, [...] retiring at several stages than all at once' (p. 92). On the one hand, this continuity of paid work may represent a way of having an extra income to deal with low pensions: 'I was interested in having my little money at the end of the week', says Lúcia (Portuguese, F, [76–80]), a retired housekeeper who worked until her seventies in this profession. This is also the case for Cândida (Portuguese, F, [81–85]), who worked as a nanny and a cleaning lady for her own daughter, giving continuity to her former work. After having retired she went back to Portugal but was persuaded by her daughter to return to Luxembourg:

> Cândida – When she became pregnant my daughter said: 'Hey mum, I need you to take care of my son! I'll pay your health insurance; I'll pay your doctor's bills. If you come back to Luxembourg, you will have room, board and everything paid!'
>
> (Portuguese, F, [81–85], living in a care home)

Cândida's situation shows that the boundaries between paid and unpaid household work are quite malleable and that the offer to work within the family can even lead to the revision of one's decision to return to the country of origin.

On the other hand, the continuity of paid work may offer a way to stay connected with the work environment, especially for individuals who liked their (higher or lower qualified) jobs. Carla (Portuguese, F, [61–65], retired tailor) continued to work from home or even to go to her previous company after retirement, because of the symbolic ties she had with her professional life:

> Carla – Because I retired but I was always there, right? [...] My boss, when she had a lot of work, she called me to go there to get some work to do at home. Sometimes I even worked there. [...] I used to go there. I used to go there a lot. I loved it.
>
> (Portuguese, F, [61–65])

Two of the more highly qualified men in our sample – Mr Schubert (German, [71–75]) and Mr Bevilaqua (Italian, [81–85]) – who worked for the EU institutions, also report a kind of continuity of work, which has made retirement more a gradual process for them. Mr Bevilacqua continued to work on various projects for several years after retiring and even today, at age 80+ years, he still develops specific studies and gives lectures. The case of Mr Schubert, who still works as a guest speaker, demonstrates that although the work is not performed as a duty within the frame of a regular employment, the type of work is characterised by its permanence:

> Mr Schubert – Basically it is not very different from the way it was before, when one also wrote texts or speeches […] within the European institutions.
> (German, M, [71–75])

Our analysis shows a clear continuity of paid work that is motivated by different reasons. These include earning additional money to compensate for low pensions, staying connected to the professional field, maintaining contact with the work environment, or even due to family duties. Comparable with the household work, it is not migration itself that influences the permanence in the paid work force, but the social positioning in which gender, class and specific contexts of migration intersect.

Discussion: work practices after retirement from a migratory life-course perspective

A broad perspective on work, as we suggest in this chapter, sheds light on the fact that most of our interviewees do not simply stop working after retirement, rather they continue with or create other forms of work to engage in (Taylor, 2004). Looking from a migratory life-course perspective at the different forms of work, we could see that the former occupation has an impact on the practices of work after retirement and their meaning. While the work that is done after retirement might be quite similar to what was done before (continuity), the meaning of it might change (e.g. when housework is provided for the family).

At the same time, housework and caring activities for the third generation might be embedded in the transnational pendulum migration that is typical for Portuguese people in our sample, and household work is presented by Italian and Portuguese interviewees as one possibility to transmit language and culture of the country of origin. However, language might be a challenge for caring when the first and third generation do not share the same language.

Concerning volunteering activities, working for one's own ethnic group represents a driving force behind the decision to formally participate. Our data also corroborate the well-known phenomenon that formal volunteering especially attracts people with higher formal education. Language capacities might also play a role although this was not explicitly mentioned by our interviewees. At the same time, we find very many informal volunteering activities for people from different ethnic backgrounds that are performed on a regular basis, especially by the Portuguese interviewees.

Our analyses from a migratory life-course perspective demonstrate the fact that the meaning of work after retirement is anchored in the biographies of the interviewees and their social positioning in which migratory and ethnic background intersect with other social categories, namely gender and class. Accordingly, further research on post-retirement practices of work of older migrants should not ignore this interrelation, and it should give visibility to a broad range of currently 'invisible' forms of work (especially those provided by women), thus situating the debate on care and social support by older migrants into a broader debate on work, including volunteer work.

Notes

1 Ethical approval was given by the Ethics Review Panel of the University of Luxembourg (ERP 13–005).
2 We use M to refer to 'male' and F to 'female'. The pseudonym is mainly a first name. However, in some cases, surnames are used preceded by the title Mr or Mrs. This was done according to the individual situations in the interview. In the quotations, '[…]' indicates an omission.

References

Alisch, M. and May, M. (2013). Formen der Selbstorganisation älterer Menschen in benachteiligten Lebenslagen als Basis 'sorgender Gemeinschaften' [Forms of self-organization of older people in disadvantaged situations as a basis of 'caring communities'. *Aus der Altersforschung, 40(3)*, 3–10. Retrieved from www.dza.de/fileadmin/dza/pdf/Heft_03_2013_Mai_Juni_2013_gekuerzt_PW.pdf.

Baldassar, L., Baldock, C. V. and Wilding, R. (2007). *Families Caring across Borders: Migration, Ageing and Transnational Caregiving*. Basingstoke/New York: Palgrave Macmillan.

Byles, J., Tavener, M., Robinson, I., Parkinson, L., Smith, P.W., Stevenson, D.,… Curryer, C. (2013). Transforming retirement: new definitions of life after work. *Journal of Women and Aging, 25(1)*, 24–44. doi:10.1080/08952841.2012.717855.

Calasanti, T. and Slevin, K. (2001). *Gender, Social Inequalities, and Aging*. Walnut Creek: Altamira Press.

Carr, D. C. and Kail, B. L. (2012). The influence of unpaid work on the transition out of full-time paid work. *The Gerontologist, 53(1)*, 92–101. doi:10.1093/geront/gns080.

Dickes, P. and Berzosa, G. (2010). *Les Compétences linguistiques auto-attribuées* [Self-assigned language competences]. (Les Cahiers du CEPS/INSTEAD 2010–19). Retrieved from www.statistiques.public.lu/catalogue-publications/cahiers-CEPS/2010/19-competences-linguistiques.pdf.

Dorfman, L. T. (2013). Leisure activities in retirement. In M. Wang (ed.), *The Oxford Handbook of Retirement* (pp. 339–353). New York: Oxford University Press.

Eichler, M. and Albanese, P. (2007). What is household work? A critique of assumptions underlying empirical studies of housework and an alternative approach. *Canadian Journal of Sociology, 32*, 227–258. Retrieved from www.jstor.org/stable/20460633.

Eichler, M. and Matthews, A. (2004). *What is Work? Looking at All Work through the Lens of Unpaid Housework*. (Manuscript). Retrieved from http://wall.oise.utoronto.ca/events/WhatisWork.pdf.

Erlinghagen, M. and Hank, K. (2005). *Participation of Older Europeans in Volunteer Work* (Working Paper 71–2005). Retrieved from https://ub-madoc.bib.uni-mannheim. de/1260/1/071_05.pdf.

Fehlen, F. and Pigeron-Piroth, I. (2009). Mondialisation du travail et pluralité des marchés du travail: L'exemple du Luxembourg. [Globalisation of work and the plurality of labour markets: the example of Luxembourg]. *ACTES du XIIièmes Journées Internationales de Sociologie du Travail.* Nancy: GREE, Université de Nancy.

Finch, J. and Groves, D. (eds) (1983). *A Labour of Love: Women, Work and Caring.* London: Routledge and Kegan Paul.

Glucksmann, M. (2005). Shifting boundaries and interconnections: extending the 'total social organisation of labour'. In L. Pettinger, J. Parry, R. Taylor and M. Glucksmann (eds), *A New Sociology of Work?* (pp. 19–36). Malden: Blackwell Publishing.

Hank, K. (2011). How 'successful' do older Europeans age? Findings from SHARE. *Journal of Gerontology: Social Sciences, 66B*, 230–236. doi:10.1093/geronb/gbq089.

Hollstein, B. (2002). *Soziale Netzwerke nach der Verwitwung. Eine Rekonstruktion der Veränderungen informeller Beziehungen* [Social networks after widowhood. A reconstruction of the changes in informal relationships]. Opladen: Leske+Budrich.

Karl, U. (2009). Learning to become an entrepreneurial self for voluntary work? Social policy and older people in the volunteer sector. In S. Maurer, T. Besley, M. Peters and S. Weber (eds), *Governmentality Studies in Education* (pp. 433–451). Rotterdam: Sense Publishers.

Martinez, I. L., Crooks, D., Kim, K. and Tanner, E. (2011). Invisible civic engagement among older adults: valuing the contributions of informal volunteering. *Journal of Cross-Cultural Gerontology, 26*, 23–37. doi:10.1007/s10823–011–9137-y.

Merla, L. (2013). Salvadoran transnational families, distance and eldercare: understanding transnational care practices in Australia and Belgium. In T. Geisen, T. Studer and E. Yildiz (eds), *Migration, Familie und soziale Lage* (pp. 295–312). Wiesbaden: VS Verlag für Sozialwissenschaften/Springer Fachmedien.

Miranda, V. (2011). *Cooking, Caring and Volunteering: Unpaid Work around the World.* (OECD Social, Employment and Migration Working Papers, No. 116). OECD Publishing. doi:10.1787/5kghrjm8s142-en.

Moen, P. (2004). Midcourse: navigating retirement and a new life stage. In J. T. Mortimer and M. J. Shanahan (eds), *Handbook of the Life Course* (pp. 269–291). New York: Springer.

Nedelcu, M. (2014, August). *Grandparents on the Move: Presence, Intergenerational Solidarities and Childcare Arrangements in Romanian Transnational Families.* Paper presented at the IMISCOE 11th Annual Conference, Madrid, Spain.

Nesteruk, O. and Price, C. A. (2011). Retired women and volunteering: the good, the bad, and the unrecognized. *Journal of Women and Ageing, 23*, 99–112. doi:10.1080/089528 41.2011.561138.

Pauly, M. (2010). Le Phénomène migratoire: une constante de l'histoire Luxembourgeoise [The migratory phenomenon: a constant in the history of Luxembourg]. In M. Pauly (ed.), *ASTI 30+: migrations, recherches, engagements* [ASTI 30+: Migration, Research, Engagement] (pp. 62–75). Luxembourg: ASTI.

Petriwskyj, A., Warburton, J., Everingham, J.-A. and Cuthill, M. (2012). Diversity and inclusion in local governance: an Australian study of seniors' participation. *Journal of Aging Studies, 26*, 182–191. doi:10.1016/j.jaging.2011.12.003.

Pettinger, L., Parry, J., Taylor, R. F. and Glucksmann, M. (eds) (2005). *A New Sociology of Work?* Malden: Blackwell Publishing.

Taylor, R. F. (2004). Extending conceptual boundaries: work, voluntary work and employment. *Work, Employment and Society, 18*, 29–49. doi:10.1177/09500170040 40761.

Wahrendorf, M. and Siegrist, J. (2011). Working conditions in mid-life and participation in voluntary work after labour market exit. In A. Börsch-Supan, M. Brandt, K. Hank and M. Schröder (eds), *The Individual and the Welfare State: Life Histories in Europe* (pp. 179–188). Heidelberg: Springer-Verlag.

10 Yearning to be free

The American dreams and ageing realities of older migrants from the USSR

Allen Glicksman

Introduction

There are approximately 58 million older (age 60+) adults living in the United States. Of those, approximately 7.4 million (13 percent) are foreign born. A bit more than half of those immigrants come from ten countries – Mexico, Philippines, Germany, Cuba, China, Canada, Italy, India, Vietnam, and Korea. Together, they reflect geography (Mexico and Canada), the history of migration to the United States (Italy, India), and America's recent political history (Cuba, Vietnam). Table 10.1 shows the proportion of older immigrants from each area of the globe; all the data is taken from the 2012 Public Use File of the American Community Survey (Ruggles *et al.*, 2010).

Table 10.2 compares the older immigrants from these areas with American born elderly. We added a row for those elders who migrated from Puerto Rico to the American mainland so that we can compare one group of internal migrants to immigrant groups. The columns report percentages of each group that: (1) completed at least one year of college; (2) reports having an Instrumental Activity of Daily Living (IADL) type disability; (3) reports having an Activity of Daily Living (ADL) type disability; 4) has an income of less than 100 percent of the Federal Poverty Level; (5) does not speak English well or does not speak English at all.

Given the size and diversity of the older foreign born population there are few if any general comparisons that can be made with U.S. born elders. As can be seen from the table there is significant diversity in years in the United States, health status, income, ability to speak English, and other domains between these groups. What should also be noted is that there is no single pattern within these groups. For example, older immigrants from the former USSR are overall the most highly educated but have the highest percent reporting an IADL limitation. The lack of a consistent pattern separating immigrants from native born means that we must also ask whether some groups of internal migrants may be more like selected immigrant groups on certain dimensions than the rest of the native-born population. For example, the Puerto Rican population has the second highest percentage of IADL impairment and the highest poverty rate, so internal migrants are clearly sometimes more disadvantaged than those arriving from foreign countries.

Table 10.1 USA: Place of origin and age for immigrants age 60 and older

County/area of origin	Approximate number of immigrants	Percent of all older immigrants to the United States	Median # years lived in the United States	Median age
Canada and Atlantic Islands	320,257	4.3	49	71
Cuba	378,599	5.1	40	72
Mexico	1,144,450	15.4	37	67
Central America and Caribbean	823,157	11.1	32	67
South America	448,794	6.1	32	67
West and Central Europe	1,418,622	19.1	50	71
East Europe	239,091	3.2	41	71
Former USSR	269,500	3.6	19	72
China	468,864	6.3	28	69
East Asia	1,142,355	15.4	30	68
Central Asia	439,844	5.9	26	67
Middle East	130,322	1.8	33	68
Africa	158,206	2.1	27	66
Pacific	35,997	0.5	37	67
Total	**7,418,058**	**100.0**	**Average: 34 years**	**Average: 69 years**

Source: All data taken from the 2012 American Community Survey IPUMS file (Ruggles *et al.*, 2010).

Table 10.2 USA: Selected characteristics of older immigrants compared to American-born elders and older Puerto Ricans (%)

County/area of origin	Education 1 year college +	Has independent living impairment	Has impairment related to daily self-care	Income less than 100% of federal poverty level	Ability to speak English not well/not at all
United States	**43**	**15**	**9**	**11**	**1**
Canada and Atlantic Islands	47	12	7	12	3
Cuba	29	20	12	23	56
Mexico	10	18	11	22	67
Central America and Caribbean	25	15	9	20	37
South America	37	13	7	15	37
West and Central Europe	40	14	8	10	10
East Europe (excluding former USSR)	35	19	11	12	28
Former USSR	61	32	22	29	50
China	44	15	7	18	59
East Asia	47	15	7	13	37
Central Asia	58	17	9	11	32
Middle East	42	21	14	20	31
Africa	57	13	7	16	18
Pacific	46	14	8	12	13
Puerto Ricans*	19	22	12	75	32

Source: All data taken from the 2012 American Community Survey IPUMS file (Ruggles *et al.*, 2010).

Note
* Puerto Ricans were added to show a group of internal migrants within the United States compared to the other groups in the table.

Is there a common thread that runs through the experience of all immigrants to the U.S.? Yes, but not in the issues of age-related health, socio-economic status, living arrangements, or even language. The common experience has to do with the process of becoming American.

What does it mean to 'become American'? In the American imagination the United States is a 'nation of immigrants' who came seeking freedom (Kennedy, 1964). Embedded in that image is the assumption that being free in the American meaning of the term is the natural desire of all humans. America, in the imagination of its citizens, is more than a place on the map – it is the expression of a basic human desire. This means that migration to the United States has significance far beyond the immediate reasons that a person might migrate – whether for economic opportunity or to escape persecution. This assumption about what it means to be American is a key element in what has been called America's 'civil religion' (Bellah, 1967). These ideas are rooted in the belief system of the English Pilgrims and Puritans whose faith tradition has shaped American civilization. This process resembles a religious conversion to the American civil faith – seeking and then holding these 'natural' and 'universal' beliefs.

It is the thesis of this chapter that the task of absorbing new immigrants to America is not simply the process of providing the resources for establishing homes and employment and education but also the transformation of the values, norms, and worldview of the immigrants. Success is measured in part depending on the success of transmitting those values. While any immigrant to a new land might be expected to adopt the language and culture of their new homeland, many Americans assume that this is a 'natural' process in that they are now 'free' to behave as natural men and women. Therefore, difficulties in the process of acculturation are seen as entirely the problem of the immigrant, and sometimes seen as a fault. This creates what may be an insurmountable problem for those who migrate in old age and may never become 'American.'

To complete this process of conversion and achieve material success one needs the time to adjust and adopt new ways of thinking, of behaving, and most importantly language. What then happens to those who migrate in old age? Persons who now face dealing with a new language, culture, and political system after a lifetime of living in very different circumstances? How does age affect the immigrant, and how does it affect the perceptions of those Americans tasked with the job of helping those ageing immigrants adjust to their new home?

We identify three key areas where migration in old age can pose challenges for successful adaptation to American life that emerge from the assumptions stated above. The roles of each of these areas will differ from group to group, but in some way all three are challenges that must be faced. They are: (1) continued identification with their country of origin and difficulty absorbing American norms and values; (2) dealing with the expectations of the individuals or agencies supporting their absorption into American society; (3) finding appropriate new roles in society and within their families. The first of these involves the immigrant herself, the second two involve the interaction of the immigrant with her new surroundings.

To examine how these areas play out in the lives of older immigrants we will use the case of older immigrants from the former USSR. As can be seen from Tables 10.1 and 10.2, the Soviets as a group have been in the U.S. for a shorter period than other groups and at the same time share with the Cubans the highest median age for those ages 60 or older. These facts make them a good example of a group of immigrants who arrived close to or already in old age.

Continued identification with their homeland

The data reported below come from a study of refugee caregivers and care recipients in four refugee communities including Soviet Jewish and Soviet Ukrainian (Glicksman, 2002). Additional information can be found in Strumpf *et al.* (2001). The study, funded by the National Institutes of Health, was designed to determine whether refugees who would be considered members of minority groups in the United States (Vietnamese and Cambodian) would face more barriers in receiving community-based social services than refugees not considered 'minority' in American society (Soviet Jews and Soviet Ukrainians). Refugees from these four groups who arrived in the United States between 1980 and 1995 were interviewed. Forty-five (45) Soviet Jewish and Soviet Ukrainian daughter and daughter-in-law caregivers were interviewed along with twenty-two (22) of the elders they cared for. Interviews included both open-ended and close-ended questions. All interviews were audio-taped, transcribed and then translated into English.

The program of the Bolshevik Party, which promised an end to physical violence against the Jews and the opening of opportunities, especially in higher education that had been closed to them, led many Jews to adopt a cautiously positive attitude toward the new regime. At first, many Jews embraced the new opportunities. For many, Russian culture seemed superior to the Jewish culture of their youth. Jews found opportunities in Soviet society and, while some Jews were persecuted in the terror of the 1930s, other Jews were part of the terror apparatus (Gitelman, 2001). 'Jewish' became a nationality that appeared on one's identity card, but without content in terms of cultural, religious, or national expression. This occurred in part because of Soviet policy and in part because shedding much of traditional Jewish life was part of becoming a Soviet citizen just as it was part of becoming American.

Because these respondents migrated in old age, they speak of their identities in the USSR in the present tense. They have not forged new identities in their new home, rather they are expatriates, living in a foreign land. The stories of their lives in the USSR are complex. On the one hand, they were given access to opportunities never enjoyed living under Tsarist rule. On the other hand, daily life in the Soviet Union could bring multiple hardships. This means that the feelings toward their homeland are best described as ambiguous, neither a rejection in favour of the freedom offered by the U.S. nor total regret that they left for a new land.

These exchanges between interviewers and respondents in the study illustrate the point:

I: How would you describe your cultural and national background?
R: You see, I consider myself to be Jewish by nationality, but culturally I am Russian because I was raised in Russian culture. I adore Russian culture, Russian opera, Russian ballet, Russian theatre, Russian actors. I adore all those. I adore Russian literature, and I can't help it.
I: Were you raised in a particular religious tradition?
R: My father died earlier, in '35. And after that, Yiddish has disappeared from my life. Completely. Besides, you have to know what my generation of Soviets has lived through. I survived three famines. I don't remember the first one. My parents told me later about it because it happened in 1921. The second famine was in the thirties [...]. The last one maybe was not so awful, but it was during the war, during our evacuation. We had a hard life at that time.

In this excerpt we see that both culture and historical events shaped the world-view and perceptions of these older migrants.

The Second World War is recognised as a turning point in the lives of many Soviet Jews. The experience of the War and the attempt to exterminate all Jews by the Nazis and their allies reawakened a sense of Jewish identity for many of these people. The reawakening of Jewish identity was one cause of a crackdown on expressions of Jewish identity starting after the Second World War. By the 1970s, the development of *détente* allowed Soviet Jews to migrate. As the ostensible reason for allowing these persons to emigrate was family reunification, older adults were always part of the migration.

Many of the elders said that they would have stayed there if not for the fact that their only child was leaving. Therefore, many left their homes because they had no choice and not from a desire to become American. The act of departure was not without stress. For some, the evacuation from Kyiv after the Chornobyl nuclear disaster brought back memories of the flight from the Nazis as they approached Kyiv in 1941.

I: What were the reasons you left your native country? How did you feel about leaving?
R1: The most important reason was radiation, to which the city was exposed and my grandchildren and my children through the Chornobyl disaster. So we were very nervous because of my children and especially my grandchildren. I didn't think about myself. I thought about my children and my grandchildren. When they offered me to emigrate, I had doubts because I thought that I could stay there. However, I would have stayed alone in (hometown) because my other son lived in Petersburg, and my sister and brother lived in Moscow. So, they talked me into emigrating with them, and I went with them. Generally it was very difficult for me to leave my homeland.

R2: I love Leningrad. And I love my native country too. That's where my child-hood has been, my youth years, my marriage, the birth of my children, all of that is understandable. But I left there without a single regret. It was more of a stepmother to me than a mother, unfortunately. Because my husband was executed, my son perished, and I mean it, although he died of a heart attack, but the endless anonymous letters during the Andropov period (the early 1980s) terrorized him, when it mattered.

The image of Russia being a stepmother rather than the traditional 'Mother Russia' is both poignant and revealing. While many of these Jews embraced Russian culture, they were well aware that Russia, and the other republics, did not always embrace them and that they were forever Jewish, not Russian. Migration was therefore neither welcomed nor forced, it simply became the only open option for many of these older adults.

American expectations

The majority of the immigrants from the USSR and its successor states were assumed to be Jewish (Altshuler, 2005). Therefore the established Jewish community in the United States was expected to create the services needed to absorb these immigrants (Kliger, n.d.). As the USSR was seen by many Americans as the antithesis of what America stands for, the expectations that immigrants from the USSR would be especially grateful to live in the U.S. was a standard assumption among American Jews.

The majority of American Jews are descended from immigrants who arrived from Eastern Europe at the end of the nineteenth century and the beginning of the twentieth. In the 2000/2001 National Jewish Population Survey 80 percent of respondents age 65+ reported that they had at least one parent not born in the United States (Glicksman and Koropeckyj-Cox, 2009). As a significant number of American Jews were the recent descendants of immigrants from Eastern Europe, we can see how the same process of 'becoming American' had affected this group as it planned to welcome yet another cohort of East European Jews.

These earlier immigrants understood that opportunities for advancement relied on them, and more importantly, their children, becoming American in language, culture, and worldview. Jewish culture had to be reinterpreted in light of what was eventually called 'The Faith of America' (Kaplan *et al.*, 1951).

The destruction of European Jewry in the Second World War was a water-shed event (Sarna, 2004). Suddenly, American Jewry was the largest and most influential Jewish community in the world. The post-war effort to establish a Jewish State galvanized much of American Jewry. But soon after Israel was established many American Jews lost interest in Jews overseas. This was even more important as the McCarthy era dawned. Fears that congressional committees investigating real and imagined Communist agents would incite anti-Jewish sentiment in the American public influenced a strong desire to demonstrate how American they had become. This process only intensified the desire to associate being Jewish and being American as virtually the same thing in regard to values and norms.

Through the mid 1960s, little attention was paid to the treatment of Jews in the Soviet Union. This situation radically changed in 1968 with the publication of the book *While Six Million Died* (Morse, 1968). This was the first book to document the failure of the American government to intervene in the Holocaust. The effect of this book on the Jewish community was profound. The sense of betrayal by Roosevelt was mixed with a sense of failure – what had the leadership of the American Jewish community done, and more importantly, not done, to secure the safety of their European brethren? To compensate for the imagined failure to save European Jewry, Soviet Jewry would have to be redeemed (Beckerman, 2010).

Through demonstrations, letter writing campaigns, visits to dissidents in the Soviet Union, and lobbying of Congress the movement supported Jewish migration from the USSR. Little was known about the actual lives of Jews in the USSR. For many American Jews, the images they held of Soviet Jewry were rooted in images of East European Jewry they found in sources that shaped the impression as to what East European Jews had been (and might still be) like. The key sources were the play *Fiddler on the Roof* (Solomon, 2013) and the book *Life is with People* (Kirshenblatt-Gimblett, 1995). Solomon's play (2013), an American adaptation of a cycle of stories written by the Yiddish author Sholom Aleichem about a dairyman named Tevye, was seen by many as an authentic recreation of the Jewish past rather than an adaptation of those stories designed to appeal to mid-century American tastes and assumptions. That image was further enhanced by *Life is with People: The Culture of the Shtetl*. First published in 1952, it has become a standard work on the topic and was greatly influential in the creation of *Fiddler*. The book was celebrated and often read as the best portrayal of East European Jewish life, a warm, appealing portrait of traditional Jewish life described and embraced by American Jews.

These images of East European Jewish life continued to permeate American Jewish thinking in spite of decades of Soviet rule and the Holocaust. American Jews were shocked that Soviet Jews were not what they expected (Markowitz, 1993). Much of the shock was caused by the fact that Soviet Jews, like American Jews, had often sought the benefits of their 'new' country (either by migration to America or by revolution in Russia) by embracing the values and norms of that country. But many American Jews had assumed that while they, the Americans, had adapted to their new homes, the Soviets were to some extent still the persons depicted in the play and book that claimed to describe their common ancestors.

Even in regard to issues that were central to experience of both Jewish communities, differences existed. The Holocaust, a defining event in both communities, was remembered in very different ways. American Jews embraced the memory of Anne Frank and the image of the good Christian couple who hid the Frank family, while for the Soviets much of the same role was taken by the journalist Vasily Grossman, whose odyssey as a correspondent with the Red Army as the war progressed lead to an awakening of his Jewish identity.

The shock turned into tension between the two communities because in many ways the Soviet immigrants were not only different than expected but engaged in behaviors that were unacceptable to American Jews. These included the Soviet tradition of a 'holiday tree' for the New Year (seen as a Christmas tree), but most critically they accepted government welfare payments, which violated the claims by the American Jewish community that 'we take care of our own' and Jews do not appear on the public dole. To American Jewish eyes, Soviet immigrants were not their imagined ancestors – either in their former lives in the USSR or the way in which they adapted to American life (Gold, 1997).

Adapting to their new society

The older immigrants had to find new communities where they could interact and try in some cases to retain the status they had in the old country. The same was true of their relation with family – how to retain status and role in a country they did not know. These efforts were especially difficult because the sources of status in the USSR were often alien to the American milieu. For example, being a veteran of the Second World War conferred prestige in the USSR, while it was much less important to Americans.

I: Could you tell me what organisations you belong to and what kinds of activities you are involved in?
R: My husband is a member of World War II veterans club.
I: Is this an immigrants' club or an American club?
R: This is immigrants' club. Americans don't care. I mean we don't have contacts because we don't understand them, and they don't understand us.

For the older woman quoted below, her moral compass remains what she learned in the Komsomol (All-Union Leninist Young Communist League), the Communist Party organization for adolescents and young adults. But to use the Komsomol as a base for belief in the United States speaks against the basic assumption of what it means to become American.

R: As far as the senior club [...] I like it there, very much so. It is very pleasant. But, you understand, the women come there only to show off their jewels, their clothes. I am sorry, but I tell you what I feel.
I: I am interested in your opinion.
R: Perhaps, that's how it should be done. Life does not stop. Perhaps, it's because my age is different. But I have never worn anything like that in my life. It was not the norm when I was part of Komsomol. And on the whole I have never been interested in trinkets. You see. But nevertheless, I am still very glad. I am there because [...] there are interesting lectures [...] I presented a lecture myself there twice which was received very well. It was dedicated to the forty-ninth anniversary of World War II [...]. It's very interesting, of course. I enjoy going there very much. But as far as friends

[...] I had tried to be with a few there, even gave them my phone number. But no one has called, and I don't either. I have not found people with similar outlook on life.

The difficulties of finding friends in a new land could be insurmountable for some. Another older survivor summed up her misery:

R: There is no one else. I am very lonely. Very much so. There are no bounds for my loneliness. I love people and everything, but I am always alone.

As with their role in community, these older adults seek a role in family that is productive and continues to confer status. In other cases, the requirements that household incomes be less than a certain amount of money forced older adults to live separately from their children in order to qualify for some programs.

I: Is your pension a part of the household income?
R: Of course it is. No doubts about it. See, I feel myself very confident because I can give them something. I can make a gift. So, I am proud of this.

While earlier generations of Jewish immigrants had a sense of having come to this country to better their lives and the lives of their children, for older Soviet immigrants the purpose of migration and whether they had done anything to further their families remained an ambiguous question. What then did they have to bequeath to their children and grandchildren? For these older adults, who will always be Soviet Jews living in America and never Americans in the full sense of the term, what of their past can be part of their children's and grandchildren's future?

But what can they pass on? One older woman spoke about teaching her granddaughter the writings of the Russian author, Alexander Pushkin. In doing this she is sharing something important to her and to the culture of her homeland in a way that teaches lessons about both. For some older immigrants, there is no cultural heritage that can be passed on to the next generations. Rather, they share a personal bond that goes generation to generation. As one middle-aged woman said of her older mother's relationship with the grandchildren:

I: Describe the types of things your children do with or for your mother.
R: They like to discuss political news with her, a newspaper article. They like to ask her about her childhood, her life. She tells them about it with pleasure, about the hard years during the war. They try to learn about her life in the past, about her family and relatives.

For some Soviet Jews the one legacy they can pass on is a personal legacy of hardship, struggle, and survival. It becomes a family legacy, especially one passed down from grandmother to daughter to granddaughter that can be shared 'with pleasure' because it provides an opportunity for generativity – to pass something on to new generations that live in a world totally foreign to the older adult. This is true even when the legacy includes tragic stories.

I: Your husband died [...]
R: No, he was executed by a firing squad [...]
I: What was the reason he was executed? What was the sentence?
R: He was accused of participating in a military plot [...] I am not a writer or journalist, but in the last few years I have written my life's history, typed it on ninety pages. It has been printed in a print shop. I have dedicated it to my grandchildren and great-grandchildren for them to know their roots (showed the manuscript). I wrote this in 1993. Before that I had written memoirs about my husband [...]

In both the wider immigrant community and within their families, the struggle to retain a meaningful role for these immigrants relies on their experience before migration. Theirs is not the story of coming to America to achieve success – rather they remain expatriates for the rest of their lives.

Conclusion

The older immigrants from the USSR did convert identity – but rather than becoming Americans, they became Russians. In the United States Jewish immigrants from Ukraine, Belarus, Lithuania, Georgia, and beyond all became Russians. What they were never accepted as in their lives they had become in their new home. How did this happen? In part because their real heritage was ignored in favor of images that fit an American perception of who immigrants are and how they should behave. By calling them 'Russian' American Jews were not only referring to the language these older immigrants spoke but to the fact that the Jews from the former Soviet Union, in the eyes of American Jews, did not seem Jewish because they failed to yearn to breath the free air of America. This is the great irony of their lives – the one thing they never were in the USSR they became here – Russians. In the end, the older Jewish Soviet immigrants have completed the process expected of all immigrants to this land – they have shed their former identities and adopted a new one, becoming in the New World what they could never achieve in the Old. But they never converted to their new identity becoming American – instead, they acquired an identity denied to them in their place of origin – they became Russian.

References

Altshuler, S. (2005). *From Exodus to Freedom: The History of the Soviet Jewry Movement.* Lanham, MD: Rowman and Littlefield Publishers.

Beckerman, G. (2010). *When They Come for Us, We'll Be Gone: The Epic Struggle to Save Soviet Jewry.* Boston: Houghton Mifflin Harcourt.

Bellah, R. N. (1967). Civil Religion in America. *Dædalus: Journal of the American Academy of Arts and Sciences, 96(1),* 1–21. doi:10.1162/001152605774431464.

Gitelman, Z. Y. (2001). *A Century of Ambivalence: The Jews of Russia and the Soviet Union, 1881 to the Present.* Bloomington: Indiana University Press.

Glicksman, A. (2002). Gods, living and dead: generativity among Soviet born elders in the United States. In C. Messikomer, J. Swazey, and A. Glicksman (eds), *Society and Medicine: Explorations of Their Moral and Spiritual Dimensions: Essays in Honor of Renée C. Fox* (pp. 43–57). New Brunswick, NJ: Transaction Press.

Glicksman, A. and Koropeckyj-Cox, T. (2009). Aging among Jewish Americans: implications for understanding religion, ethnicity, and service needs. *The Gerontologist, 49,* 816–827. doi:10.1093/geront/gnp070.

Gold, S. J. (1997). Community formation among Jews from the former Soviet Union in the US. In N. Lewin-Epstein, Y. Ro'I, and P. Ritterband (eds), *Russian Jews on Three Continents: Migration and Resettlement* (pp. 261–283). Portland, OR: Frank Cass.

Kaplan, M. M., Williams, J. P., and Kohn, E. (1951). *The Faith of America; Prayers, readings, and songs for the celebration of American holidays.* New York: H. Schuman.

Kennedy, J. F. (1964). *A Nation of Immigrants.* New York: Harper and Row.

Kirshenblatt-Gimblett, B. (1995). Introduction. In M. Zborowski and E. Herzog (eds), *Life is with People: The Culture of the Shtetl* (pp. ix–xlviii). New York: Schocken.

Kliger, S. (n.d.). *Russian-Jewish Immigrants in the U.S: Social Portrait, Challenges, and AJC Involvement.* Retrieved from www.ajcrussian.org/site/apps/nlnet/content2.aspx?c=chLMK3PKLsF&b=7718799&ct=11713359.

Markowtiz, F. (1993). *A Community in Spite of Itself: Soviet Jewish Émigrés in New York.* Washington, D.C.: Smithsonian Institute Press.

Morse, A. D. (1968). *While Six Million Died: A Chronicle of American Apathy.* New York: Random House.

Ruggles, S., Alexander, J. T., Genadek, K., Goeken, R., Schroeder, M. B., and Sobek, M. (2010). *Integrated Public Use Microdata Series: Version 5.0* (Machine-readable database). Minneapolis: University of Minnesota.

Sarna, J. D. (2004). *American Judaism: A History.* New Haven: Yale University Press.

Solomon, A. (2013). *Wonder of Wonders: A Cultural History of Fiddler on the Roof.* New York: Metropolitan Books.

Strumpf, N. E., Glicksman, A., Goldberg-Glen, R. S., Fox, R. C., and Logue, E. H. (2001). Caregiver and elder experiences of Cambodian, Vietnamese, Soviet Jewish, and Ukrainian Refugees. *International Journal of Aging and Human Development, 53,* 233–252. doi:10.2190/PXUG-J0T8-DGUK-08MD.

Part III

Elderly care in the context of migration

11 Migrant homecare workers in elder care

The state of the art

Esther Iecovich

Introduction

The purpose of this chapter is to review the current literature on migrant home-care workers (MCW) in elder care and highlight the various aspects of this fast-spreading phenomenon. In fact, labour migration in elder care has become a global and multifaceted issue. This is a critical matter for all involved: the MCWs migrating to provide caring labour, their families who were left in the care of others for extended periods of time, the economy and manpower drain, creating care deficiencies in the sending countries, as well as their care recipients in the receiving countries and institutions in which they work. It is not surprising that during the past decade we have witnessed an abundance of publications addressing the intersection between population ageing, the growing needs and demand for home-based long-term care services, and the pivotal role played by MCWs.

The chapter contains four parts: first, population ageing and the growing needs for home-based long-term care are described. The second part presents a theoretical approach to understanding the migration of care workers and policies on MCWs. The third part relates to roles performed by MCWs and the quality of their relationships with their care recipients and families. The fourth part describes the MCWs' working conditions and difficulties. Finally, challenges and implications for policy and research will be discussed.

Population ageing and long-term care needs

Population ageing is a global issue, affecting most Western and developed countries. The global current life expectancy at the age of 60 for females is 21 years and is higher in American and European Regions (24 and 23, respectively), and 19 years for males, and is higher in Western Pacific and American Regions (20 and 21, respectively) (WHO, 2013). Projections for the next 40 years foresee an increase in the older population with one of every five persons projected to be aged 60+. The greatest increase is projected in the layer aged 80+, suggesting that the older population itself is rapidly ageing and more people will be functionally dependent (WHO, 2011). The number of centenarians world-wide is growing even faster, and is projected to increase from approximately 343,000 in 2012 to 3.2 million by 2050 (United Nations, 2012).

With the ageing of the population the demand for home-based long-term care services is increasing accordingly. To this one should add the health service policies to shorten hospital stays to constrain costs so that older people are sent home before they are completely healed, and the fact that responsibility for their care then falls upon their families (Degiuli, 2007). Concurrent changes in family structure and roles have reduced availability, ability, and motivations to meet their multiple, complex, and varied needs. These changes include a decline in co-residency between generations, decrease in the number of potential family caregivers due to decreasing fertility rates, more women joining the labour force, and increased rates of divorce resulting in single-parent families (e.g. A. Anderson, 2012; Di Rosa *et al.*, 2012). Thus many women are preoccupied with balancing work and caregiving, while increasing life expectancies have increased the duration of caregiving to older family members. These changes have left a great number of countries with a care-deficit and increased reliance on formal care, in particular homecare services.

Although there are differences in welfare regimes between countries with regard to elder care, their common policy is to enable ageing in place to constrain public expenditures on institutional long-term care and match the preferences of the older person and their families (B. Anderson, 2012). To meet these goals, more than 30 per cent of the total public long-term care funding is spent on homecare services (Simonazzi, 2009). Thus, most Western ageing countries are moving towards homecare and demand for care labour is increasing rapidly, but facing problems in recruiting workers to meet the increasing demand. It should be noted that manpower shortage in elder care includes a variety of care workers: domestic care, professional homecare services and professional residential workers such as nursing homes. This chapter focuses on homecare workers. However, the shortage in local homecare workers has propelled many Western ageing countries to recruit MCWs from developing countries. Migration occurs in a context of increasing globalisation, with labour mobility being a significant element of this process. Migrant labour is also a cost-effective alternative to the purchase of homecare services, in particular live-in care.

Migration labour: theory and policies

The push-pull paradigm of migration reflects the neoclassical economics paradigm and is based on principles of utility maximisation, rational choice, and factor-price differentials between regions and countries (King, 2012; Lee, 1966). This relates to macro and micro levels: at the macro-economic level, migration is to rich countries where there is labour shortage and higher salaries than in the countries of origin. At the micro-economic level, migration is the result of rational decisions made by individuals who weigh the pros and cons of moving relative to staying.

Piore (1979), in his seminal book *Birds of Passage*, argues that labour migration is primarily driven by the pull that filling labour supply entails rather than push factors. It is the demand for certain types of cheap labour that is the dominant force. This is linked to the presence of a dual labour market in developed countries: a primary labour market of secure and well-paid jobs for native workers, and a secondary labour market of low-skill, low-wage, insecure jobs in the service sector. Piore found that migrant workers were typically over-represented in jobs that had low social status, were characterised by hard or unpleasant working conditions, had limited chances of job mobility, and involved an informal, highly personal relationship between employer and employee. This reasoning is in line with regard to MCWs in elder care. They tend to cost less; they are prepared to work long hours and perform live-in jobs; they are dependent on their employers to get a visa and/or work permit, restrict-ing them from changing jobs. This dependency is in particular true when the MCWs are illegal residents in the hosting country and are willing to accept poor employment conditions (Cangiano *et al.*, 2009; Lutz, 2011).

In other words, the push factors are those that drive people to migrate from their countries because they experience poverty, unemployment, and other social and economic problems. The pull factors are those that attract people to emigrate to developed and rich countries because they believe that in the destination countries they will have better opportunities to earn money and to send remittances to their families. What will finally influence the decision of the potential MCW to emigrate are the perceptions of the push-pull factors and the extent to which the pull factors are strong enough to encourage the poten-tial MCW to go through the migration process. However, Gordon (1995) has challenged this assumption and suggests that wider political and historical pro-cesses account for labour migration in both sending and receiving countries, as will be discussed later.

Policies on MCWs in elder care

Migration in the long-term care industry is a widespread phenomenon, which reflects the changes associated with the globalisation of the international economy and the growing interdependence between countries. MCWs compose a growing share of homecare workers in many ageing countries in North America, Europe, and the Mediterranean area (Browne and Braun, 2008; Lamura *et al.*, 2008), although data on MCWs is unreliable due to difficulties in obtain-ing data on undocumented workers. MCWs come from a wide ethnic and cul-tural spectrum – i.e. the Philippines, Eastern European countries, Africa, and South America. However, their proportions among homecare workers vary from 18 to 27 per cent in English-speaking countries such as Britain, Ireland, Canada, and the US (Cangiano *et al.*, 2009; Lowell *et al.*, 2010) to over 70 per cent in Italy (Di Rosa *et al.*, 2012). France, the Netherlands, and Sweden seem to rely least on MCWs because substantial public spending has resulted in a largely native workforce, which is well paid and highly trained (Simonazzi, 2009; van Hooren, 2012). With the increasing needs for elder care, this sector of workers is expected to grow accordingly (Eborall *et al.*, 2010; Fraher *et al.*, 2009). For example, in the UK the proportion of MCWs more than doubled within one decade and is projected to increase significantly (Cangiano and Shutes, 2010).

States play an important role in the shaping of demand for MCWs. The share of MCWs in elder care depends on a multiplicity of contextual factors including: local migration control policies (e.g. the extent to which there are difficulties obtaining residence and/or work permits, immigration legacies, policies toward irregular migrant, quotas); welfare regimes (e.g. social-democratic, familialistic vs. liberal regimes, long-term care policies and allowances, cash vs. in-kind, universal vs. means-tested benefits, degree of balance between state vs. market); labour market policies (e.g. regulation of the labour market, marketisation of care provision workforce, demand and supply, recruitment and retention, wage policies, women in the labour force); and families' obligations and responsibilities (Simonazzi, 2009; van Hooren, 2012). For example, in England, the increased contracting-out of care provision led to the expansion of a private sector that now includes 76 per cent of the homecare agencies, whereas in Nordic countries public services are the dominant form of homecare provision and the share of MCWs is very low (Shutes and Chiatti, 2012).

Although countries constitute their forms of 'care regime' and shape their level of reliance on MCWs, migrant care labour can be found in all welfare regimes: liberal, social democratic, and even in familialistic care regimes in countries such as Spain, Italy, Japan, and Korea (Michel and Peng, 2012). Yet, while cross-national convergences are clear, the processes by which these are travelled are varied because they are rooted in different histories, cultures, politics, and practices in care work and migration (Williams, 2012; Williams and Brennan, 2012). Specifically, the intersection between policies related to care, migration, and employment regimes reflects the divergence and convergence across countries and the specific policies regarding migrant care labour in the field of elder care (Shamir, 2013; Williams, 2012).

The policy choices made by countries actually changed the interaction between the institutions of the state, the family, and the market, and the role of each institution in the provision of elder care. For example, the provision of cash long-term care benefits in countries such as Austria, Italy, and Spain, on the one hand, and marketisation of care services and lack of immigration regulation on the other hand, facilitated and shaped the heavy reliance on MCWs in these countries (Shutes and Chiatti, 2012). Countries vary in their policies regarding the employment of MCWs; in some countries the families directly recruit and employ the care workers (e.g. Italy), whereas in other countries (e.g. UK and Israel) care agencies employ the MCWs. However, in some cases these policy areas may suffer from lack of coordination and concordance, reflecting ambiguity and ambivalence towards migrant care work.

Tasks performed by MCWs

Care work includes both 'caring about' and 'caring for', which implies both 'hands on' bodily and emotional work (Huang *et al.*, 2012). Many employers prefer to hire MCWs because they are believed to be committed to caring for elder clients (Martin *et al.*, 2009). MCWs are perceived to be more willing to do hard and shift work than local workers; are highly qualified, reliable, polite, respectful, and compassionate to older people; and provide good quality of care, despite the low wage and low status (Hussein *et al.*, 2011; Spencer *et al.*, 2010).

A distinction should be outlined between *live-in* elder care work, which requires cohabitation with the care recipients and being available around the clock, and *live-out* elder care work, which is usually defined by the number of care hours a day. These different jobs generate different types of relationships and different scopes of tasks performed by the care workers, as well as different expectations from their employers (Degiuli, 2007). However, MCWs' jobs, in particular live-in jobs, are very intensive. They perform a great number of domestic tasks including cooking, cleaning, and shopping; personal care including medication administration and help with the most intimate daily routines; companionship; and surveillance (Degiuli, 2007; Di Rosa *et al.*, 2012; Doyle and Timonen, 2009; Iecovich, 2010). In Italy, for example, live-in MCWs more frequently perform tasks connected with medicine administration, shopping, and help with indoor mobility compared to live-out care workers. In addition, MCWs also provide personal assistance in hospitals when their care recipients are hospitalised (Di Santo and Ceruzzi, 2010). This amount of work increases whenever the care recipient is severely physically dependent, bed-ridden, or cognitively impaired. Indeed, many of the MCWs take care of cognitively impaired and frail older adults and are involved in heavy care tasks. The presence of MCWs is a key to sustaining the lives of a great number of families who otherwise would collapse under the caregiving burden or would look for institutional care.

In fact, the employment of MCWs enabled families to delegate most burdensome care activities, leaving the family to focus more on emotional support and management of care. Several studies (e.g. Ayalon, 2009; Iecovich, 2010) that examined the roles and tasks performed by migrant live-in workers in Israel found that family carers did not relinquish their role in providing care to their elderly relatives, but rather their roles changed by assuming the role of care managers and taking care of finances, while delegating the more intimate personal care tasks and housekeeping tasks to the MCWs. Indeed, the care provided by MCWs was found to significantly alleviate family caregiving burdens and enabled them to work and be productive (Chiatti *et al.*, 2013; Ostbye *et al.*, 2013).

However, care work is not just instrumental help or body work. It is also emotional work, although care plans concentrate predominantly upon the provision of reproductive labour and inhibit the creation of nurturing relationships between care providers and recipients (Datta *et al.*, 2010). Care is a dyadic and reciprocal process that includes the care recipients and their care providers; it is therefore the quality of relationships between them that is so essential for caregiving. Previous studies reported that older clients described the relationship with their homecare workers as 'false kinship', 'one of the family', or as 'fictive kin' (e.g. Cox and Narula, 2003; Piercy, 2001). However, when all these relate to live-in MCWs, the borders between work and caring becomes blurred (Ungerson, 1999) and the relationships between them becomes a crucial factor that affects the quality of care (Hanley *et al.*, 1991).

Quality of relationships is also pivotal for both the MCWs' job satisfaction (Iecovich, 2011) as well as for the satisfaction of the care recipients and their families with the quality of care (Cangiano and Shutes, 2010; Walsh and Shutes, 2013). Studies (e.g. Ayalon, 2009) showed that when care providers cohabited with care recipients, they tended to develop closer family-like relationships compared to those who were live-out care workers. However, poor quality of relationships can result in poor job satisfaction of the MCWs, intentions to leave, turnover, and abuse of the care recipient. MCWs are also dependent on the quality of relationship because poor relationships may lead to dismissal and difficulties in finding better jobs.

Work conditions and difficulties of MCWs

In line with Piore's (1979) paradigm, MCWs are more likely to accept poor employment conditions, which in turn reinforce the undesirability of these jobs, enabling employers to drive down wages and working conditions. MCWs have no bargaining power and accept such wages and jobs, which are still preferable to the poverty and unemployment in their homelands (Lutz, 2011; Samers, 2010). There is evidence that many MCWs find themselves in situations where their employers possess most of the power, leaving them limited grounds to negotiate the terms of their employment and living conditions, which can adversely affect their mental and physical health (Pyle, 2006). Although MCWs often migrate because the wages promised abroad are higher than what they could earn at home, the wages they receive are relatively low and the fringe benefits they are entitled to are not preserved.

In addition, in some countries they have to pay the recruitment agencies, who want to recoup the costs of placing the worker abroad, a significant amount of money that they have to borrow and repay, forcing many to stay with the same employer even when they are abused and exploited. In Israel, for example, recruiters in the sending countries demand an average of US$6,000 for their services and provide high interest loans to cover their travel expenses; thus repayment of their debt may take several months, putting them in a situation akin to debt bondage, and reducing their ability to leave their employer (Shamir, 2013). This makes them convenient employees, but it also makes them vulnerable to exploitation.

Studies conducted in various countries, such as England, Ireland, and Canada, revealed that MCWs' exposure to discrimination, racism, abuse, and exploitation were prevalent (Doyle and Timonen, 2009; Meintel *et al.*, 2006; Stevens *et al.*, 2012). Visible markers such as skin colours, and cultural and language differences are sources leading to racism and discrimination of MCWs (Bowyer, 2009; Johnstone and Kanitsaki, 2008). To these one should add that caring labour is mostly a gender-based issue; that is, the majority of MCWs are women from lower income regions or countries (Fujisawa and Colombo, 2009). Women globally are taking on more responsibilities to earn income, and this has given rise to their transnational movement into care work (Lutz, 2011). Governments in some developing countries even encourage workers to migrate for employment and count on female migrants, to send remittances home (Blue, 2004).

Furthermore, as mentioned above, the nature of care work – at the employer's home – and care that is associated with close relationships make MCW particularly vulnerable to exploitation. This can create problems including poor working conditions, such as excessive work demands or being on call continuously with no additional cost to the employer, with little time to themselves (Bourgeault *et al.*, 2010; Lutz, 2011). Furthermore, in many cases there is no written contract or the contract is written in a language in which the care worker is not proficient, or the job description is too vague and allows employers to constantly reframe the terms of the work relationship. MCWs, who are afraid of losing their jobs, very often comply with their employers' requirements (Degiuli, 2007). All these can jeopardise good quality care provided to the most vulnerable frail older people (Cangiano *et al.*, 2009) and even result in their abuse by their MCWs. In addition to these economic difficulties, MCWs experience psychological, social, and physical difficulties and distress. They also have to cope with feelings of loneliness as a result of separation from their families (Ayalon and Shiovitz-Ezra, 2010; Baldassar, 2008; Chowdhury and Gutman, 2012), having limited opportunities to interact with others and experiencing difficulties in creating social bonds because being confined to the homes of their care recipients and their caregiving burden, as with family caregivers, can negatively affect their health (De la Cuesta-Benjumea and Roe, 2013).

Although MCWs' migration can be understood as a way to improve the livelihoods of their families and enable their children to have better education by sending remittances, it also has harmful social and emotional ramifications for both themselves and the children they leave behind, because parental absence is often experienced with a sense of loneliness and abandonment, an issue that has been barely studied (Salazar-Parreñas, 2003). The impact of migration on the wider family network has resulted in the establishment of other informal support structures to fill the arising gaps in child care and care for older family members (Hoff *et al.*, 2010). A study that examined the economic, social, and emotional consequences of the migration of Sri Lankan female MCWs found that emotional, behavioural, social, mental, and health problems were reported in children who were separated from their mothers, although they kept several channels of communication between them (Ukwatta, 2010). These complex situations can cause much emotional strain to their mothers who work abroad.

Conclusions

The future demand for MCWs is likely to continue to grow because of the demographic shift in ageing societies. MCWs are projected to continue playing a pivotal role in enabling functionally disabled older adults to age-in-place and meet their complex and varied needs, decreasing caregiving burden on their family caregivers, and closing a growing shortage in local homecare workers. It is therefore clear that there is likely to remain a significant reliance on migrants. However, the increasing demand for home-based long-term care is becoming more evident and calls for policy makers to challenge and address several core policy issues. Similar to the complex nature of care provision, care deficit is not a single policy issue but rather a result of fragmentation and divergence of immigration, employment, and elder care policies. Intersects between these policies shape different policies and strategies with regard to recruitment of MCWs. However, the growing numbers of MCWs cannot be understood outside of the social care system, policy regulations, and culture of care within which they work. This suggests that the employment of MCWs is a multifaceted and multidimensional issue, and as such it has to be addressed. Therefore, divergent policies on migration, employment, and elder care should converge to establish a comprehensive policy in this regard.

There is need to improve MCWs' work conditions and regulate this workforce (Gallart et al., 2013). Human rights NGOs in various countries espouse protecting this group of vulnerable workers to prevent abuse and exploitation by recruitment and manpower agencies as well as by the families of care recipients, but their help is only a drop in the ocean. Therefore sending countries should negotiate bilateral or multilateral agreements with receiving countries that include worker protections. In addition, MCWs need emotional and social support. This can be obtained by enabling them to maintain relationships with their families through communication technologies, albeit at a distance and at very low cost (Baldassar 2007, 2008), such as communication centres, visits to their countries to meet with their families, as well as enabling them to establish social networks in the receiving countries. All these are necessary to provide relief of caregiving burden, promote their well-being, and consequently improve quality of care provided to their care recipients. But to assure quality of care it is necessary to increase wages, provide training opportunities, and improve the image of long-term care work. Improving all these may attract more local workers to this field. It is therefore in the interest of all parties involved to improve the work conditions of this sector of homecare workers.

From the perspective of research, although the past decade yielded an abundance of studies that highlighted various aspects connected to MCWs, labour immigration is one of the most controversial public policy issues in affluent countries. Therefore, there is still need to learn and have a deeper understanding about this significant sector of the care workforce and the implications of their potential future contribution. These include comparative examination of the intersection between migration, employment, and elder care policies and its implications on the economy, supply, and demand of long-term care, and the impact of immigration policies on continuity of care across countries. Taking into account that we are dealing with the rights of two vulnerable people – older care recipients and their MCWs – who are both susceptible to abuse, exploitation, mistreatment, and discrimination, there is need for a better understanding of the circumstances in which all these arise, and the interventions that should be developed to address and challenge these problems. However, these issues have not yet received the appropriate attention in the literature and merit further investigation. In other words, further research is needed on the intersection between migration, employment, and elder care policies in order to help policy makers to get a more comprehensive perspective on these issues. This will help them to determine the appropriate policies to address this complex and multifaceted issue.

References

Anderson, A. (2012). Europe's care regimes and the role of migrant care workers within them. *Journal of Population Ageing, 5*, 135–146. 10.1007/s12062–012–9063-y.

Anderson, B. (2012). Who needs them? Care work, migration and public policy. *Cuadernos de Relaciones Laborales, 30*, 45–61. doi:org.10.5209/rev_CRLA.2012.v30. n1.39113.

Ayalon, L. (2009). Family and family-like interactions in households with round-the-clock paid foreign carers in Israel. *Ageing & Society, 29*, 671–686. doi:10.1017/ S0144686X09008393.

Ayalon, L. and Shiovitz-Ezra, S. (2010). The experience of loneliness among live-in Filipino homecare workers in Israel: implications for social workers. *British Journal of Social Work, 40*, 2538–2559. doi:10.1093/bjsw/bcq050.

Baldassar, L. (2007). Transnational families and support: the relationship between truth and distance. *Identities: Global Studies in Culture and Power, 14*, 385–409. doi:10.1080/10702890701578423.

Baldassar, L. (2008). Missing kin and longing to be together: emotions and the construction of co-presence in transnational relationships. *Journal of Intercultural Studies, 29*, 247–266. doi:10.1080/07256860802169196.

Blue, S. A. (2004). State policy, economic crisis, gender, and family ties: determinants of family remittances to Cuba. *Economic Geography, 80*, 63–82. doi:10.1111/ j.1944–8287.2004.tb00229.x.

Bourgeault, I. L., Parpia, R., and Atanackovic, J. (2010). Canada's live-in caregiver program: is it an answer to the growing demand for elderly care? *Journal of Population Ageing, 3*, 83–102. doi:10.1007/s12062–010–9032–2.

Bowyer, B. T. (2009). The contextual determinants of Whites' racial attitudes in England. *British Journal of Political Science, 39*, 559–586. doi:10.1017/S0007123409000611.

Browne, C. V. and Braun, K. L. (2008). Globalization, women's migration, and the long-term care workforce. *The Gerontologist, 48*, 16–24. doi:10.1093/geront/48.1.16.

Cangiano, A. and Shutes, I. (2010). Ageing, demand for care and the role of migrant care workers in the UK. *Journal of Population Ageing, 3*, 39–57. doi:10.1007/ s12062–010–9031–3.

Cangiano, A., Shutes, I., Spencer, S., and Leeson, G. (2009). *Migrant care workers in ageing societies: research findings in the United Kingdom*. Retrieved from www.esds. ac.uk/doc/6920%5Cmrdoc%5Cpdf%5C6920report.pdf.

Chiatti, C., Di Rosa, M., Melchiorre, M. G., Manzoli, L., Rimland, J. M., and Lamura, G. (2013). Migrant care workers as protective factor against caregiver burden: results from a longitudinal analysis of the EUROFAMCARE study in Italy. *Aging & Mental Health, 17*, 609–614. doi:10.1080/13607863.2013.765830.

Chowdhury, R. and Gutman, G. (2012). Migrant live-in caregivers providing care to Canadian older adults: an exploratory study of workers' life and job satisfaction. *Journal of Population Ageing, 5*, 215–240. doi:10.1007/s12062–012–9073–9.

Cox, R. and Narula, R. (2003). Playing Happy Families: rules and relationships in au pair employing households in London, England. *Gender, Place and Culture, 10*, 333–344. doi:10.1080/0966369032000153304.

Datta, K., McIlwaine, C., Evans, Y., Herbert, J., May, J., and Wills, J. (2010). A migrant ethic of care? Negotiating care and caring among migrant workers in London's low-pay economy. *Feminist Review, 94*, 93–116. doi:10.1057/fr.2009.54.

Degiuli, F. (2007). A job with no boundaries: home eldercare work in Italy. *European Journal of Women's Studies, 14*, 193–207. doi:10.1177/1350506807079010.

De la Cuesta-Benjumea, C. and Roe, B. (2013). The experience of family care-givers and migrant paid care-givers' relief of burden: a contrasted qualitative analysis. *Ageing & Society*. Advance online publication. doi:10.1017/S0144686X13000044.

Di Rosa, M., Melchiorre, M. G., Lucchetti, M., and Lamura, G. (2012). The impact of migrant work in the elder care sector: recent trends and empirical evidence in Italy. *European Journal of Social Work, 15*, 9–27. doi:org/10.1080/13691457.2011.56 2034.

Di Santo, P. and Ceruzzi, F. (2010). *Migrant Care Workers in Italy: A Case Study*. Vienna: European Centre for Social Welfare Policy and Research. Retrieved from www.euro.centre.org/data/1278594833_93987.pdf.

Doyle, M. and Timonen, V. (2009). The different faces of care work: understanding the experiences of the multi-cultural care workforce. *Ageing & Society, 29*, 337–350. doi:10.1093/sp/jxp026.

Eborall, C., Fenton, W., and Woodrow, S. (2010). *The State of the Adult Social Care Workforce in England*. Leeds: Skills for Care.

Fraher, E., Carpenter, J., and Broome, S. (2009). Health care employment and the current economic recession. *North Carolina Medical Journal, 70*, 331–336. Retrieved from www.ncmedicaljournal.com/wp-content/uploads/NCMJ/Jul-Aug-09/Fraher.pdf.

Fujisawa, R. and Colombo, F. (2009). *The Long-Term Care Workforce: Overview and Strategies to Adapt Supply to a Growing Demand*. Paris: Organisation for Economic Co-operation and Development. Retrieved from http://search.oecd.org/official-documents/displaydocumentpdf/?doclanguage=en&cote=delsa/elsa/wp2/hea(2009)1.

Gallart, A., Cruz, F., and Zabalegui, A. (2013). Factors influencing burden among non-professional immigrant caregivers: a case-control study. *Journal of Advanced Nursing, 69*, 642–654. doi:10.1111/j.1365–2648.2012.06049.x.

Gordon, I. (1995). Migration in a segmented labour market. *Transactions of the Institute of British Geographers, 20*, 139–155. doi:10.2307/622428.

Hanley, R. J., Wiener, J. M., and Harris, K. M. (1991). Will paid home care erode informal support? *Journal of Health Politics, Policy and Law, 16*, 507–521. doi:10.1215/03616878–16–3–507.

Hoff, A., Feldman, S., and Vidovicova, L. (2010). Migrant home care workers caring for older people: fictive kin, substitute, and complementary family caregivers in an ethnically diverse environment. *International Journal of Ageing and Later Life, 5(2)*, 7–16. doi:10.3384/ijal.1652–8670.10527.

Huang, S., Yeoh, B. S. A., and Toyota, M. (2012). Caring for the elderly: the embodied labour of migrant care workers in Singapore. *Global Networks, 12*, 195–215. doi:10.1111/j.1471–0374.2012.00347.x.

Hussein, S., Stevens, M., and Manthorpe, J. (2011). What drives the recruitment of migrant workers to work in social care in England? *Social Policy and Society, 10*, 285–298. doi:10.1017/S1474746411000029.

Iecovich, E. (2010). Tasks performed by primary caregivers and migrant live-in homecare workers in Israel. *International Journal of Ageing and Later Life, 5(2)*, 53–75. Retrieved from www.ep.liu.se/ej/ijal/2010/v5/i2/a03/ijal10v5i2a03.pdf.

Iecovich, E. (2011). What makes migrant live-in home care workers in elder care be satisfied with their job? *The Gerontologist, 51*, 617–629. doi:10.1093/geront/gnr048.

Johnstone, M.-J. and Kanitsaki, O. (2008). Cultural racism, language prejudice and discrimination in hospital contexts: an Australian study. *Diversity in Health and Social Care, 5*, 19–30. doi:10.1177/1043659609340803.

King, R. (2012). *Theories and Typologies of Migration: An Overview and a Primer.* Sweden, Malmö: Malmö Institute for Studies of Migration, Diversity and Welfare. Retrieved from www.mah.se/upload/Forskningscentrum/MIM/WB/WB%203.12. pdf.

Lamura, G., Mnich, E., Nolan, M., Wojszel, B., Krevers, B., Mestheneos, L., and Dohner, H. (2008). Family carers' experiences using support services in Europe: empirical evidence from the EUROFAMCARE study. *The Gerontologist, 48*, 752–771. doi:10.1093/geront/48.6.752.

Lee, E. S. (1966). A theory of migration. *Demography, 3(1)*, 47–57. Retrieved from www.jstor.org/stable/2060063.

Lowell, B. L., Martin, S., and Stone, R. (2010). Ageing and care giving in the United States: policy contexts and the immigrant workforce. *Population Ageing, 3*, 59–82. doi:10.1007/s12062–010–9029-x.

Lutz, H. (2011). *The New Maids: Transnational Women and the Care Economy.* London: Zed Books.

Martin, S., Lowell, B. L., Gozdziak, E. M., Bump, M., and Breeding, M. E. (2009). *The Role of Migrant Care Workers in Aging Societies: Report on Research Findings in the United States.* Washington, D.C.: Georgetown University. Retrieved from http://www12.georgetown.edu/sfs/docs/20101201_Elder_Care_Report.pdf.

Meintel, D., Fortin, S., and Cognet, M. (2006). On the road and on their own: autonomy and giving in home health care in Quebec. *Gender, Place and Culture, 13*, 563–580. doi:10.1080/09663690600859059.

Michel, S. and Peng, I. (2012). All in the family? Migrants, nationhood, and care regimes in Asia and North America. *Journal of European Social Policy, 22*, 406–418. doi:10.1177/0958928712449774.

Ostbye, T., Malhotra, R., Malhotra, C., Arambepola, C., and Chan, A. (2013). Does support from foreign domestic workers decrease the negative impact of informal caregiving? Results from Singapore survey on informal caregiving. *Journals of Gerontology, Series B: Psychological Sciences and Social Sciences, 68*, 609–621. doi:10.1093/geronb/gbt042.

Piercy, K. W. (2001). 'We couldn't do without them!' The value of close relationships between older adults and their nonfamily caregivers. *Generations, 25(2)*, 41–47.

Piore, M. J. (1979). *Birds of Passage: Migrant Labour and Industrial Societies.* New York: Cambridge University Press.

Pyle, J. L. (2006). Globalization and the increase in transnational care work: the flip side. *Globalizations, 3*, 297–315. doi:10.1080/14747730600869938.

Salazar-Parreñas, R. (2003). The care crisis in the Philippines: children and transnational families in the new global economy. In B. Ehrenreich and A. R. Hochschild (eds), *Global Woman: Nannies, Maids and Sex Workers in the New Economy* (pp. 39–54).

158   E. Iecovich

New York: Metropolitan Books. Retrieved from http://educ.jmu.edu/~brysonbp/337/ GlobalWomanPhilippines.pdf.
Samers, M. (2010). *Migration*. London: Routledge.
Shamir, H. (2013). Migrant care workers in Israel: between family, market and state. *Israel Studies Reviews, 28*, 192–209. doi:http://dx.doi.org/10.3167/isr.2013.280212.
Shutes, I. and Chiatti, C. (2012). Migrant labour and the marketisation of care for older people: the employment of migrant care workers by families and service providers. *Journal of European Social Policy, 22*, 392–405. doi:10.1177/0958928712449773.
Simonazzi, A. (2009). Care regimes and national employment models. *Cambridge Journal of Economics, 33*, 211–232. doi:10.1093/cje/ben043.
Spencer, S., Martin, S., Bourgeault, I. L., and O'Shea, E. (2010). *The Role of Migrant Care Workers in Ageing Societies: Report on Research Findings in the United Kingdom, Ireland, Canada and the United States*. Geneva: International Organization for Migration. Retrieved from http://publications.iom.int/bookstore/free/MRS41.pdf.
Stevens, M., Hussein, S., and Manthrope, J. (2012). Experiences of racism and discrimination among migrant care workers in England: findings from a mixed-methods research project. *Ethnic and Racial Studies, 35*, 259–280. doi:10.1080/01419870.2011.574714.
Ukwatta, S. (2010). Sri Lankan female domestic workers overseas: mothering their children from a distance. *Journal of Population Research, 27*, 107–131. doi:10.1007/s12546-010-9035-0.
Ungerson, C. (1999). Personal assistants and disabled people: an examination of a hybrid form of work and care. *Work Employment and Society, 13*, 583–600. doi:10.1177/09500179922118132.
United Nations (2012). *Population Ageing and Development 2012*. Retrieved from www.un.org/esa/population/publications/2012WorldPopAgeingDev_Chart/2012PopAgeingandDev_WallChart.pdf.
van Hooren, F. J. (2012). Varieties of migrant care work: comparing patterns of migrant labour in social care. *Journal of European Social Policy, 22*, 133–147. doi:10.1177/0958928711433654.
Walsh, K. and Shutes, I. (2013). Care relationships, quality of care and migrant workers caring for older people. *Ageing & Society, 33*, 393–420. doi:10.1017/S0144686X11001309.
Williams, F. (2012). Converging variations in migrant care work in Europe. *Journal of European Social Policy, 22*, 363–376. doi:10.1177/0958928712449771.
Williams, F. and Brennan, D. (2012). Care, markets and migration in a globalising world: Introduction to the Special Issue. *Journal of European Social Policy, 22*, 355–362. doi:10.1177/0958928712449777.
WHO (World Health Organization) (2011). *World Report on Disability*. Geneva: WHO. Retrieved from http://whqlibdoc.who.int/publications/2011/9789240685215_eng.pdf.
WHO (World Health Organization) (2013). *World Health Statistics 2013*. Geneva: WHO. Retrieved from http://apps.who.int/iris/bitstream/10665/81965/1/9789241564588_eng.pdf.

12 The employment of migrant workers in Italy's elder care

Opportunities and challenges

Francesco Barbabella, Mirko Di Rosa,
Maria Gabriella Melchiorre and Giovanni Lamura

Introduction

Italy is one of the countries in which the role of migrants in providing everyday long-term care (LTC) to frail older people has reached an extensive and almost 'systemic' character. This is due to the combined effect of a traditionally weak provision of formal LTC services, on the one hand, and of the increased use – at national and local levels – of cash-for-care schemes. The latter trend has been certainly in line with the *familistic* tradition of the Italian welfare state, and partly nurtured also by the lack of a strong political will to implement a more structured – but organisationally also more demanding – response to LTC challenges. During the 1990s, the increase of cash allowance coverage had been matching the phenomenon of rising migration to the country – mainly unmanaged – for covering positions as domestic workers and care workers privately employed by dependent people and their families. This led to a change in the traditional family-based welfare approach, characterising Italy and most Mediterranean countries (Ferrera, 1996), into what some observers have later defined as the *migrant-in-the-family care model* (Bettio *et al.*, 2006; van Hooren, 2012).

The aim of this chapter is to discuss the main opportunities and challenges currently raised by the phenomenon of migrant care workers (MCWs) privately employed by Italian families for assisting dependent older people living in the community. At first, a brief introduction to the main features of the Italian LTC system is provided, together with an analysis of the role played by MCWs. A second part includes main issues and consequences arising from the employment of MCWs in the Italian context, in terms of both main related opportunities and challenges at different level (micro, meso and macro). Finally, closing remarks give an overview of future perspectives and possible policy options available to improve MCWs' competences and social integration in Italy as a destination country.

Italian long-term care context and the role of migrant care workers

Italy is one of the most aged countries in the world, with over 20 per cent of its population being 65 years old or over (and almost 10 per cent – i.e. 6.1 million –

over 75 years old) (Barbabella *et al.*, 2013), and all projections suggesting that the number of older Italians will continue growing in the future (ISTAT, 2014a). As a consequence, despite the longer life span in good health experienced by most Italians, the absolute number of those needing assistance in everyday life (currently representing 14 per cent of the older population) will increase as well, reaching at least 2.4 million in 2030 (Chiatti *et al.*, 2011).

While many European countries have been reforming their LTC systems in the last two decades – adopting more appropriate policy measures to tackle the challenges deriving from population ageing – no comprehensive reform of the Italian LTC system has been concretely planned. The formal LTC system is therefore currently addressing the phenomenon with old-fashioned measures. Among these, the most relevant is the 'Care Allowance' (*Indennità di Accompagnamento*, IA), a universal and unrestricted care allowance of about €500 per month (up to €750 for certain types of disability). It was introduced in 1980 and is provided by the Italian state to anybody who is fully dependent upon others' help, after a need assessment by local committees. The number of its beneficiaries has significantly increased in the last decade, skyrocketing from 5.5 per cent of the older population in 2001 to 12.5 per cent in 2010 (Barbabella *et al.*, 2013; Gori and Lamura, 2009). As no new policies are responsible for this trend, other reasons exist beyond mere demographic factors, such as for instance a high discretion in granting this allowance (recipients are assessed by over 100 provincial committees using no common standardised criteria across the country). This contributed to a certain extent of misuse in the provision of the IA, especially in the poorest regions, where it has partly ended up becoming a form of income support, rather than disability-related measure (Gori, 2012).

While Italian care allowance coverage is certainly among the most generous across Europe and beyond (Da Roit and Le Bihan, 2010), the same cannot be stated with regard to in-kind supports, such as home and institutional care. The former is provided through two main different programmes: the 'Integrated Home Care' (*Assistenza Domiciliare Integrata*, ADI), granted mainly in the form of nursing care by local health authorities, and the 'Home Help' (*Servizio di Assistenza Domiciliare*, SAD), ensured by municipalities and mainly consisting of household and personal care. Together, the two programmes reach 5.6 per cent of the population over 65 years old, with a significant increase in the last 20 years (from 2 per cent in the early 1990s), mostly due to the positive trend of ADI (Barbabella *et al.*, 2013; Gori and Lamura, 2009). Still, care intensity remains quite low, as ADI recipients receive home visits for just over 20 hours per year on average (with strong regional inequalities), which represents a very small amount of care if compared to other European countries (Garms-Homolová *et al.*, 2012), though similar to figures in other Mediterranean countries (Melchiorre *et al.*, 2010). Also regarding the SAD, this programme has tended over time to be restricted to a smaller number of recipients with the most severe care needs. Finally, as to institutional care, the share of dependent older people accessing nursing homes and residential facilities is stable at a quite low level (just below 2 per cent), with a trend to focus on the frailest people (Barbabella *et al.*, 2013; Gori and Lamura, 2009). This confirms once again that, as already shown by comparative studies (e.g. Pavolini and Ranci, 2008; Rodrigues *et al.*, 2012), the overall provision of in-kind formal services by the Italian welfare state is very limited if compared to other European countries (especially in the Nordic, Continental and Anglo-saxon care regimes: see Simonazzi, 2009), whereas it is in line with other Mediterranean countries.

As anticipated, in the last three decades very few policy attempts have been undertaken to reform the LTC system described above. Among these, we can mention some more general laws in the health care sector which – in the early 1990s – reformed the organisation of local health authorities and introduced efficiency and standard quality indicators (Leg. Decrees 502/1992 'Riordino della disciplina in materia sanitaria' and 517/1993 'Modificazioni al D. Lgs. 502/1992'). Also, the social care reform accomplished in 2000 can be mentioned, since it aimed at introducing, among other things, regional social plans, quality standards for social services and a series of requisites for residential facilities (Law 328/2000 'Legge quadro per la realizzazione del sistema integrato di interventi e servizi sociali'). However, these measures represented no real in-depth reform of the Italian LTC system, and their impact was very limited, as the Italian context remained characterised by a lack of formal services and the predominance of cash-for-care schemes perpetuating a familistic reliance on informal care.

Recently, however, the potential availability of the latter source to provide informal support has been partly affected by an increase in the number of women in the age group 55–64 (who traditionally represent the bulk of informal elder care) in the labour market, which has grown from 16.4 to 33.1 per cent between 2000 and 2013 (ISTAT, 2014b), despite the economic crisis which has been heavily affecting the country since 2008. Notwithstanding, familistic attitudes of Italian households, as revealed by different European surveys (European Commission, 2007), do not seem to have been affected by these trends. This fact, in combination with the strong cash-orientation of the Italian welfare system, has indirectly encouraged Italian families to find new solutions to address the challenge of dependent older people living in the community, especially through the private employment of migrant care workers (MCWs).

Growing phenomenon of migrant care work at home

The size of a peculiar home care market based on privately hired assistants has reached impressive numbers, as shown by official statistics reporting as many as 872,000 domestic workers (a category which includes mostly, but not only, MCWs) in 2010, of which 711,000 had a foreign nationality (Ministero del Lavoro e delle Politiche Sociali, 2012), compared to 180,000 and 35,000 respectively in 1991. These numbers should be integrated with those concerning the 'parallel' market of undeclared MCWs employed without a contract. In this sense, recent estimates indicate that the total number of privately hired care assistants in Italy is around 830,000, of which 750,000 are MCWs and only one-third have a regular contract (Pasquinelli, 2013).

Given the lack of professional requirements to enter this market, the great majority of MCWs has no formal qualification in care and/or nursing (Pasquinelli, 2013). As for their countries of origin (Ministero del Lavoro e delle Politiche Sociali, 2012), they primarily come from Eastern Europe – Romania in the first place (covering alone about one-quarter of the workforce), but also from Ukraine, Poland and Moldova – Latin America (in particular from Peru) and the Philippines. Of all those privately employed by households, over 80 per cent of those coming from non-EU countries are women.

Some evidence shows that, on average, in Italy MCWs work twice as many hours as those contractually agreed (Paletti, 2010), almost half of them working more than nine hours per day (Chiatti *et al.*, 2013a). This is tacitly accepted by many MCWs themselves, who often have poor language skills, are not aware of their rights and experience a context of occupational (and often also housing) segregation and precarious legal status (Villosio and Bizzotto, 2011). Notwithstanding, a relevant number of MCWs considers Italians to be 'kind' or 'friendly', and reports to be treated well or very well by the family they work for (UniCredit Foundation, 2013), in 60 per cent of cases feeling treated even as a family member (IREF, 2007).

Concerning the legislative framework regarding MCWs, it is necessary to distinguish between citizens from the European Union (EU) and workers from non-EU countries. The employment of migrants from other EU member states is certainly facilitated by the current European legislation concerning the free movement of EU citizens, who can move and work in Italy (as is also the case in all other EU member states) and benefit from the same opportunities granted to national workers, so that employers (i.e. older people and households) can directly hire them with no additional restrictions.

People from non-EU countries need instead both a visa and a stay permit to work in Italy (as elsewhere in the EU). If the migrant is still in his/her country of origin, the Italian employer should apply to the local immigration office for a working permit for the person, who can then enter Italy and apply for a stay permit for work to the local police headquarters. However, the possibility to apply in this case depends upon the annual 'flows-decree', which sets both a maximum number of non-EU nationals to be hired and the specific sectors and requirements of open positions. For many migrants from non-EU countries, the common solution is to enter Italy with a regular visa and then find a job through informal networks (e.g. relatives, friends or acquaintances of their ethnic group who are already present in Italy). However, a remarkable number of migrants is still able to enter Italy even without a visa or a stay permit, or to continue to stay even after visas and permits have expired. For future developments it should be noted that, since September 2013 (Law 97/2013 'Disposizioni per l'adempimento degli obblighi derivanti dall'appartenenza dell'Italia all'Unione europea'), non-EU citizens with an EU stay permit of at least five years can access permanent working positions in Italian public organisations (including those active in the LTC sector), in principle making it easier for such migrants to move from undeclared or temporary positions to permanent ones in the formal sector.

Opportunities and challenges related to migrant care work

In order to gain a better understanding of this phenomenon in the Italian LTC context, it is useful to analyse in greater depth the motivations driving Italian families to employ MCWs (Degiuli, 2010), often on a live-in basis. Among the reasons most frequently mentioned by Italian family carers are certainly the wishes 'to ensure constant care' and 'to keep the older family member at home', combined with the possibility of 'keeping on working' and 'safeguarding my own family', in the light of the current 'lack of appropriate alternatives' (FLM, 2011; Spano, 2006). These reasons on the recipients' side can be reformulated in terms of a series of opportunities for the Italian LTC system as a whole.

First, the private employment of MCWs has been relieving family carers of dependent older people from the most burdensome care activities, especially in case of a live-in solution (Di Rosa *et al.*, 2012). Recently, therefore, Italian families have been shifting towards MCWs not only for heavier care tasks (i.e. housework and personal care), but also more delicate ones (like medicine administration). In this way, professional home care services have re-focused more and more on restricted care segments, such as more sophisticated personal care and transportation, while families have concentrated particularly on emotional and organisational activities. Furthermore, if compared to other European citizens, Italians maintain a relatively familistic approach towards elder care. Institutionalisation rates are kept very low also thanks to MCWs' contribution, and this is highly appreciated as Italians have clearly shown their preference for ageing in place, rather than moving to assisted living facilities (European Commission, 2007).

Another opportunity concerns the control over expenditure for LTC. The cash-for-care programme, together with the fact that MCWs often live-in with the older person to ensure 24-hour supervision, clearly contributes to keep overall costs low. This is explained by three further factors: the remarkable wage differentials between Italy and the migrants' countries of origin; the fact that migrants are in most cases illegally employed, with no payment of due taxes and social protection duties; and the availability of specific fiscal incentives for those employing MCWs with regular contracts, allowing savings up to €480 per year (incentives which were introduced with the aim of discouraging undeclared work). The combined effect of all these factors makes this solution economically very convenient, when compared to the alternative of institutionalising the older person in nursing home settings, where monthly user fees usually range between €1,000 and €2,000 per month (Pesaresi and Brizioli, 2009). This represents also a relief to the overall LTC system, as the cash-for-care scheme is on the whole cheaper than other solutions, such as home and residential care services.

Finally, as population ageing continues and the availability of public care services cannot expand due to financial constraints, family carers' stress and burden remains a major, unsolved public health issue. Anxiety, depression, a diminished social life, loss of self-esteem, and a decline in job performance are some of the problems with which burdened caregivers, mainly women, find themselves struggling (Ho *et al.*, 2009; MacNeil *et al.*, 2010). The evidence suggests also that carers' burden might be a contributory factor even for elder abuse (Soares *et al.*, 2010). In this respect, the employment of a MCW seems to represent the only effective measure able to prevent or reduce such a burden (Chiatti *et al.*, 2013b), thus reflecting the crucial role played by these workers in Italy. On the other hand, these findings raise important equity issues since, unlike public welfare services (which in Italy are usually provided on a universal, means-tested basis to all people in need), private home care by MCWs is increasingly becoming the preferred care option for families with higher socio-economic status.

Issues under discussion and to be solved

Besides the mentioned benefits, the widespread employment of MCWs raises a series of challenges at different levels. One of the most important issues is the progressive narrowing of services to the frailest users. The matching of an increasing care demand by older people's families, on the one hand, and the supply of cheap care work offered by migrants reaching Italy to escape poverty in their countries of origin, on the other hand, is challenging the traditional role played by professional LTC services. These services are being partly crowded out by MCWs in most usual care tasks. The services are also reacting very slowly to the growing request for a more targeted training and integration of MCWs into the existing formal care system. This might, however, be partly compensated by a bridging effect, i.e. the trend to a more frequent use of formal care services by older people who can count on family carers, who act as advocates and mediators in acquiring such formal services (Geerlings *et al.*, 2005). This is likely to apply also to private care work, as confirmed by the fact that carers employing MCWs are relieved in heavier tasks and can be more effective as care managers, thus reporting a more frequent use of formal services (Di Rosa *et al.*, 2013).

The risk of abuse and neglect is another relevant aspect. Relationship among MCWs, older people cared for and family carers may be very problematic, due to cultural and linguistic aspects, and in this context both MCWs and the older people they care for may be involved in reciprocally abusive situations. As for the MCWs, they are generally very vulnerable to abusive employment practices (e.g. non-payment of wages, poor living and working conditions) given the isolated and unprotected nature of domestic work (ILO, 2013), thus often suffer from exclusion from basic rights and social protection. Cases of abuse towards MCWs, including sexual violence, are in fact frequent and not always punished (Potalivo, 2013).

Sometimes older people, too, report being harassed and threatened by privately hired MCWs (Melchiorre *et al.*, 2012). There is still little concern and attention to this aspect, although some observers estimate that the prevalence of abuse should not be less than 20 per cent of all cases (Salvioli, 2007), this including cases of thefts perpetrated by MCWs in the house of the assisted older person (Sgritta and Deriu, 2009). A recent study – investigating the 'double direction' of violence in the caregiving relationship as a complex reality of abuses in the home involving MCWs, family carers and cared-for older persons (Ligabue, 2010) – reports that abusive acts are perpetrated in 35 per cent of cases by MCWs (mainly physical and psychological abuse), while the latter report abuse (mainly sexual molesting behaviours and verbal aggression) by both family carers (29 per cent) and by older people (23 per cent). Stress related to heavy working conditions by the MCWs and cognitive pathologies and social isolation by the cared-for older people represent in this respect crucial risk factors, as does forced cohabitation, thus showing the relevance of adopting appropriate training, information and counselling efforts to support all involved parties (MCWs, families and professional carers).

From a labour market perspective, a major problem associated with the widespread employment of MCWs by private households is the large extent of undeclared work. Recent estimates suggest that over 26 per cent of them do not possess a stay permit or a working permit, while over 36 per cent are regularly registered as residents but provide paid care without a contract (Pasquinelli, 2013). Traditionally, two main tools have been used to fight undeclared work: fiscal incentives and ex-post legalisations. Fiscal incentives have been made available to care recipients and families employing MCWs, under the requirement that they are hired through a regular contract (Law 342/2000 'Misure in materia fiscale' and Law 296/2006 'Disposizioni per la formazione del bilancio annuale e pluriennale dello Stato'). The main policy option has been, however, the ex-post legalisation of those employed without having even a stay permit, by means of decrees (seven in total since 1997), allowing them and their employers to regularise their positions with no legal consequences. Numbers are impressive: in 2002 a total of 350,000 domestic workers, including MCWs, were legalised, about 295,000 in 2009 and over 134,000 in 2012 (Pasquinelli and Rusmini, 2013; Lamura *et al.*, 2014). In addition, the government has set annual quotas for migrant workers from non-EU countries, which are usually exceeded by the number of applications. However, in the last few years, available positions have significantly decreased, mainly due to the recent financial crisis, dropping from 65,000 positions in 2007 to 14,000 in 2012 and 30,000 in 2013 (Lamura *et al.* 2014).

A crucial issue – which has, however, had a marginal role in the Italian debate so far – concerns the risk of care drain in migrants' own countries of origin. This refers to the danger that although the children and/or older parents whom MCWs' leave behind might be better off financially, they can also be more socially deprived and could end up being cared for by already frail grandmothers (Tolstokorova, 2007; HelpAge International, 2008; Pantea, 2012). In fact, as Bettio *et al.* (2006) argue, transfers can be seen as just one side of the 'care drain' story in Italy, the other one being women's care work burden (as economic emancipation drives the behaviour of both Italian and immigrant women, similarly to the path followed by a far less familistic society such as the United States). Another problem is that of the mental health challenges that affect several migrant women returning back home after long years of isolated, unhealthy life as care workers abroad (Tolstokorova, 2007). Finally, it should be mentioned that destination countries might save remarkable amounts of money in terms of education and training costs, which have been borne by migrant's countries of origin (Sriskandarajah, 2005).

Final remarks

The opportunities and challenges discussed above indicate the urgency to carry out in-depth reforms of the Italian LTC sector in order to improve the quality of life of frail older people, of MCWs and of family carers (including caregiving and working conditions of these latter two groups), and to build a more sustainable, equal and efficient LTC system. One of the crucial steps needed entails improving care quality by strengthening the integration of privately paid MCWs with professional carers and health professionals (Tidoli, 2006). While most of the initiatives undertaken in Italy have focused so far on enhancing the quality of the care provided by MCWs only (e.g. by means of training courses), a more appropriate and coordinated approach would require such courses to be better connected with initiatives on other fronts. Among these, an often proposed measure – implemented only in a fragmented and sporadic way by local care providers – is that of introducing a public register of MCWs. This would offer families the possibility of accessing information in an easy and transparent way, providing a freedom of choice which is usually strongly limited when one relies on the traditional 'word-of-mouth' search. Through these registers, MCWs could be provided with a certification of their professional status, of the knowledge they have gained through courses and of the skills they have acquired in the workplace (Pasquinelli and Rusmini, 2013).

The Italian government has not yet designed any articulated programme at state level to improve both working conditions and care quality provided by the MCWs privately hired by households, albeit experts and policy analysts have been discussing in depth about these issues for at least a decade, addressing in particular the following three topics (Pasquinelli and Rusmini, 2013): (1) the training of both MCWs and family carers to improve caregiving skills and the quality of care provided; (2) an improved integration of both MCWs and family carers in the network of formal services; and (3) a more controlled and integrated use of care allowances.

The commitment that Italy will demonstrate in trying to achieve these objectives, and also by financing home care in a more accredited and articulated way, will be a clear indicator of the country's ability to provide decent living conditions for frail elderly, their family carers and MCWs, and to prevent abuse or neglect, phenomena which are most likely to occur when both the family and MCWs feel to be inadequately supported by the formal care system (Di Rosa *et al.*, 2010). Moreover, a 'transnational integration' of policies in both source and destination countries could be helpful to compensate the care drain of MCWs and contribute to transform it, at least partially, in a care gain, by building on the informal networks existing between migrants and non-migrants, also taking into account the need for labour force in the home care sector existing within the EU (Lamura *et al.*, 2014). The aim should be to stimulate the 'return' of a certain amount of 'welfare' to source societies in the form of transnational caregiving, in addition to traditional remittances (Boccagni, 2008). Current policy perspectives in Italy suggest, however, that there is still a long way to go in this respect.

References

Barbabella, F., Chiatti, C., Di Rosa, M. and Gori, C. (2013). La bussola di N.N.A.: lo stato dell'arte basato sui dati [A compass of long-term care in Italy: a state-of-the-art based on evidence]. In Network Non Autosufficienza (ed.), *L'assistenza agli anziani non autosufficienti in Italia: 4° Rapporto* [Long-term care to older people: 4th Report] (pp. 11–28). Santarcangelo di Romagna: Maggioli Editore. Retrieved from www.maggioli.it/rna/2012/pdf/rapporto2012-assistenza_anziani.pdf.

Bettio, F., Simonazzi, A. and Villa, P. (2006). Change in care regimes and female migration: the 'care drain' in the Mediterranean. *Journal of European Social Policy, 16*, 271–285. doi:10.1177/0958928706065598.

Boccagni, P. (2008). *Oltre il* care drain? *Opportunità e limiti di un approccio 'win-to-win' al rapporto tra migrazioni e welfare. Il caso ecuadoriano* [Beyond the care drain? Opportunities and limits of a 'win-to-win' approach concerning the relation between migration and welfare: the Ecuadorian case]. Paper presented at the annual conference of ESPAnet Italia 'Le politiche sociali in Italia nello scenario europeo', Ancona (Italy). Retrieved from www.espanet-italia.net/conferenza2008/paper_edocs/C/5-Boccagni.pdf.

Chiatti, C., Barbabella, F., Lamura, G. and Gori, C. (2011). La 'bussola' di N.N.A.: lo stato dell'arte basato sui dati [A compass of long-term care in Italy: a state-of-the-art based on evidence]. In Network Non Autosufficienza (ed.), *L'assistenza agli anziani non autosufficienti in Italia: 3° Rapporto* [Long-term care to older people: 3rd Report] (pp. 13–33). Santarcangelo di Romagna: Maggioli Editore. Retrieved from www.maggioli.it/rna/2011/pdf/rapporto2011-assistenza_anziani.pdf.

Chiatti, C., Di Rosa, M., Barbabella, F., Greco, C., Melchiorre, M. G., Principi, A., Santini, S. and Lamura, G. (2013a). Migrant care work for elderly households in Italy. In J. Troisi and H.-J. von Kondratowicz (eds), *Ageing in the Mediterranean* (pp. 235–256). Bristol: Policy Press.

Chiatti, C., Di Rosa, M., Melchiorre, M. G., Manzoli, L., Rimland, J. M. and Lamura, G. (2013b). Migrant care workers as protective factor against caregiver burden: results from a longitudinal analysis of the EUROFAMCARE study in Italy. *Aging and Mental Health, 17*, 609–614. doi:10.1080/13607863.2013.765830.

Da Roit, B. and Le Bihan, B. (2010). Similar and yet so different: cash-for-care in six European countries' long-term care policies. *The Milbank Quarterly, 88*, 286–309. doi:10.1111/j.1468–0009.2010.00601.x.

Degiuli, F. (2010). The burden of long-term care: how Italian family care-givers become employers. *Ageing & Society, 30*, 755–777. doi:10.1017/S0144686X10000073.

Di Rosa, M., Barbabella, F., Chiatti, C., Melchiorre, M. G. and Lamura G. (2013). Private Employment of Home Care Workers and Use of Health Services by Disabled Older People in Italy. *Euroregional Journal of Socio-Economic Analysis, 1*, 33–42. Retrieved from http://eurjsea.ro/archive/001/I001-4.pdf.

Di Rosa, M., Melchiorre, M. G. and Lamura, G. (2010). I servizi domiciliari tra reti informali e assistenti familiari [Home care between informal networks and privately-employed care assistants]. In Network Non Autosufficienza (ed.), *L'assistenza agli anziani non autosufficienti in Italia: 2° Rapporto* [Long-term care to older people: 2nd Report] (pp. 181–197). Santarcangelo di Romagna: Maggioli Editore. Retrieved from www.maggioli.it/rna/2010/pdf/rapporto2010-assistenza_anziani.pdf.

Di Rosa, M., Melchiorre, M. G., Lucchetti, M. and Lamura, G. (2012). The impact of migrant work in the elder care sector: recent trends and empirical evidence in Italy. *European Journal of Social Work, 15*, 9–27. doi:10.1080/13691457.2011.562034.

European Commission (2007). *Health and long-term care in the European Union* (Special Eurobarometer 283/Wave 67.3). Brussels: European Commission.

Ferrera, M. (1996). The 'Southern Model' of welfare in Social Europe. *Journal of European Social Policy, 6*, 17–37. doi:10.1177/095892879600600102.

FLM (Fondazione Leone Moressa) (2011). *Quali badanti per quali famiglie?* [Which Migrant Care Workers for Which Families?]. Mestre: Fondazione Leone Moressa. Retrieved from www.fondazioneleonemoressa.org/newsite/wp-content/uploads/2012/06/Quali-badanti-per-quali-famiglie_completo.pdf.

Garms-Homolová, V., Naiditch, M., Fagerström, C., Lamura, G., Melchiorre, M. G., Gulácsi, L. and Hutchinson, A. (2012). Clients in focus. In N. Genet, W. Boerma, M. Kroneman, A. Hutchinson and R. B. Saltman (eds), *Home Care across Europe: Current Structure and Future Challenges* (pp. 55–70). Copenhagen: WHO Regional Office for Europe. Retrieved from www.euro.who.int/__data/assets/pdf_file/0008/181799/e96757.pdf.

Geerlings, S. W., Pot, A. M., Twisk, J. W. R. and Deeg, D. J. H. (2005). Predicting transitions in the use of informal and professional care by older adults. *Ageing & Society, 25*, 111–130. doi:10.1017/S0144686X04002740.

Gori, C. (2012). Home care in Italy: A system on the move, in the opposite direction to what we expect. *Health and Social Care in the Community, 20*, 255–264. doi:10.1111/j.1365–2524.2011.01052.x.

Gori, C. and Lamura, G. (2009). Lo scenario complessivo [An overview of long-term care services]. In Network Non Autosufficienza (ed.), *L'assistenza agli anziani non autosufficienti in Italia: Rapporto 2009* [Long-term care to older people in Italy: Report 2009] (pp. 17–34). Santarcangelo di Romagna: Maggioli. Retrieved from www.maggioli.it/rna/pdf/rapporto2009-assistenza_anziani.pdf.

HelpAge International (2008). *Grandparents and Grandchildren: Impact of Migration in Moldova*. Chisinau: Help Age International. Retrieved from www.helpage.org/download/4c48e4e033f77/.

Ho, S. C., Chan, A., Woo, J., Chong, P. and Sham, A. (2009). Impact of caregiving on health and quality of life: a comparative population-based study of caregivers for elderly persons and noncaregivers. *The Journals of Gerontology: Series A: Biological Sciences and Medical Sciences, 64*, 873–879. doi:10.1093/gerona/glp034.

ILO (International Labour Office) (2013). *Domestic Workers across the World: Global and Regional Statistics and the Extent of Legal Protection*. Geneva: ILO. Retrieved from www.ilo.org/wcmsp5/groups/public/--dgreports/--dcomm/--publ/documents/publication/wcms_173363.pdf.

IREF (Istituto di Ricerche Educative e Formative) (2007). *Il welfare 'fatto in casa'* ['Home-Made' Welfare]. Rome: IREF. Retrieved from www.irefricerche.it/File/Rapporto_Il_welfare_fatto_in_casa_DEF.pdf.

ISTAT (2014a). *GeoDemo – Database ISTAT: bilancio demografico e proiezioni* [Database of the Italian Institute of Statistics: Demographic Balance and Projections] (Data set). Retrieved from www.demo.istat.it.

ISTAT (2014b). *I.Stat – Database ISTAT: lavoro* [Database of the Italian Institute of Statistics: Labour] (Data set). Retrieved from http://dati.istat.it.

Lamura, G., Chiatti, C., Barbabella, F. and Di Rosa, M. (2014). *Filling the Gap in Long-Term Professional Care through Systematic Migration Policies: Synthesis Report.* Luxembourg: Publications Office of the European Commission. Retrieved from http://ec.europa.eu/social/BlobServlet?docId=11602&langId=en.

Law 328/2000 Legge quadro per la realizzazione del sistema integrato di interventi e servizi sociali [Framework law for the fulfilment of an integrated system of social interventions and services].

Law 342/2000 Misure in materia fiscale [Measures on fiscal matters].

Law 296/2006 Disposizioni per la formazione del bilancio annuale e pluriennale dello Stato [Dispositions for the arrangement of annual and multi-year balance of the State].

Law 97/2013 Disposizioni per l'adempimento degli obblighi derivanti dall'appartenenza dell'Italia all'Unione europea [Dispositions for the fulfilment of obligations derived from Italy's membership to European Union].

Leg. Decree 502/1992 Riordino della disciplina in materia sanitaria [Reorganisation of the healthcare sector].

Leg. Decree 517/1993 Modificazioni al D. Lgs. 502/1992 [Modifications to Leg. Decree 502/1992].

Ligabue, L. (2010). *Progetto DIADE: attività svolte ed elementi emersi dal progetto* [DIADE Project: Activities Carried out and Results Emerged from the Project]. Paper presented at the Conference on 'Double direction of violence in the caregiving relationship', Reggio Emilia (Italy). Retrieved from www.informanziani.it/docs/LL.pdf.

MacNeil, G., Kosberg, J. I., Durkin, D. W., Dooley, W. K., DeCoster, J. and Williamson, G. M. (2010). Caregiver mental health and potentially harmful caregiving behavior: the central role of caregiver anger. *The Gerontologist, 50*, 76–86. doi:10.1093/geront/gnp099.

Melchiorre, M. G., Chiatti, C. and Lamura, G. (2012). Tackling the phenomenon of elder abuse in Italy: a review of existing legislation and policies as learning resource. *Educational Gerontology, 38*, 699–712. doi:10.1080/03601277.2011.608610.

Melchiorre M. G., Di Rosa M., Chiatti C. and Lamura G. (2010). Italia ed Europa a confronto [A comparison between Italy and Europe]. In Network Non Autosufficienza (ed.), *L'assistenza agli anziani non autosufficienti in Italia: 2° Rapporto* [Long-Term Care to Older People: 2nd Report] (pp. 199–206). Santarcangelo di Romagna: Maggioli Editore. Retrieved from www.maggioli.it/rna/2010/pdf/rapporto2010-assistenza_anziani.pdf.

Ministero del Lavoro e delle Politiche Sociali (2012). *Secondo rapporto annuale sul mercato del lavoro degli immigrati* [Second Annual Report on the Labour Market of Immigrants]. Rome: Direzione Generale dell'Immigrazione e delle Politiche di Integrazione. Retrieved from www.integrazionemigranti.gov.it/archiviodocumenti/lavoro/Documents/II_Rapporto_immigrati_2012.pdf.

Paletti, F. (2010). *Le lavoratrici di cura immigrate nella provincia di Massa Carrara* [Migrant Care Workers in the Province of Massa Carrara]. Paper presented at the Conference ESPAnet 'Welfare and Federalism', Napoli (Italy). Retrieved from www.espanet-italia.net/conferenza2010/programma/edocs/2E/2E_Paletti.pdf.

Pantea, M.-C. (2012). Grandmothers as main caregivers in the context of parental migration. *European Journal of Social Work, 15*, 63–80. doi:10.1080/13691457.2011.562069.

Pasquinelli, S. (2013). Le badanti in Italia: quante sono, chi sono, cosa fanno [Migrant care workers in Italy: how many they are, who they are, what they do]. In S. Pasquinelli and G. Rusmini (eds), *Badare non basta: Il lavoro di cura: attori, progetti, politiche* [Caring is Not Enough: Care Work: Actors, Projects, Policies] (pp. 41–55). Rome: Ediesse.

Pasquinelli, S. and Rusmini, G. (2013). Il punto sulle badanti [A discussion about migrant care workers]. In Network Non Autosufficienza (ed.), *L'assistenza agli anziani non autosufficienti in Italia: 4° Rapporto* [Long-Term Care to Older People: 4th Report] (pp. 93–112). Santarcangelo di Romagna: Maggioli Editore. Retrieved from www. maggioli.it/rna/2012/pdf/rapporto2012-assistenza_anziani.pdf.

Pavolini, E. and Ranci, C. (2008). Restructuring the welfare state: reforms in long-term care in Western European countries. *Journal of European Social Policy, 18*, 246–259. doi:10.1177/0958928708091058.

Pesaresi, F. and Brizioli, E. (2009). I servizi residenziali [Residential care services]. In Network Non Autosufficienza (ed.), *L'assistenza agli anziani non autosufficienti in Italia: Rapporto 2009* [Long-Term Care to Older People in Italy: Report 2009] (pp. 53–68). Santarcangelo di Romagna: Maggioli Editore. Retrieved from www.maggioli.it/rna/pdf/rapporto2009-assistenza_anziani.pdf.

Potalivo, A. (2013). Assistenza familiare e immigrazione: L'inclusione finanziaria [Home care and immigration: financial inclusion]. *Webzine dell'Associazione Nuovo Welfare, 4*, 5–8. Retrieved from www.nuovowelfare.it/nuovoWelfare/store/fileStore/File/WOL/Anno%202013/WOL%20maggio-giugno%202013.pdf.

Rodrigues, R., Huber, M. and Lamura, G. (eds) (2012). *Facts and Figures on Healthy Ageing and Long-Term Care. Europe and North America.* Vienna: European Centre for Social Welfare Policy and Research. Retrieved from www.euro.centre.org/data/LTC_Final.pdf.

Salvioli, G. (2007). Gli anziani e le badanti [Older people and migrant care workers]. *Giornale di Gerontologia, 2*, 59–61. Retrieved from www.sigg.it/public/doc/GIORNALEART/883.pdf?r=0,3763331.

Sgritta, G. B. and Deriu, F. (eds) (2009). *La violenza occulta: Violenza, abusi e maltrattamenti contro le persone anziane* [The Hidden Violence: Violence, Abuse and Maltreatment towards Older People]. Rome: Edizioni Lavoro.

Simonazzi, A. (2009). Care regimes and national employment models. *Cambridge Journal of Economics, 33*, 211–232. doi:10.1093/cje/ben043.

Soares, J. J. F., Barros, H., Torres-Gonzales, F., Ioannidi-Kapolou, E., Lamura, G., Lindert, J.,... Stankunas, M. (2010). *Abuse and Health among Elderly in Europe.* Kaunas: Lithuanian University of Health Sciences Press.

Spano, P. (2006). *Le convenienze nascoste: Il fenomeno badanti e le risposte del welfare* [The Hidden Conveniences: The Phenomenon of Migrant Care Workers and Measures from the Welfare State]. Portogruaro: Nuova Dimensione.

Sriskandarajah, D. (2005). *Migration and Development.* Geneva: Global Commission on International Migration. Retrieved from http://iom.ch/jahia/webdav/site/myjahiasite/shared/shared/mainsite/policy_and_research/gcim/tp/TP4.pdf.

Tidoli, R. (2006). Le metamorfosi dell'assistenza domiciliare [Changes in home care]. *Prospettive Sociali e Sanitarie, 2*, 6–10.

Tolstokorova, A. (2007). *Effect of External Labour Migration on Ukrainian Family: 'Poisoned Gift' or 'Dream Realized'?* Paper presented at the international conference 'New Migration Dynamics: Regular and Irregular Activities on the European Labour Market' of University of Nice Sophia Antipolis, Nice (France).

UniCredit Foundation (2013). *Indagine sull'assistenza familiare in Italia: Il contributo degli immigrati* [Survey on Home Care in Italy: The Contribution of Migrants]. Bergamo: CPZ. Retrieved from www.unicreditfoundation.org/content/dam/ucfoundation/documents/publications/Report_immigrazione.pdf.

van Hooren, F. J. (2012). Varieties of migrant care work: comparing patterns of migrant labour in social care. *Journal of European Social Policy, 22*, 133–147. doi:10.1177/0958928711433654.

Villosio, C. and Bizzotto, G. (2011). *Once There Were Wives and Daughters, Now There are Badanti. Working in Home Elderly Care in Italy is Still an Informal, Unqualified and Unrecognised Occupation* (Walqing Social Partnership Series 2011.14). Moncalieri: Walqing Social Partnership. Retrieved from www.walqing.eu/fileadmin/download/external_website/WALQING_SocialPartnershipSeries_2011.14_ElderlyCare_ITA.pdf.

13 More diversity, better quality of care

Constructions of professional identity and work culture among migrant care workers in Denmark

Tine Rostgaard

Introduction[1]

Many ageing countries are facing the challenge of how to attract and retain workers to the Long-Term Care (LTC) sector, as work here is often regarded as physically and mentally challenging. A common response in many countries has been to recruit migrant care workers (Colombo *et al.*, 2011). So far, most studies of migrant care work have focused on countries applying strategies of transnational and often unmanaged migration, tolerating or even relying on low-skilled and undeclared migration, such as Italy (Di Rosa *et al.*, 2012), where migrant care work is predominantly unregulated and taking place in an informal setting. In contrast, there have been fewer studies of countries applying managed care migration strategies in a setting with formal care sector employment, as in Denmark, which is the focus of this chapter. Here, the main feature of the public social service model is that the responsibility for the organisation, provision and financing of care traditionally lies in the public sector (Anttonen and Sipilä, 1996). LTC constitutes one of the cornerstone welfare services, with continuous popular support and relatively generous service provision, providing home care for 14 per cent and nursing home care for 4 per cent of all persons over age 65. Service provision is highly regulated and primarily provided by professional staff. More than 70 per cent of nursing home and home help staff have received 1–3 years of formal training (Rostgaard *et al.*, 2011; Leon *et al.*, 2014). A central factor for the continuation of this rather labour-intensive system is, thus, the availability of qualified care workers. This helps account for the interest in attracting persons of migrant background to seek work in this sector.

In Denmark, one in ten care workers in the LTC sector now has a migrant background. The recruitment into the LTC sector is primarily aimed at persons already living in the country. There is the very explicit assumption that if 3–4 per cent of the migrant population currently outside of the labour market were to pursue an education in social care and 75 per cent of these persons were to complete their studies, the problem of recruitment to the sector would be overcome (FOA, 2008). But the interest in attracting migrants to the care sector spans more than addressing a staff shortage. Inherent to the recruitment strategy are specific assumptions concerning the professional identity and work culture of the care workers with migrant backgrounds, which is assumed to favour the LTC sector as such and older persons needing care in general. This emphasises the cultural orientation and natural caring skills of migrants, which should be a motivational factor for taking work in the LTC sector and ensure the provision of a substantially different form of care, more akin to traditional care rationality.

Drawing on the theoretical notion of 'Otherness', the chapter critically discusses this assumption by investigating the institutionalised thinking about professional identity and work culture, as this is brought forward in the expressions by key actors, such as the care workers with migrant and non-migrant backgrounds, as well as middle and top managers. In particular, the motives for taking up training and work in the LTC sector are investigated, as is the understanding of care culture, quality and skills. The chapter will begin by describing the data set and theoretical framework before investigating whether the recruitment strategies match individual motivations of care workers of migrant background. Finally, we investigate the assumptions about good quality care and care competences and how they match the recruitment strategy for migrant care work.

Methodology: data and definitions

The analysis is based on ten individual and six focus group interviews with frontline care workers, middle level and top management from the LTC sector in three municipalities in Denmark – Elsinore, Greve and Vejle – all experienced in recruiting migrant care workers. In addition, a survey was carried out among 1,035 frontline LTC workers from ten Danish municipalities, including the mentioned three. Municipalities were in general chosen, on the basis of their active approach to recruiting migrant care workers, the size of the care sector and the share of migrants in the local population. Care staff with a migrant background were oversampled in the survey. 'Migrant background' is defined as having a first- or second-generation migrant background; that is, that oneself or both of one's parents were born outside Denmark, using the definition applied by Statistics Denmark (2013). 'Danish background' is defined as persons – regardless of their place of birth – who have at least one parent who was born in Denmark (or in Greenland, the Faroe Islands or Iceland, as our purpose is to capture linguistic and ethno-cultural differences). Register data is applied in order to identify migrant status. Migrant care workers are further divided into Western background and non-Western background.[2]

Of the respondents, 50.3 per cent were of Danish origin, 11.6 per cent of Western migrant origin and 38.1 per cent of non-Western migrant origin. In total, slightly more than half of the respondents (52.4 per cent) represented the Nordic countries, 80 per cent of whom came from Denmark. 8.8 per cent of all of the respondents came from Africa, 8.5 per cent from the Middle East, mainly Iran, Iraq or Turkey, 8.9 per cent from South East Asia, such as the Philippines, Thailand or Vietnam, and 5.7 per cent were from Eastern Europe, mainly Poland.

Of the 1,350 care workers participating in the survey, 8.3 per cent were men and 91.7 per cent women, which reflects the general gender division among care workers. The proportion of men was slightly but not significantly higher for care workers with Western backgrounds (10.0 per cent) and non-Western backgrounds (13.2 per cent). Finally, a study of various policy documents has been carried out in order to investigate the understandings and institutionalisation of migrant care work.

Theoretical framework: the discursive construction of 'Otherness'

The chapter critically investigates the assumptions behind the discursive construction of professional identity and work culture of care workers with migrant backgrounds in a sector, which is relatively new to multicultural dynamics. The analysis draws on the post-colonial notion of 'Otherness', as forwarded first and foremost by Said (1978). The shaping of 'Otherness' is believed to take place as people deal with culture by making statements about it, authorising views of it, describing it or ruling over it (Said, 1978). Inspired by the work of Prasad and Prasad (2002), these representations of 'Otherness' are believed to be expressed in organisational milieus and sustained through a series of institutional arrangements, which support specific ways of thinking about ethnicity. How the organization is 'doing ethnicity' may, despite all good intentions, create stereotypical perceptions about individuals based on their shared cultural or national identity (Lill, 2007). When we use certain descriptions of each other, different identities are generated and we start acting upon them as well. Doing ethnicity when caring for older people refers to how, for example, colleagues respond to and talk about cultural differences among each other (Lill, 2007).

The conceptualization of the 'Other' is seen as an expression of something that goes against the norm and the expected and accepted, discursively creating binary groups of the dominant in-group ('us', the 'self') and the dominated out-group ('them', 'Other') (Pio and Essers, 2014). In this sense, it is often considered in the literature to be an appropriating discourse with an inherent power relation, where the 'Other' is summarised as something which is inferior, something 'deficient, backward, primate or in other ways denigrated and diminished' (Westwood, 2001, p. 242). However, rather than seeing the creation of 'Otherness' as simply a construction of subordination, which negatively simplifies and reduces the individual, the chapter will investigate the many forms that 'Otherness' might also assume. This will be done both in the sense of understanding the agency which is exerted by the care workers with migrant backgrounds, and also in order to understand how the conceptualisation of 'Otherness' at the institutional and organisational levels is seen to contribute to the functioning of the organisation.

Motivation to work with care

The LTC sector in Denmark has been targeted as a labour market sector with great potential for the recruitment of migrant women and low-skilled migrants in particular, not least because of the practical elements in the care education and work performance:

> Education to Social and Health Care Helper [SOSU helper] and to Social and Health Care Assistant [SOSU assistant] … may be relevant to refugees and immigrants in that there are practically oriented courses in an area of employment which is expected to experience a shortage of trained manpower in the future.
>
> (Ministry of Education, 2003, p. 11, author's translation)

Many recruitment initiatives have been taken in order to increase the intake of migrant students to LTC education. And the interest in acquiring an LTC education has been generally high – and higher than among Danish born – among the migrant population (Teknologisk Institut, 2004). This means that 22 per cent of SOSU (Social- og Sundheds-uddannelses Centret, Danish basic health care college) students currently have migrant backgrounds, up from 15 per cent in 2006. In comparison, as of 2013, first- and second-generation migrants made up 10.7 per cent of the population (Statistics Denmark, 2013). Moreover, local job centres have targeted the migrant population as a potential LTC labour supply (Beskæftigelsesministeriet, 2007).

With the practical orientation and need for labour, the LTC sector is thus perceived as an attractive sector in which to work by a proportionally higher share of people with a migrant background than with a Danish background. Are there other motivational factors? The recruitment strategies are marked by more or less direct assumptions about the migrant carer's cultural orientation, which should also make them more motivated to work in this sector. As Lill (2007) notes, the dominant discourse related to LTC work is that the main motivation to work in the sector is an interest in working with older people rather than the wages or status. Maria, a care worker of Western migrant origin, acknowledges how it is the interpersonal relationships, the sense of being able to help and expressions of gratitude that provide a sense of satisfaction: 'It is really lovely with the older people. They're very happy when you help them.'

The first question to be examined is if the motives for seeking work in the sector are generally shared by those of Danish and migrant origins alike. Overall, the survey data confirms that the interest in working with older people is a general trait among care workers, with 82 per cent indicating this to be the main motivational reason to work in the sector (Table 13.1). Looking across the ethnic divide, however, there are no indications that migrant care workers should be more motivated by an interest in working with older people. On the contrary, care workers from other Western countries are significantly less likely to mention this reason (73.7 per cent, 'agree to a very high or high degree'), than

Table 13.1 Denmark: Motivational factors for seeking LTC work – migrant/non-migrant background (per cent)

	To a very high degree	To a high degree	To some degree	To a lesser degree	Not at all	Do not know	N	Level of significance
Interest in working with older people								
Western	41.5	32.2	15.3	5.9	4.2	0.8	118	**
Non-Western	43.6	41.3	13.1	1.0	0.3	0.8	383	
Danish	41.8	40.2	14.1	2.8	0.8	0.4	505	
Total, weighted	41.9	40.1	14.1	2.7	0.8	0.4	1,009.2	
Easy to find work								
Western	20.2	29.4	25.7	7.3	16.5	0.9	109	*
Non-Western	22.8	31.8	26.6	7.2	9.5	2.0	346	
Danish	15.3	27.9	26.5	13.9	14.6	1.8	452	
Total, weighted	16.0	28.2	26.5	13.2	14.3	1.8	904.6	
Care education (SOSU) is of short duration								
Western	9.7	8.7	25.2	17.5	32.0	6.8	103	**
Non-Western	10.3	20.5	26.3	14.8	18.1	10.0	331	
Danish	9.3	12.6	24.5	18.4	29.4	5.8	429	
Total, weighted	9.4	13.1	24.7	18.1	28.6	6.1	859.0	
Possibility to advance in management								
Western	3.8	7.5	11.3	13.2	55.7	8.5	106	**
Non-Western	1.2	6.1	11.6	17.3	46.8	17.0	329	
Danish	3.2	3.6	9.9	17.6	58.5	7.2	443	
Total, weighted	3.1	3.9	10.1	17.5	57.6	8.0	884.4	

	To a very high degree	To a high degree	To some degree	To a lesser degree	Not at all	Do not know	N	Level of significance
Possibility for further education within the field								
Western	15.0	15.9	29.9	14.0	23.4	1.9	107	
Non-Western	23.6	27.7	18.2	9.5	12.7	8.4	347	
Danish	14.2	19.6	26.9	15.6	19.6	4.2	450	
Total, weighted	14.9	20.1	26.3	15.1	19.2	4.5	900.8	
Wages								
Western	1.9	11.3	18.9	22.6	45.3	0.0	106	***
Non-Western	4.1	12.3	29.2	28.7	22.2	3.5	342	
Danish	2.2	5.7	17.0	24.1	49.9	1.1	453	
Total, weighted	2.3	6.3	18.0	24.4	47.7	1.3	905.0	
Status								
Western	3.8	9.4	17.0	16.0	50.9	2.8	106	***
Non-Western	4.3	14.2	27.5	20.7	21.6	11.7	324	
Danish	1.1	4.1	14.6	22.0	52.2	5.9	437	
Total, weighted	1.4	5.0	15.6	21.8	49.9	6.3	872.6	
Referred by job centre								
Western	1.9	1.0	3.8	3.8	85.7	3.8	105	***
Non-Western	2.1	4.0	7.0	3.7	75.8	7.3	327	
Danish	0.7	0.9	2.5	2.3	91.1	2.5	437	
Total, weighted	0.8	1.1	2.9	2.4	89.8	2.9	873.0	

care workers with a Danish background (82 per cent) or a non-Western migrant background (84.9 per cent).

Conversely, care workers with a Western background are more likely to point out the opportunity to advance to a management position as a motivational factor (11.3 per cent 'agree to a very high or high degree', compared to non-Western migrants 8.3 per cent and Danish background 6.8 per cent). More importantly overall, and in particular for migrant care workers with a non-Western background, the SOSU education is considered a stepping stone towards further education (30.9 per cent Western, 51.3 per cent non-Western, 33.8 per cent Danish background), presumably due to the possible integration of the SOSU and nursing degrees. And, as mentioned earlier, the fact that the SOSU education is relatively short, compared to other Danish educational pathways, is particularly attractive to care workers with a non-Western background (30.8 per cent 'agree to a very high/high degree', compared to 18.4 per cent among Western and 21.9 per cent among Danish care workers) (Table 13.1).

Other traditional motivational factors, including wages and status, are overall less important for the respondents in the survey, but with significant differences across the ethnic divide. Migrant care workers are generally more likely to mention wages as a motivational factor, especially non-Western migrants (13.2 per cent Western, 16.5 per cent non-Western, 7.9 per cent Danish background). Likewise, status plays a greater motivational role for migrant carers – and again for non-Western migrants in particular (13.2 per cent Western, 18.5 per cent non-Western, 5.2 per cent Danish background) (Table 13.1). One of the respondents explains how status is an important reason for seeking training and work in this sector, particularly for care workers of non-Western origins, which she associates with a newfound sense of independence and expression of agency among this group of relatively young women:

> There has been some kind of change. It's as though these women are more in charge of their own lives and say: 'This is what I want!' At least we have one who says that all the time. Great girl. It doesn't bother her; all she wants is to finish this education. And then her hubby can shout and yell as he pleases, and take care of the home and children in the meantime.
>
> (Karin, nursing home manager, Danish origin)

Another particular motivation for seeking work in the care sector is the direct referral from the local job centre as part of the national and local recruitment strategy. Few respondents in the survey actually mention this as being their reason for working with LTC, but with differences related to ethnical background nevertheless. The migrant workers with a non-Western background are those who are most likely to refer to this as a motivational factor (2.9 per cent Western, 6.1 per cent non-Western, 1.6 per cent Danish background) (Table 13.1).

This also becomes evident with the focus group interviews, where many care workers with a migrant background explain how their initial interest was evoked by the job centre. Husna, who initially took work as a cleaner at a nursing home on advice from the job centre, gradually became interested in training in the social and health care field:

> Then I went over there [to the job centre] and found work as a cleaner ... then I could see what they were doing, or how they are ... I saw every day how they work with older people and I was cleaning! They're having a nice time with the older people ... so I thought 'what am I doing?', and then, well then I need to get education as well ... I need to try it! And then I called the school.
>
> (Husna, care worker, non-Western origin)

While the interest in working with older people is thus generally acknowledged but by no means more predominant among care workers with a migrant background, other motives may prevail. The LTC sector appears to offer better opportunities for advancement than some other sectors, but again depending on migrant origin, appealing more to migrant carer workers with Western origins. Conversely, migrant care workers with non-Western backgrounds are especially motivated by the possibility of using the SOSU education as a stepping-stone to further education, and they are also more likely to refer to the wages and status as motivational factors.

Care cultures and quality of care

Another important assumption behind the recruitment strategy is that the increased recruitment of migrant care workers to the LTC sector will improve the care quality. This final section will therefore focus on the issue of care culture and its association with care quality. Care culture refers to the norms, values and traditions as well as the assumptions about 'natural' or given competences. Assumptions about ethnicity and care often include certain hierarchies and discourses, which dictate how we evaluate an individual's competences and working skills. As noted by Williams and Gavanas (2008), for example, care workers with a Muslim background were considered the lowest in the hierarchy in Spain on the grounds that it was assumed that they had a poor work ethic due to their upbringing and religion. Similarly, care migrants from South America were thought of as kind but slow.

In this study, we find that the general assumption as expressed in official documents is also that migrant origins ensure certain working skills and competences. First, there is the general expectation that migrant care workers will be more likely to accommodate the need for culture-sensitive and culture-specific care. There is reason to believe that there will be increasing numbers of older persons with migrant backgrounds in the near future who will require care, also due to shifts in the norms regarding family obligations, which put pressure on the provision of public care (e.g. Styrelsen for Social Service [The National Board of Social Services], n.d.). The mere fact that one might be speaking another language or have non-Danish origins is often considered a quality in itself, as one is assumed to possess greater cross-cultural communication skills. As stated in a report from Copenhagen municipality, Copenhagen being one of the areas currently experiencing a real increase in the number of older persons with an ethnic minority background: 'Bilingual care workers are popular among older migrants with poor language skills, also due to the intercultural competences which the bilingual care workers possess' (Abelskov, 2007, p. 10, author's translation). Thus, migrant care workers may be expected to act as interpreters, regardless of whether their linguistic and cultural background matches the background of the older person in question requiring assistance.

This indicates that these care workers in particular – and to a higher degree than those with Danish origins – are assumed able to offer cross-cultural care; that is, that care provision is adapted to be universal as well as culture-specific needs; in other words, care provision which is meaningful and in accordance with different culturally based ways of living and beliefs (Leininger, 1999). Second, there is also the specific assumption that migrant care workers will bring certain values with them, including greater respect for older persons. This is reflected in recruiting materials from the Ministry of Integration:

> We need your skills. As a youngster with an immigrant background, you have specific values, which you have acquired from your upbringing and traditions for strong family ties. You are also raised in a care culture with emphasis on respect for older people. With these distinctive values, you can help to improve the quality of care and level of professionalism in the LTC sector.
>
> (Ministry of Integration, n.d., author's translation)

The same argument is often heard in the interviews, as expressed by Lone, a nursing home manager of Danish origin: 'I fundamentally believe that those girls who are with us, and who are not Danish – they tend to show a little more respect for older people'. The issue of showing respect was also covered in the survey and was a care skill and quality item generally supported among the care workers, but with an ethnic distinction (Table 13.2). Overall, 86.1 per cent said displaying respect for the older person was an important skill to 'a very high degree', but only 72.4 per cent among the non-Western care workers (compared to 90.5 per cent of those with Western and 87.1 per cent with Danish backgrounds). Likewise, when asked whether they themselves possess the skill to show respect, care workers with non-Western backgrounds again stand out by stating that they possess such skills to a lesser degree (to 'a very high degree': 82.1 per cent Western, 70.1 per cent non-Western, 73.0 per cent Danish background). It is not possible to determine whether or not this reflects that this skill is in fact valued less or if it reflects a concern over the inability to show respect due to organisational and resource factors. The assumption that migrant care workers value respect higher is not recognised, however, particularly among those with a non-Western background, nor is it highlighted as a core competence.

Table 13.2 Denmark: Showing respect as a quality item and personal competence (per cent)

	To a very high degree	To a high degree	To some degree or less	Do not know	N	Level of significance
I value this quality item						
Western	90.5	8.6	0.9	0.0	116	***
Non-Western	72.4	24.7	2.9	0.0	380	
Danish	87.1	12.1	0.4	0.4	504	
Total, weighted	86.1	13.0	0.6	0.4	1,006.4	
I myself possess this quality competence						
Western	82.1	17.1	0.9	0.0	117	*
Non-Western	70.1	25.6	4.0	0.3	371	
Danish	73.0	25.6	1.0	0.4	503	
Total, weighted	73.0	25.4	1.2	0.4	1,003	

Nevertheless, the construction of a care culture and related competences often refer specifically to the issue of respect. As the following quotes illustrate, however, it is not a general assumption, but rather only related to the group of non-Western migrant care workers due to their cultural background. As a nursing home manager explains, this group of care workers can become frustrated when family members are not there for an older person's needs, which they interpret as a lack of respect:

> We have had some residents who might not have had the best relationship with their children. They [migrant care workers] could not grasp this at all. Well, it was so foreign to their culture … you simply couldn't. You might say that this reflects their 'caring-gene' [*omsorgsgen*], right? Because they're used to looking after their older family members. So they find it disrespectful that others don't do the same, right?
>
> (Katrine, nursing home manager, Danish origins)

This assumption about the special 'caring gene' is reflected in several of the interviews with care workers and managers with Danish origins. As a care worker with such a background explains:

> If I work with a Turk, they have an entirely different approach than I do. Well, not that they provide better care but they do it in a different way. They appreciate providing care in a whole different way than I would. So maybe they just have some kind of mentality which makes them want to help other people.
>
> (Karina, care worker, Danish origins)

Or like another nursing home manager comments:

> They display incredible care for older people, because it is part of their upbringing to care for older people in a whole different way than we have ever learned. So for many of them, it is not just an education. It comes to them naturally.
>
> (Else, nursing home manager, Danish origins)

The underlying understanding in these quotes is that a specific work skill or competence is being identified, something that is valued in the organisation and among colleagues. The assumption nevertheless creates a notion of 'us' and 'them', generating a culturally conditioned distance between care workers of various ethnic origins (Torres, 2010). It is also an assumption which contributes to de-professionalising the understanding of care competences, which a skilled care worker should possess and which contributes to a divide according to migrant background. The care workers with non-Western migrant backgrounds thus qualify themselves via their 'natural' ability to care, whereas care workers with Danish origins together with care workers hailing from other Western countries are expected to become qualified through training and practice.

Finally, there is the assumption that employing more care workers with migrant backgrounds will stimulate greater diversity in the production of care, going beyond culture-sensitive and culture-specific care, thus adding a universal dimension to care production. This is in accordance with what Abelskov writes: 'Apart from being a necessity in order to accommodate this large group of older people, diversity in the LTC sector is also a way to add both a cultural and a human value' (Abelskov, 2007, p. 18, literature study produced for Copenhagen municipality, author's translation). Employing migrant care workers in the LTC sector is therefore believed to add an extra dimension to the benefit of the organisation as such and all older people, regardless of their ethnic origin.

Both the care workers and managers with Danish origins reflect on the quality of care and how the recent reform of LTC care has transformed Danish care culture, transgressing from the valued 'warm hands' towards a more cold, instrumental and New Public Management (NPM) dominated care regime (Rostgaard, 2012). This NPM inspired regime is in sharp contrast to what is often conceived to be 'traditional' caring skills, or what Waerness has termed 'rationality of caring': the combination of situational and shared knowledge, experience and skill, with the willingness and ability to place oneself in the position of another (Anttonen and Zechner, 2011; Waerness, 1984). Their encounter with care workers with migrant origins provides an opportunity to praise the rationality of caring and to express their hopes that the entry of migrant care workers may help redeem this somewhat:

> They haven't forgotten the care dimension which us Danes tend to have forgotten somewhat. They manage the 'warm' stuff ... I wouldn't say some of our own ... but I sometimes experience they forget about caring, and we see this less often with the ethnic girls.
>
> (Karin, nursing home manager, Danish origin)

Again, migrant care workers are positively singled out for performing according to a care culture, which may be difficult to practice in a rationalised and resource-focused care system but which nevertheless is highly praised. This perspective constructs a general assumption of quality in care which is seen as a relation and social interaction between two or more persons; or that which in Tronto's (1993) work is termed 'care ethics', involving not only caring *for*, but also caring *about*. In this manner, caring is considered to be more than instrumental work; it is also the (often time-consuming) relation work and creating relations, i.e. creating a trustful relation with the cared-for and working with the emotional aspects also. This identification of difference, however, also raises questions regarding the right approach to caring. Is it a (sufficient) qualification to be caring? And is it possible to be too caring to perform a job professionally within a resource-restrained care system? Some care workers with Danish origins point out that this approach is time-consuming and sets excessive standards and expectations: 'They're very caring and motherly and cuddly. Although it may take a lot of time' (Rikke, care worker, Danish origin); 'Yeah, it gets to be too much sometimes, right. Because you need to take care not to spoil the older person too much – 'cause then they expect this from all of us' (Birte, care worker, Danish origin). Here, that which is identified as a special approach to caring whilst acknowledged as a core value is also presented as somewhat problematic in that it goes against the rationalised, resource-focused care system.

Conclusion

The Danish strategies to recruit migrants into LTC go beyond the direct purpose of overcoming the shortage of 'warm hands'. They are also intended to strengthen quality of care by ensuring that care workers and care production reflect the increasingly multi-cultural societal context. Overall, this recruitment strategy has proven successful in that the share of students with migrant backgrounds entering SOSU education programmes has increased dramatically. Consequently, more care work in Denmark will most likely be provided in the future by care workers with migrant backgrounds. A number of the assumptions behind the recruitment strategy are, however, questionable, one being that migrant care workers are particularly motivated by their specific and culturally based caring and work abilities. Although the interest in working with older people constitutes a general and main motivational factor for all care workers in the study, regardless of their ethnic origins, it is not a motive singled out by care workers with migrant backgrounds. On the contrary, migrant care workers with a Western background are less likely to indicate this as a motive. This most likely reflects how the entry of migrants into the care education and work sector is largely determined by the job opportunities found in this sector more than anything else. It is possible to find work in this sector, and it provides opportunities for career advancement for some while providing a stepping-stone for others towards more attractive educational qualifications. For the non-Western migrants in particular, employment in the LTC sector provides some measure of status, and the wages are appreciated. Again, it may to some degree be the actual situation of being in work and being paid that is attractive to this particular group of women and part of their search for independence.

Another assumption is that, via what is assumed to be a specific care culture, migrant care workers may contribute to the development of the quality of care by providing more culture-sensitive and culture-specific care. There is even the expectation that the employment of migrant care workers will contribute to the creation of greater overall diversity in care; and by this, reaching beyond the culture-specific and adding something universal to the care sector; and more specifically, that their supposedly greater respect for older people is an asset to the sector. There is thus the notion that migrant care workers due to their specific care culture will be able to add new and important values to the sector, and that their work performance is based on fundamentally different values than is the work carried out by care workers with Danish origins. This means that the recruitment of migrant care workers is presented as a positive contribution to the sector, not least in the midst of the concerns over the standardisation and rationalisation the sector has undergone.

The entry of migrant care workers and their particular care ethic is presented perhaps somewhat romantically as an opportunity to return to a more traditional care ethic. More critical perspectives are also present, however, in that it is questioned whether that which seems to be a more caring approach is compatible with the available time and resources.

The identified contrast between Danish and migrant cultures of care is, however, also contributing to the 'us-them' distinction, in particular singling out the care workers with non-Western backgrounds. It furthermore contributes to the understanding that care competences in the group of migrants are 'natural' competences that do not require training in the field to learn. In this way, care competences are generalised across individual approaches and given an ethnic dimension; consequently, they tend to lose their professional meaning. This again relates in particular to non-Western migrants. Not only does this assumption devalue migrants' skills (as being non-professional), it paradoxically also looks to their skills as a central component in the development of a better LTC system.

Notes

1 The chapter is based on the findings in Rostgaard *et al.*, 2011.
2 Western countries: all 25 EU countries, plus Andorra, Iceland, Liechtenstein, Monaco, Norway, San Marino, Switzerland, the Vatican State, Canada, USA, Australia and New Zealand. Non-Western countries: the remaining countries.

References

Abelskov, C. (2007). *Litteratur- og erfaringsstudie: ældreplejen og ældre med etnisk minoritetsbaggrund* [Literature and Experience Study: Eldercare and Elderly with Ethnic Minority Background]. København: Sundheds- og Omsorgsforvaltningen Københavns Kommune.

Anttonen, A. and Sipilä, J. (1996). European social care services: is it possible to identify models? *Journal of European Social Policy, 6*, 87–100. doi:10.1177/095892879600600201.

Anttonen, A. and Zechner, M. (2011). Theorising care and care work. In Pfau-Effinger, B. and Rostgaard, T. (eds) *Care, Work and Welfare in Europe* (pp. 15–34). Houndmills: Palgrave Macmillan.

Beskæftigelsesministeriet (2007). *Bekendtgørelse af lov om en aktiv beskæftigelsesindsats* [Act on Active Employment]. København: Beskæftigelsesministeriet.

Colombo, F., Llena-Nozal, A., Mercier, J. and Tjadens, F. (2011). *Help Wanted? Providing and Paying for Long-Term Care*. Paris: OECD. Retrieved from www.oecd.org/health/longtermcare/helpwanted.

Di Rosa, M., Melchiorre, M. G., Lucchetti, M. and Lamura, G. (2012). The impact of migrant work in the elder care sector: recent trends and empirical evidence in Italy. *European Journal of Social Work, 15*, 9–27. doi:10.1080/13691457.2011.562034.

FOA (Fag og Arbejde) (2008). *Førtidspension blandt FOAs medlemmer* [Early Retirement among FOA Members]. København: FOA.

Lill, L. (2007). *Att göra etnicitet: inom äldreomsorgen*. Avhandling [Doing Ethnicity: In Eldercare]. Malmø: Malmö Högskola.

Leininger, M. M. (1999). What is transcultural nursing and culturally competent care? *Journal of Transcultural Nursing, 10(9).* doi:10.1177/104365969901000105.

Leon, M., Ranzi, C. and Rostgaard, T. (2014). Pressures towards and within universalism: conceptualising change in care policy and discourse. In M. Leon (ed.), *Care Regimes in Transitional European Societies* (pp. 11–33). Houndmills: Palgrave Macmillan.

Ministry of Education (2003). *Rapport fra den tværministerielle arbejdsgruppe* [Report of the Inter-Ministerial Task Group]. København: Undervisningsministeriet.

Ministry of Integration (n.d.) *Brug for alle unge.* Retrieved from http://brugforalleunge.dk/sosu.

Pio, E. and Essers, C. (2014). Professional migrant women decentering Otherness: a transnational perspective. *British Journal of Management.* In press. doi:10.1111/1467-8551.12003.

Prasad, A. and Prasad, P. (2002). Otherness at large: identity and difference in the new globalized organizational landscape. In I. Aaltio and A. J. Mills (eds), *Gender, Identity and the Culture of Organizations* (pp. 57–71). London: Routledge.

Rostgaard, T. (2012). Quality reforms in Danish home care: balancing between standardisation and individualisation. *Health and Social Care in the Community, 20,* 247–254. doi:10.1111/j.1365–2524.2012.01066.x.

Rostgaard, T., Bjerre, L., Sørensen, K. and Rasmussen, N. (2011). *Omsorg og etnicitet: Nye veje til rekruttering og kvalitet i ældreplejen* [Care and Ethnicity: New Ways of Recruitment and Quality in Elderly Care] (SFI Report No. 11:16). København: SFI.

Said, E. W. (1978). *Orientalism: Western Conceptions of the Orient.* London: Routledge & Kegan Paul.

Statistics Denmark (2013). *Indvandrere i Danmark 2013* [Immigrants in Denmark 2013]. København: Danmarks Statistik.

Styrelsen for Social Service [The National Board of Social Services] (n.d.). *Ældre etniske borgeres syn på alderdommen og den danske ældrepleje* [Older Ethnic Citizens' Views on Old Age and Danish Elderly Care]. Retrieved from www.servicestyrelsen.dk/filer/aeldre/etniske-mindretal/1909.pdf.

Teknologisk Institut (2004). *Mangfoldige sundhedsuddannelser* [Diverse Health-Educations]. København: Teknologisk Institut.

Torres, S. (2010). Etnicitet och invandrarskap: relevanta begreppsliga och teoretiska perspektiv för äldrevård och omsorgsforskning [Ethnicity and immigrant status: relevant conceptual and theoretical perspectives for eldercare and care-research]. In S. Torres and F. Magnússon (eds), *Invandrarskap, äldrevård och omsorg* [Migrantship and Eldercare] (pp. 222–243). Malmö: Gleerups.

Tronto, J. C. (1993). *Moral Boundaries: A Political Argument for an Ethic of Care.* New York: Routledge.

Wærness, K. (1984). The rationality of caring. *Economic and Industrial Democracy, 5,* 185–211.

Westwood, R. (2001). Appropriating the 'other' in the discourses of comparative management. In R. Westwood and S. Linstead (eds), *The Language of Organization* (pp. 241–282). London: SAGE.

Williams, F. and Gavanas, A. (2008). The intersection of child-care regimes and migration regimes: a three-country study. In H. Lutz (ed.), *Migration and Domestic Work: A European Perspective on a Global Theme* (pp. 13–27). Aldershot: Ashgate.

14 The perceived differences in the recognition of migrant care workers' credentials in Germany

Johanna Krawietz and Stefanie Visel

Introduction

In view of the growing female employment rate, ageing societies, and the decline in the benefits offered by the welfare state, European countries are attempting to make up for deficits in care (Dussault *et al.*, 2009; Gerlinger and Schmucker, 2007) by employing migrants in geriatric care and nursing. International research into care focused for a long time on migrants working in private households, investigating the living and working conditions of migrants responsible for child care, elderly care, and housework. However, the transnationalisation of elderly care (Torres, 2013) is not limited to private households. A growing proportion of workers in nursing homes and the health services possess credentials acquired abroad (Connell, 2008; Kofman and Raghuram, 2006; Yeates, 2009). Recently, Germany too has made efforts to recruit non-EU migrants to work in care and nursing, by means of bilateral agreements. At the same time, some sending countries are offering special preparation courses for migrant care workers. With this in mind, Kofman and Raghuram (2006) warn that the research focus on informality makes it easy to overlook other forms of work and the presence of qualified migrants on the labour market. They criticise the fact that research into care migration is confined to the unqualified sector of private households, and call for the recognition of the qualified care work carried out in the institutional sector. In doing so they point out that migrants are not only employed as domestic workers in elderly people's private households but provide care at state-run or private institutions as well. Yeates (2009), too, calls for transnational care migration and concepts such as global care chains to be used and taken into account in the case of qualified migrants, with the analysis of global care chains extended to include 'skilled migrant care workers' (Gabriel, 2011, p. 42) and other forms of care work such as 'health, educational, sexual and religious' (ibid.) care. Here, state regulations play a major role, not only for recruitment but also for certification and admission to care labour markets. However, it is known from research into nurse migration and from studies of various professions that migration often involves 'brain waste' (Vouyioukas and Liapi, 2013; or for Germany: Englmann and Müller, 2007). This means that qualifications are not always recognised, and migrants work at a level below their actual qualifications.

In this chapter, we concentrate on qualified migrants working for care institutions, hospitals, nursing homes, and care service providers in Germany, focusing on the macro and meso levels of nurse migration in Germany. This chapter refers to migrants who have completed their nursing training abroad. The term 'nurses' is used here to cover the regulated German professions 'Altenpfleger' (geriatric nurse) and 'Gesundheits- und Krankenpfleger' (registered general nurse). The 'geriatric nurse' career profile does not exist in most countries, and most migrants arrive with general nursing training. Often, however, the foreign-educated general nurses are specifically recruited to work as geriatric nurses in Germany.[1] The aim of this chapter is to analyse how foreign nursing credentials are recognised by German institutions. In the first sections, we present the role played by the state in the transnationalisation of nurse migration. Immigration rules and recognition procedures for nurses are a decisive factor in whether internationally qualified migrants can work in the care sector. In the next two sections, we concentrate on empirical case examples, featuring the professional care suppliers and educational institutions, illustrating how the recognition of migrant care workers' credentials takes place. From our data we develop the hypothesis that the recognition of qualifications is delayed or prevented by the construction of nursing differences. These lead to migrants being undervalued and deskilled.

Immigration regulations

In contrast to other countries, for a long time there was no active recruitment policy for nurses in Germany.[2] Only recently bilateral agreements have been signed with certain selected countries to recruit skilled workers in the field of nursing and care. In Germany until 2013, non-EU nurses could only be placed in jobs through the Federal Employment Agency (Bundesministerium für Wirtschaft und Technologie, BMWi 2012). Nurses from Serbia, Bosnia and Herzegovina, and the Philippines were first recruited in 2012. According to the federal government, 398 nurses have been recruited so far (Deutscher Bundestag, 2013). Since 2012, the Federal Employment Agency has also been concentrating increasingly within the EURES (European Employment Services) network on finding jobs for skilled workers from southern European countries particularly badly affected by the financial crisis (Portugal, Spain, Greece, and Italy) (Deutscher Bundestag, 2013).[3] Only very recently changes in immigration policy have taken place, described here in brief.

One of the fundamental freedoms guaranteed to EU nationals within the European Union is full freedom of movement for workers. Since May 2011, workers from Central and Eastern European countries[4] (CECs) have enjoyed full freedom of movement in Germany, and since 1 January 2014 this has also applied to Bulgaria and Romania. There has, however, been no great rush; instead, nurses have tended to move to other countries in the European Union, such as Scandinavia and the UK (Merda, 2012). Experts believe that this is related to the bureaucratic recognition process, the late opening of the German labour market, and the low earnings opportunities compared with other EU countries (Gerlinger and Schmucker, 2007; Merda, 2012). Before the full freedom of movement for workers, citizens from the new member states were allowed to set up their own businesses under the EU Services Directive, and there were exceptions for seasonal workers (Gerlinger and Schmucker, 2007).

Residence and working permits for nurses (and workers in general) from outside Europe are strictly regulated. In 2013, a number of policies were introduced to make it easier for non-EU citizens with non-academic vocational credentials to work in Germany. Permits for nurses from outside Europe are regulated in the Ordinance on the Admission of Foreigners for the Purpose of Taking up Employment (BeschV). According to Section 30 of BeschV, with the approval of the employment services, nurses can be given a residence permit allowing them to take up employment (Janda, 2013), if there is a shortage of skilled workers in their profession (which is the case for nurses and geriatric nurses at the moment), they have a binding job offer, and their qualifications have been recognised as equivalent to German qualifications. Another way of employing non-EU nurses is an agreement between the Federal Employment Agency and the employment agency of the country of origin. This also requires an assessment by the authorities that the qualifications gained abroad are equivalent to the corresponding German qualifications. Agreements of this type are currently held with Serbia, Bosnia and Herzegovina, Tunisia, and the Philippines.

The EU Blue Card regulates the residence and working status of highly qualified non-EU workers in EU countries. It came into force on 1 August 2012 in Germany. Nurses are not explicitly mentioned in the German implementing act, but the EU Blue Card does offer an opportunity for training non-EU workers. This indirectly opens up a route to recruitment (BAMF, 2013).

Recognition procedure

Migrant nurses' access to the German labour market depends not only on immigration regulations but also on the official recognition of qualifications gained abroad. Nursing and health services are known as 'regulated professions', requiring official permission to use the titles 'geriatric nurse' or 'registered general nurse' and thus carry out skilled work in that field. In contrast to many other countries, nurses in Germany are usually trained for three years within the vocational system, with theoretical and practical elements. The content and length of courses are set out in codes of practice. While general nursing courses with a chance to specialise are common international practice, specialised training as a geriatric nurse is specific to Germany (BMWi, 2012). However, a general nursing course can also lead to a job in care for the elderly.[5] The processes we examine below are those regulating admission as a registered general nurse.[6]

One significant indication that Germany now intends to open its arms to qualified migrants is the new law to improve the assessment and recognition of professional and vocational education and training qualifications acquired abroad (Federal Recognition Act), which came into force on 1 April 2012. Knuth (2012) points out that the lawmakers' main intention was to deal with the lack of skilled workers. Thus, the purpose of the law, as described in Section 1, 'serves to improve the use of professional qualifications acquired abroad so that holders of such qualifications can find work commensurate with those qualifications on the German labour market' (Federal Recognition Act, official translation).[7] The Federal Recognition Act is the first law granting persons with non-EU domiciles the right to have their qualifications reviewed. The old, abstruse bureaucratic system meant that processes of deskilling often took place because qualifications were not recognised, as shown by various studies targeting different occupational groups (Bauder, 2005; Englmann and Müller, 2007). It is the first time that the right to review one's qualification has been unrelated to nationality. To have their qualifications recognised, applicants need to have their papers translated and state-certified, and submit them to the authorities in question.[8] For nursing this means a curriculum vitae, training documents, confirmation of occupational experience, a medical certificate, and confirmation of aptitude. The authorities check the number of hours and subjects involved to see whether there are any significant differences from the German code of practice. If the authorities do not find any significant differences, permission can be granted to use the occupational title. If there are significant differences, migrants may provide proof that compensatory measures have been taken (in the form of an exam or a course attended for up to three years). The costs involved in taking these steps[9] may be paid by the job centre, though on a discretionary basis. At the end of the course there is an examination, which, if passed, means the worker can use the occupational title.

For EU citizens, credentials are recognised on the basis of EU Directive 2005/36/EC. This stipulates that the occupational credentials of general care nurses must automatically be recognised. The member countries are, however, given the chance to stipulate the minimum level of qualifications required, to maintain the quality of work carried out within their territory (see Art. 14, Directive 2005/36/EC). Moreover, recognition is only automatic if the certificate was acquired after the country in question joined the EU. For the eight new EU countries in Central and Eastern Europe, along with Bulgaria, Romania, and Croatia, this regulation has a particularly negative effect.

Data and methods

The findings in this chapter are based on 18 qualitative interviews with professional care suppliers, the competent authorities as well as employment centres, educational institutions, and migrant information centres. The examples used in this chapter come from interviews with people running 'compensatory measures' to train migrants, and with nursing managers at institutions providing in- and outpatient care. They are part of the research project 'Border Crossing Work in a Service Mix – Developments and Challenges of Professional Elderly Care', financed by the Ministry for Science and Culture of Lower-Saxony and based at the University of Hildesheim. The empirical data were analysed using the methodology of Grounded Theory (Strauss, 1998), using the data to generate theoretical concepts of the phenomenon.

The construction of nursing differences during the recognition process

In an ongoing study (Krawietz and Visel, 2014) it was shown that for a large number of applicants the qualifications were not recognised as equivalent and the applicants had to take part in adaption courses. In the field of nursing recognition, the reasons interviewees give for qualifications not being recognised is that migrants have different nursing skills from those required in Germany. Below, interview extracts are used to show how the participants construct and explain these differences in nursing, and the consequences involved for migrants.

Status and professional differentiation

A different professional self-image and understanding of the job are cited by the interviewees as reasons why qualifications are not being recognised. This is reflected in the different tasks that nursing involves. Migrants are said to have a more medical and technical understanding of nursing. They are said to be responsible for a greater proportion of 'medical treatment'. In contrast, 'basic care' and nursing procedures are taken on by assistants. The construction of different nursing skills is also linked to a different professional status. Nurses with training abroad are said to have greater responsibility in their jobs and delegate tasks to different occupational groups. The following interview extract points out the medical skills of nurses trained abroad and the higher professional status this involves:

> In many countries nursing does not play the same role; instead, their understanding of the job means assisting doctors rather than looking after patients at the bedside and coming into direct contact with them. That is done by assistants and family members; in any case it is not necessarily part of how they see their job at all.
>
> (Training provider)

The following quote shows that difference is determined by a more medical and managerial understanding of their job:

> Nurses in Poland and Russia don't care for patients like we do every morning, making up beds, providing basic care and nursing, etc.; they have more of a managerial function, sending off other assistants and saying 'Now you go and make up the beds and take care of the patients; and provide basic care and nursing duties'. They are more in charge of administration, management and medical treatments: bandages, checking vital signs, injections, etc.
>
> (Care service manager)

According to the interviewee's description, nurses have more authority in their countries of origin, i.e. more room to carry out certain treatments. The activities the care service manager describes as basic care and nursing procedures are taken on by different groups of assistants in the workers' native countries. In those countries, the work that falls under nursing in Germany is carried out by untrained workers or informally, by family members: groups which from a professional point of view occupy a lower position in the hierarchy than professional nurses.

At the same time, the migrants seeking recognition are said to have deficits in basic nursing and care skills. These relate to activities involving close physical contact such as washing, making up beds, and serving food. They are said not to be able to carry out these activities, as they have not learned them in their native countries. These deficits are demonstrated by the following extract from an interview with a training provider in a recognition course:

> I have nurses who have never made up a bed in their lives; that are what we do in the first week here in the recognition course: patient contact, making up beds, care, and nursing; basic care and nursing procedures. How do I wash and dress people, how do I change incontinence aids? [...] Recognition is quite different, so their continuing education or training is of a totally different kind, which is why they can't make up a bed. That isn't meant to be nasty: it's just not part of their training modules at all.
>
> (Training provider)

Migrants are said not to be capable of the basic care and nursing skills linked to lower-status care work. The activities mentioned involved physically intimate care and direct interaction with patients. Migrants with foreign qualifications are said not to possess these skills. This line between care and medicine forms a hierarchy of the activities carried out by nurses in Germany and other countries. In this comparison, the self-image of German nurses is set apart as unique, based on the high proportion of basic care and nursing practice. Migrants with foreign qualifications are said not to possess these skills. Under the German code of practice, certain tasks which migrants are allowed to carry out in their countries of origin fall under the doctors' monopoly. On the other hand, some jobs, which they need to be able to do in Germany, are carried out by assistants or family members in the countries of origin.

Deskilling

The ascribed nursing differences and the higher status in the occupational hierarchy are not without consequences for migrants. The differences are linked to a deskilling of their qualifications. The differences named are used to show that foreign trained nurses cannot simply start working in Germany. Instead they have to start out by learning basic care and nursing skills during training and practical work when they apply for recognition of their qualifications. They have to be prepared for their work and need therefore to attend specially designed courses (compensatory measures or adaption courses). Thus, the differences act as a rationale to justify why, despite their high-level of training and work experience in their native countries, applicants have to re-learn nursing in Germany. A typical example, which points to experiences of deskilling and is often brought up in the context of the recognition of nursing occupations, is the *feldsher. Feldsher* is the term for a health care professional in the post-Soviet states. Their training falls somewhere between nurses and physicians, and they are widespread in rural areas. The difficulties which people in the field of nursing recognition have in categorising the profession *feldsher* are a clear demonstration of deskilling. This training provider reports on the process through which the *feldshers* are deskilled:

> Well, we sometimes have to deal with *feldshers* here; they have different training in Russia; they're the Russians that come from former Soviet Republic states. It wasn't recognised for a long time here in Germany; they weren't recognised, until they found out that the *feldshers* sometimes had a higher level of training than nurses; it's an additional course above that. Something like a paramedic; in Russia you're trained in nursing then you have one or one and a half years more as a kind of paramedic. Some of them are nurses who travel from door to door doing actual medical diagnosis; they can prescribe medicine, they can take blood samples, all that. They've even done births themselves, though they aren't midwives, not trained ones. So they're well above the level of nurses, and at first they weren't recognised here [...]. At first it was really difficult, they weren't recognised, ended up somewhere in a home as an assistant.
>
> (Training provider)

The deskilling of *feldshers* can be seen clearly from the contrast between the different occupational fields. In their countries of origin, with their nursing training they were able to carry out tasks corresponding to those of a doctor, whereas in Germany they remained in care for the elderly, with its lower status and lower pay. The fact that the migrants act as 'assistants' shows that they are not able to work within the limits of their qualifications in Germany, where their qualifications can only be downgraded to the field of nursing assistants,[10] a precarious area with lower qualifications. Another nursing manager also describes in a statement the devaluation nursing differences imply:

> Well, they are stuck at this status of being care assistants and in fact it's the same as taking the first housewife I come across on the street, sending her on a five-day course, a limited range of basic treatment procedures, administering medicine, putting on tights. And she does the same jobs here as people who've studied for five years there, worked ten years in a hospital, for example, here not.
>
> (Care service manager)

The skills which applicants have upon arrival cannot be valued at the original level of their qualifications. Instead, putting migrants in the category of nursing assistants deskills their occupational qualifications. The interviewee stresses that without their qualifications being recognised, migrants might be able to work 'here' as nursing assistants, though they have training and work experience which allow them to work in a higher position in their native countries. The interviewee illustrates the experience of deskilling by comparing the group of migrants who arrive with training and experience from their countries of origin ('there') with housewives, a group of people who only attend a short course. Both groups are to take on the same tasks as nursing assistants. It shows that less value is placed on the migrant group, with no formal qualifications. When migrants apply to have their qualifications recognised, they are essentially devalued, despite the professionalism linked to their training in medicine and at university. At the same time, basic care and nursing skills are also devalued in the example assuming that they can be acquired within five weeks, in a short course. This short period of time is in turn contrasted with the one-year catch-up qualification for migrants.

Consequently, another care service manager reports: 'Because they [the migrants, J.K./S.V.] are expected to forget everything they were once allowed to do; everything they are able to do' (Nursing manager). From her point of view, the competencies that the migrants have learned in their native countries and carried out as part of their work and their old fields of responsibility are of no or less value in Germany. For this reason, applicants are advised to forget them as soon as possible. This suggested strategy of forgetting implies that the nursing skills learned by migrants in their native countries are of no use in Germany or might even constitute a disadvantage.

Conclusion

This chapter focused on the transnationalisation of care work in nursing occupations requiring a state permit. Based on the observation that research into care and migration has long been limited to informal care work in private households, this chapter analysed qualified migrants' access to nursing occupations and the recognition of their credentials, based on the example of Germany. To this end a description was provided of the current political and legal situation as regards access to nursing and the recognition of credentials.

The recognition of credentials in nursing acquired abroad was investigated by studying the way in which the interviewees justified the practice of recognition. It was established that various differences were used to explain why recognition was refused or delayed. The justifications offered are connected to different skills and a different professional status. It emerged that the interviewees' justifications are related to categorisation problems: making the skills which migrants have on arrival fit into the context of German nursing. When credentials are not recognised, this leads to migrants being devalued and deskilled.

Moreover, the specific justifications given in the field of nursing were differences in basic care and medical treatments. These differences can be explained as distinguishing nursing from other medical professions (Bollinger, 2012). They are a disadvantage for the highly qualified migrant nurses. The constructed differences in nursing claim foreign trained nurses lack precisely the communicative and physical work skills. The medical and technical leaning of migrant training, meanwhile, is used as a reason to devalue them on the labour market in their field and 'only' employ them as nursing assistants.

Ambivalences are also revealed when the results are seen in the light of the lack of skilled workers in the field of nursing, which has been the subject of public discussion in Germany, and new recruitment programmes launched by the German government based on bilateral agreements with several countries. This points out the discrepancy between public *talk* about how to tackle the lack of skilled workers and the paucity of *action* (Brunsson, 1989) taken to recognise migrants' devalued credentials.

Notes

1 If it is important to distinguish between the two fields, this is explicitly mentioned.
2 However, there was a special recruitment programme for Eastern European EU citizens who are known as 'home helps' to work in private households with those in need of care, run by the Federal Employment Agency.
3 The German government set up the special 'MobiPro-EU' programme to help young people from the European Union take up occupations suffering from labour shortages, including nursing, in Germany. See the website: www.thejobofmylife.de/de.
4 The CEC countries, which joined the European Union back in 2004 as part of EU expansion, include Estonia, Latvia, Lithuania, Poland, Slovakia, Slovenia, the Czech Republic, and Hungary.
5 Whereas the other direction, employing a state-recognised geriatric nurse as a general care nurse, is not possible.
6 There are plans to introduce general nursing training in Germany combining the three occupations 'general care nurse', 'paediatric nurse', and 'geriatric nurse' into one regulated profession (Bund-Länder-Arbeitsgruppe Weiterentwicklung der Pflegeberufe, 2012).
7 See Act concerning the Assessment of Equivalence of Professional Qualifications, Part 1, Section 1. Retrieved from www.anerkennung-in-deutschland.de/media/bqfg_englisch.pdf.
8 These authorities vary from one federal state to the next and from one profession to the next. There is currently no central office for testing or recognition. For occupations in nursing and the health services, the authorities concerned are responsible for issuing certificates to all graduates, e.g. the regional education authorities (Sommer, 2014).
9 Courses cost between 1,000 and 2,000 euros.
10 According to figures published in the WSI Collective Agreement Archive, geriatric care assistants and nursing assistants occupy the last two places on the list of all nursing occupations. See www.lohnspiegel.de/main/zusatzinformationen/pflegeberufe.

References

BAMF (Bundesamt für Migration und Flüchtlinge) (2013). *Studying and Working in Germany: A Brochure on the Legal Requirements of Residence for Third-Country Nationals*. Nürnberg: BAMF. Retrieved from www.bamf.de/SharedDocs/Anlagen/EN/Publikationen/Broschueren/bildung-und-beruf-in-deutschland.pdf?__blob=publicationFile#page=16.

Bauder, H. (2005). Institutional capital and labour devaluation: the non-recognition of foreign credentials in Germany. *European Journal of Economics and Economic Policies: Intervention, 2(1)*, 75–93. doi:10.4337/ejeep. 2005.01.09.

BMWi (Bundesministerium für Wirtschaft und Technologie) (2012). *Chancen zur Gewinnung von Fachkräften in der Pflegewirtschaft* [Opportunites for Recruiting Skilled Workers in the Care Sector]. Berlin: BMWi.

Bollinger, H. (2012). Profession – Dienst – Beruf: Der Wandel der Gesundheitsberufe aus berufssoziologischer Perspektive [Profession – service – job: the change in health professions from the perspective of the sociology of professions]. In H. Bollinger, A. Gerlach and M. Pfadenhauer (eds), *Gesundheitsberufe im Wandel: Soziologische Beobachtungen und Interpretationen* (3rd edn) (pp. 13–30). Frankfurt a. M.: Mabuse.

Brunsson, N. (1989). *The Organization of Hypocrisy: Talk, Decisions and Actions in Organization.* Chichester: Wiley.

Bund-Länder-Arbeitsgruppe Weiterentwicklung der Pflegeberufe (2012). *Eckpunkte zur Vorbereitung des Entwurfs eines neuen Pflegeberufegesetzes* [Cornerstones for Preparing a Draft for a New Law Regulating Care Occupations]. Retrieved from www. bmg.bund.de/fileadmin/dateien/Downloads/P/Pflegeberuf/20120301_Endfassung_Eckpunktepapier_Weiterentwicklung_der_Pflegeberufe.pdf.

Connell, J. (ed.) (2008). *The International Migration of Health Workers.* New York: Routledge.

Deutscher Bundestag (2013). *BT-Drucksache 17/14716* [BT Printed Paper 17/14716]. Retrieved from http://dipbt.bundestag.de/dip21/btd/17/147/1714716.pdf.

Directive 2005/36/EC of the European Parliament and of the Council of 7 September 2005 on the Recognition of Professional Qualifications. Retrieved from http://eurlex. europa.eu/LexUriServ/LexUriServ.do?uri=OJ:L:2005:255:0022:0142:en:PDF.

Dussault G., Fronteira, I. and Cabral, J. (2009). *Migration of Health Personnel in the WHO European Region.* Lisbon: WHO Report. Retrieved from www.euro.who.int/__ data/assets/pdf_file/0010/95689/E93039.pdf.

Englmann, B. and Müller, M. (2007). *Brain Waste: Die Anerkennung von ausländischen Qualifikationen in Deutschland* [Brain Waste: The Recogniton of Foreign Qualifications in Germany]. Augsburg: Tür an Tür – Integrationsprojekte GmbH. Retrieved from www.migranet.org/images/PDF/brain%20waste.pdf.

Gabriel, C. (2011). Migration and globalized care work: the case of internationally educated nurses in Canada. In R. Mahon and F. Robinson (eds), *Feminist Ethics and Social Policy: Towards a New Global Political Economy of Care* (pp. 39–59). Vancouver: University of British Columbia Press.

Gerlinger, T. and Schmucker, R. (2007). Transnational migration of health professionals in the European Union. *Cadernos de Saúde Pública, 23*, 184–192. doi:10.1590/ S0102–311X2007001400008.

Janda, C. (2013). Feminisierte Migration in der Krise? Pflegearbeit in Privathaushalten aus aufenthalts-, arbeits- und sozialrechtlicher Perspektive [Feminised migration in crisis? Care work in private households from the perspective of residence, labor and social legislation]. *Ethik und Gesellschaft: Ökonomische Zeitschrift für Sozialethik, 7(2)*, 1–35. Retrieved from www.ethik-und-gesellschaft.de/mm/EuG-2-2013_Janda. pdf.

Knuth, M. (2012). Berufliche Anerkennung und Erwerbsintegration von Eingewanderten [Occupational recognition and job integration of immigrants]. In A. Bolder, R. Dobischat, G. Kutscha and G. Reutter (eds), *Beruflichkeit zwischen institutionellem Wandel und biographischem Projekt* (pp. 127–151). Wiesbaden: VS.

Kofman, E. and Raghuram, P. (2006). Gender and global labour migrations: incorporating skilled workers. *Antipode, 38*, 282–303. doi:10.1111/j.1467–8330.2006.00580.x.

Krawietz, J. and Visel, S. (2014). 'Die examinierten Praktikanten': Differenzkonstruktionen in der Anerkennung von ausländischen Pflegequalifikationen [Certified interns: constructed differences in the recognition of foreign care credentials]. In J. Krawietz and S. Visel (eds), *Prekarisierung transnationaler Care-Arbeit: Ambivalente Anerkennung* (pp. 82–95). Münster: Westfälisches Dampfboot.

Merda, M. (2012). Den Blick über den Tellerrand wagen [Looking beyond one's own nose]. *Häusliche Pflege, 11*, 20–25.

Sommer, I. (2014). Die Müh(l)en der staatlichen Anerkennung: Selektionsmechanismen der Umwandlung 'ausländischer' in 'deutsche' Pflegefachkräfte zwischen Berufsrecht und Anerkennungspraxis [The efforts of stately recognition: mechanisms of conversion from 'foreign' into 'German' nurses between professional law and practice of recognition]. In J. Krawietz and S. Visel (eds), *Prekarisierung transnationaler Care-Arbeit: Ambivalente Anerkennung* (pp. 56–81). Münster: Westfälisches Dampfboot.

Strauss, A. L. (1998). *Grundlagen qualitativer Sozialforschung* [Basics of qualitative research] (2nd edn). Paderborn: UTB.

Torres, S. (2013). Transnationalism and the study of aging and old age. In C. Phellas (ed.), *Aging in European Societies: Healthy Aging in Europe* (pp. 267–281). New York: Springer.

Vouyioukas, A. and Liapi, M. (2013). Coping with deskilling: strategies of migrant women across European societies. In F. Anthias, M. Kontos and M. Morokvasic-Müller (eds), *Paradoxes of Integration: Female Migrants in Europe* (pp. 79–96). Heidelberg: Springer.

Yeates, N. (2009). *Globalizing Care Economies and Migrant Workers: Explorations in Global Care Chains*. Basingstoke: Palgrave Macmillan.

Index

Page numbers in *italics* denote tables, those in **bold** denote figures.

For Product Safety Concerns and Information please contact our EU
representative GPSR@taylorandfrancis.com
Taylor & Francis Verlag GmbH, Kaufingerstraße 24, 80331 München, Germany

9 780367 869168